CW01261201

Lifelong Learning Book Series

Volume 32

Series Editors
Karen Evans, UCL, Institute of Education UCL, London, UK
Natasha Kersh, Education, Practice & Society, University College London, London, UK

Editorial Board Members
Andrew Brown, Insitute of Education UCL, London, UK
Chiara Biasin, University of Padova, Padova, Italy
Richard Desjardins, University of California Los Angeles, Los Angeles, CA, USA
Kitty te Riele, Peter Underwood Centre, University of Tasmania, Hobart, Australia
Yukiko Sawano, University of the Sacred Heart, Shibuya-ku, Japan
Maria Slowey, Dublin City University, Higher Education Research Centre, Dublin, Ireland
Maurice Taylor, Faculty of Education, University of Ottawa, Ottawa, ON, Canada
Ann-Charlotte Teglborg, Ecole Supérieure Commerce Paris, Paris, France
Rebecca Ye, Stockholm University, Norrköping, Östergötlands Län, Sweden
Dayong Yuan, Beijing Academy of Educational Sciences, Beijing, China

Competing visions and paradigms for lifelong learning co-exist at national as well as international levels. The fact that one 'official' discourse may be dominant at any one time does not mean that other ways of thinking about learning throughout the life course have disappeared. They are alive and well in a range of critical traditions and perspectives that retain their power to engage and persuade.

Lifelong learning is presented in this Series in all its versatility. Accordingly, lifelong learning is referred to as an idea, a concept, an approach, a method, a programme, a strategy, even a philosophy or worldview. Similarly, the approaches to lifelong learning presented in the Series are sometimes philosophical, sociological, economic, psychological or educational, and frequently multi-disciplinary. Common foci are the practices of individual, organisational and collective learning as well as the development of people, communities and societies.

The Series promotes critical, evidence-informed exploration of problems, themes and issues in the evolving field of lifelong learning. Each volume is firmly based on high quality scholarship and a keen awareness of both emergent and enduring issues in practice and policy. Our mission is to engage scholars, practitioners, policy makers and professionals with new insights from international research and practice, and to provoke fresh thinking and innovation in lifelong learning. Contributions that highlight previously under-researched groups, countries and territories are strongly encouraged.

The Lifelong Learning Series aims to bring together established authors building on a strong platform of previous work to develop their themes and positions, with new generation authors bringing novel ideas and perspectives. We welcome contributions from multi-disciplinary research collaborations that approach contemporary and emerging global and local challenges in creative ways.

Through advocacy of broad, diverse and inclusive approaches to learning throughout the life course, the series aspires to be a leading resource for researchers and practitioners who seek to rethink lifelong learning to meet the challenges and opportunities of the 21st Century.

The Lifelong Learning Book Series complements the Third International Handbook of Lifelong Learning https://link.springer.com/referencework/10.1007/978-3-031-19592-1 with an elaboration of specific topics, themes and case studies in greater depth than is possible in the Handbook.

Jan Kalenda

Formation of Adult Learning Systems in Central Europe

Springer

Jan Kalenda
Faculty of Humanities
Tomas Bata University in Zlín
Zlín, Czech Republic

ISSN 1871-322X ISSN 2730-5325 (electronic)
Lifelong Learning Book Series
ISBN 978-3-031-59826-5 ISBN 978-3-031-59827-2 (eBook)
https://doi.org/10.1007/978-3-031-59827-2

© The Editor(s) (if applicable) and The Author(s), under exclusive license to Springer Nature Switzerland AG 2024

This work is subject to copyright. All rights are solely and exclusively licensed by the Publisher, whether the whole or part of the material is concerned, specifically the rights of translation, reprinting, reuse of illustrations, recitation, broadcasting, reproduction on microfilms or in any other physical way, and transmission or information storage and retrieval, electronic adaptation, computer software, or by similar or dissimilar methodology now known or hereafter developed.

The use of general descriptive names, registered names, trademarks, service marks, etc. in this publication does not imply, even in the absence of a specific statement, that such names are exempt from the relevant protective laws and regulations and therefore free for general use.

The publisher, the authors and the editors are safe to assume that the advice and information in this book are believed to be true and accurate at the date of publication. Neither the publisher nor the authors or the editors give a warranty, expressed or implied, with respect to the material contained herein or for any errors or omissions that may have been made. The publisher remains neutral with regard to jurisdictional claims in published maps and institutional affiliations.

This Springer imprint is published by the registered company Springer Nature Switzerland AG
The registered company address is: Gewerbestrasse 11, 6330 Cham, Switzerland

If disposing of this product, please recycle the paper.

In memory of my beloved teacher and role model, František Znebejánek (†2021). Some people should teach forever!

Series Editors' Note

The Lifelong Learning Book Series was launched in 2004 and, by 2024, had published 31 volumes on topics of international significance. The series continues to contribute to cross-cultural dialogue by exploring and sharing research and new perspectives on topics related to Lifelong Learning and its intersections with social, economic, and cultural developments.

Over the past 30 years, the processes of formation and development of cross-national patterns of Adult Learning Systems (ALSs) in Central Europe (CE) have been characterised by their multidimensional complexities, influenced by both historical and contemporary trends in the region. The book captures these complexities and offers a fresh perspective on the relationship between lifelong learning and long-term institutional transformations.

This book is the first in the series to explore in-depth how institutional settings in Central European countries have formed, evolved, and contributed to overall participation in Adult Education and Training (AET), specifically shedding light on the complex interplay between ALSs formation and resulting differences in AET participation. This monograph purposefully adopts a comparative lens to explore emerging policies and practices in post-socialist countries and to explain cross-national variations in the region, with a specific focus on four countries: the Czech Republic, Hungary, Poland, and Slovakia. The book addresses a gap in research on the topic in this region and offers a comprehensive mapping of the development of ALSs in Central Europe after the fall of the Berlin Wall.

To explore the complex interplay between individuals, governments, employers, and public policies that shape ALSs, the book develops an innovative analytical approach defined as 'constructing ALSs from below', where typologies of adult learning systems evolve as a result of the interaction of empirical data and sensitive concepts related to the main features of ALS. This approach enables the capturing of key quantitative features of these systems to understand their cross-national differences. To further advance the approach and uncover qualitative aspects within these systems and their transformations over time, the author employs an analytical framework rooted in the theories of historical institutionalism (Mahoney & Thelen, 2010, 2015; Verdier, 2018).

The country-specific exploration of the formation pathways of the Czech Republic, Hungary, Poland, and Slovakia is truly enriching, providing insight into both the institutional dynamics and the unique construction of ALSs, covering the period from 1989 to 2019. The author offers an illustrative consideration of the sequence of the formation process, while highlighting potential path dependencies, institutional complementarities, and critical junctures in their evolution. The novel Global Adult Learning Space (GALS) framework devised for investigating these systems further strengthens the comparative analysis, allowing for the examination of not only the characteristics of CE ALSs but also their relation to other selected European ALSs. What makes this analysis particularly engaging is that the innovative theoretical approach adopted in this book is always grounded in available data and focuses on explaining the variability among related empirical structures and processes. This analytical perspective enables the evaluation of a range of pertinent aspects in each country's context. It also contributes to a comparative approach to encourage policy learning among different countries of the former Soviet Bloc and beyond. This approach allows for understanding how different social settings and actions of key stakeholders have contributed to the formation of both similar and different forms of ALSs, enabling a better understanding of participation levels and patterns in AET.

This volume makes an original and timely contribution to the series. In summary, the monograph offers valuable policy recommendations and outlines future directions for the development of adult learning systems in the region. A key strength is the comparative approach to the formation of Adult Learning Systems across time and space, particularly in the context of under-researched countries in relation to this topic. The book will be of interest across national and international audiences, including both academics and policymakers.

University College London
London, UK
March 2024

Natasha Kersh
Karen Evans

Preface

This book caters to all who share my fascination with lifelong learning, big structures, and long-term institutional transformations. The following pages tell the story of these three overlapping topics, somewhere on the borders of adult education research, comparative education, politics, and historical institutionalism. I aim to recount the evolution of adult learning systems within four Central European countries (Hungary, the Czech Republic, Slovakia, and Poland) from the post-communist era to the onset of the COVID-19 pandemic. This narrative will illustrate that, despite starting from a similar institutional framework and facing comparable societal challenges, each of these countries has embarked on a distinct formation trajectory, culminating in uniquely different adult learning systems. In addition to this critical analysis, I introduce concepts such as the Global Adult Learning Space (GALS) to further enrich comparative adult education research. My aspiration is that this book will serve as a valuable resource for fellow researchers aligned with this field of study.

This text is a coincidence of three unforeseen developments that have significantly influenced my life, shaping me both as a researcher and as an individual. Firstly, since 2015, I have developed a keen interest in the macro-social dynamics underpinning the transformation of adult education systems. Secondly, in 2021, I experienced the profound loss of my dearest mentor and role model, František Znebejánek, to whom I had pledged to dedicate a book. His constant, albeit often subtle, encouragement was pivotal in advancing my scientific journey further than I could have imagined without his guidance (I have missed you so much). Thirdly, the generous support from the Fulbright Commission enabled me to spend a year at the University of California, Los Angeles, where I had the opportunity to work on this manuscript under the best guidance I could imagine.

In addition to expressing my gratitude to the Fulbright Commission for its support (Grant: *Political Economy of Adult Learning Systems in Central Europe: From their Emergence to Liberalisation, 2022-03-21*), I must extend my heartfelt thanks to Professor Richard Desjardins. During my research stay at UCLA, he became not only a great mentor but also a critical reader of my book, offering insightful comments and constructive critiques on all versions of this manuscript. His influence permeates numerous aspects of this book. My appreciation also goes out to the students and postdoctoral researchers from the School of Education and Information Studies at UCLA, who engaged in thoughtful discussions about my project. Furthermore, I am indebted to Professor Ellen Boeren for her enduring support, sage advice, and constant encouragement. Additionally, I am thankful to Tomáš Karger for his valuable feedback on one of the manuscript's later versions, whose insights are always highly esteemed. Finally, my thanks extend to my 'research commando'—Ilona Kočvarová, Jitka Vaculíková, and Hana Zouharová—for enhancing my daily work life beyond my expectations. I could not wish for better colleagues.

Zlín, Czech Republic   Jan Kalenda

Contents

Part I Introduction

1 The Objective of the Book 3
   1.1 Content of the Publication 4
   1.2 Significance of AET...................................... 5
   1.3 Adult Learning Systems................................... 6
   1.4 Un-systemic Nature of ALSs.............................. 6
   1.5 Adult Education and Training 7
   1.6 Participation Constraints 9
   1.7 Central Europe: Spatial-Temporal Framework 10

Part II Theory

2 Typologies of ALS 15
   2.1 Two Theoretical Approaches to ALSs 16
      2.1.1 Typologies Built from Above........................ 17
      2.1.2 Critique of ALSs Typologies Built from Above 29
      2.1.3 Typologies Built From Below 33
      2.1.4 Two Types of Theorising Regarding ALSs 38

3 Participation Theories in AET................................ 41
   3.1 Theoretical Approaches to Participation 41
      3.1.1 Macro Social Mechanism 43
      3.1.2 Meso Social Mechanisms 43
      3.1.3 Microsocial Factors 45
   3.2 Global Empirical Trends 47

4 Barriers to Participation in AET.............................. 49
   4.1 Types of Barriers 49
   4.2 Current Findings 51

Part III Analytical Approach and Methodology

5　General Analytical Approach.................................. 55
　5.1　Global Adult Learning Space (GALS):
　　　Mapping Quantitative Features of ALSs 56
　5.2　Institutional History: Mapping Qualitative Features of ALSs..... 60
　　　5.2.1　Coordination Side 61
　　　5.2.2　Supply Side 62
　　　5.2.3　Demand Side 62
　5.3　Sensitive Concepts.. 63
　　　5.3.1　Critical Junctures................................. 63
　　　5.3.2　Coalitions... 63
　　　5.3.3　Path Dependency 64
　　　5.3.4　Diffusion, State Capacity and Weak Institutions......... 65
　　　5.3.5　Pace and Sequencing of ALSs Formation 65
　　　5.3.6　Drift and Conversion 66
　　　5.3.7　External Pressure on Institutions..................... 66

6　Methodology 69
　6.1　Large-N Quantitative Analysis.............................. 70
　　　6.1.1　Available Data 70
　　　6.1.2　Measuring Adult Participation....................... 71
　　　6.1.3　Limits of Secondary Data and their Availability 72
　6.2　Small-N Qualitative Analysis............................... 72
　　　6.2.1　Data Used... 73

Part IV Formation Paths of ALSs in CE

7　Hungary... 79
　7.1　Early Formation Period: The 1990s.......................... 79
　　　7.1.1　The Coordination Side of ALS:
　　　　　Toward the Withdrawal of the State.................... 80
　　　7.1.2　The Supply Side of ALS:
　　　　　Birth of Deregulated AET Market..................... 81
　　　7.1.3　The Demand Side of ALS:
　　　　　Inherited Social Structure 82
　7.2　Development Phase: The 2000s............................. 83
　　　7.2.1　The Coordination Side of ALS:
　　　　　Introducing a Legislative and Regulative Framework..... 83
　　　7.2.2　The Supply Side of ALS:
　　　　　From Free to Segmented Market...................... 85
　　　7.2.3　The Demand Side of ALS:
　　　　　Increasing Demand among High-Skilled Adults.......... 86
　7.3　Late Phase: The 2010s..................................... 87
　　　7.3.1　ALS Coordination Side:
　　　　　Turn to Centralisation and Specialisation 87

		7.3.2	The Supply Side of ALS:	
			From Segmented to Directly Regulated Market	89
		7.3.3	The Demand Side of ALS:	
			Slowdown of Social Transformation	
			with High Demand for Low-Skilled Work...............	89
8	**The Czech Republic**			91
	8.1	Early Formation Period: The 1990s........................		91
		8.1.1	The Coordination Side of ALS:	
			The Transition from Socialism to Capitalism	91
		8.1.2	The Supply Side of ALS: Quick Birth of Free Market	93
		8.1.3	The Demand Side of ALS: Structural Constraints........	93
	8.2	Development Phase: The 2000s...........................		94
		8.2.1	The Coordination Side of ALS:	
			Attempts to Regulate AET Field	94
		8.2.2	The Supply Side of ALS:	
			Expansion and Regulation of the Supply...............	97
		8.2.3	The Demand Side of ALS:	
			Remaining Structural Constraints	98
	8.3	Late Formation Phase: The 2010s		98
		8.3.1	The Coordination Side of ALS:	
			Step Back to Deregulation..........................	99
		8.3.2	The Supply Side of ALS: Toward Highly	
			Differentiated and Employers-Oriented Market	100
		8.3.3	The Demand Side of ALS:	
			Limited Acceleration in Demand.....................	101
9	**Slovakia**			103
	9.1	Early Formation Period: The 1990s........................		103
		9.1.1	The Coordination Side of ALS:	
			Decentralisation of AET	103
		9.1.2	The Supply Side of ALS: Emergence	
			of a Deregulated Market	104
		9.1.3	The Demand Side of ALS: Socioeconomic Constraints ...	105
	9.2	Development Period: The 2000s		106
		9.2.1	The Coordination Side of ALS:	
			Introducing a Weak Form of Regulation	107
		9.2.2	The Supply Side of ALS:	
			Growth of the Uncoordinated Market	108
		9.2.3	The Demand Side of ALS: Stagnated Demand	109
	9.3	Late Formation Phase: The 2010s		110
		9.3.1	The Coordination Side of ALS:	
			Attempts in an Extension of Regulation	110
		9.3.2	The Supply Side of ALS: Growth of Employers'	
			Supply of AET...................................	111
		9.3.3	The Demand Side of ALS: Improving	
			Conditions for AET Demand........................	112

10 Poland ... 115
- 10.1 Early Formation Period: The 1990s ... 115
  - 10.1.1 The Coordination Side of ALS: The Transition from Socialism to Capitalism ... 115
  - 10.1.2 The Supply Side of ALS: Formation of State-Dominant AET Market ... 117
  - 10.1.3 The Demand Side of ALS: Structural Constraints and Slow Transformation ... 117
- 10.2 Development Phase: The 2000s ... 118
  - 10.2.1 The Coordination Side of ALS: Differentiation and Specialisation ... 119
  - 10.2.2 The Supply Side of ALS: Strengthening of FAE Provision ... 121
  - 10.2.3 The Demand Side of ALS: Strong Constraints ... 122
- 10.3 Late Formation Phase: The 2010s ... 123
  - 10.3.1 The Coordination Side of ALS: Vocationalisation and Homogenisation ... 123
  - 10.3.2 The Supply Side of ALS: Persistent Pattern ... 124
  - 10.3.3 The Demand Side of ALS: Slow Rise in Demand ... 125

Part V CE ALSs in Global Adult Learning Space

11 Vertical Axis: Volume of Participation ... 129
- 11.1 Participation in AET with a 12-Month Referential Period ... 129
- 11.2 Participation in AET with a 4-Weeks Referential Period ... 131
- 11.3 Getting Closer to the EU? ... 134
- 11.4 Participation in AET Based on Training Hours ... 136

12 First Horizontal Axis: The Extensification of AET ... 139

13 Second Horizontal Axis: Orientation Toward FAE ... 143
- 13.1 Long-Term Trends in FAE ... 143
- 13.2 Changes in the Role of FAE ... 146

14 Third Horizontal Axis: Employers' Support of NFE ... 149
- 14.1 Long-Term Trends in Job-Related NFE ... 149
- 14.2 Uneven Paths of CE ALSs ... 153

15 Fourth Horizontal Axis: Public Provision of NFE ... 157
- 15.1 Public Provision of NFE ... 157
- 15.2 Pathways of CE ALSs ... 159

16 Fifth Horizontal Axis: Demand for AET ... 161
- 16.1 Perceived Demand for AET ... 161
- 16.2 Adults with No Demand for AET ... 163
- 16.3 A Decline in No Demand for AET in CE ALS ... 164

Summary of Part V

Part VI Patterns of Participation and Barriers in CE ALSs

17 Participation Patterns in AET 173
 17.1 Participation Based on Age 174
 17.2 Participation Based on Gender............................ 175
 17.3 Participation Based on the Highest Attained Education 177
 17.4 Participation Based on Economic Status 179
 17.5 Participation Based on Occupation Status 181

18 Barriers to Participation in AET 187
 18.1 Commonalities in Barriers 187
 18.2 Differences in Barriers 189
 18.3 Barriers Among Those Who Did Not Want to Participate 190

Summary of the Part VI

Part VII Discussion and Conclussion

19 Three Stages of ALSs Formation in CE 201
 19.1 Years of Transition (1989–2003) 202
 19.2 Years of Accession (2004–2012) 203
 19.3 Years of Economic Recovery (2013–2019) 204
 19.4 Multidimensionality and Multipath of Institutional Change 205

20 Key Drivers of ALSs Formation in CE 207
 20.1 Europeanisation of ALSs Matters, but...................... 207
 20.2 National Policy Matters, but... 209
  20.2.1 Institutional Instability
   and Secondary Priority of AET 211
 20.3 Social Structure Matters, but.............................. 211
  20.3.1 Matthew Effect and Partial Democratisation 213
 20.4 Dependent Market Capitalism Matters, but.................. 214
 20.5 Welfare State Policy Matters, but.......................... 215

21 Conclusion 217
 21.1 Summary 217
 21.2 Policy Recommendations................................. 220
 21.3 Future Directions 223

References 227

Abbreviations

ABE	Adult Basic Education
AES	Adult Education Survey
AET	Adult Education and Training
AGE	Adult General Education
AHE	Adult Higher Education
ALE	Adult Liberal Education
ALS	Adult Learning System
ALSs	Adult Learning Systems
ALMP	Active Labour Market Policy
CE	Central European/Central Europe
CEDEFOP	European Centre for Development of Vocational Training
CME	Coordinated Market Economy
DMC	Dependent Market Capitalism
EC	European Commission
EE	Eastern Europe, Eastern European
EU	European Union
FAE	Formal Adult Education
FDI	Foreign Direct Investment
GALS	Global Adult Learning Space
HRD	Human Resources Development
HRM	Human Resources Management
IFL	Informal Learning
ISCED	International Standard Classification of Education
ISCO	International Standard Classification of Occupation
LME	Liberal Market Economy
MEYS	Ministry of Youth, Education and Sport
NFE	Non-formal Education
NFE-Voc	Non-formal Vocational Education
NGO	Non-governmental Organisation
OECD	Organisation for Economic Co-operation and Development

PIAAC	Programme for the International Assessment of Adult Competencies
UNESCO	United Nations Educational, Scientific and Cultural Organization
VET	Vocational and Educational Training
VoC	Variety of Capitalism
WSR	Welfare State Regimes

List of Figures

Fig. 2.1	Institutions in the subspheres of the political economy in the 1990s	30
Fig. 2.2	Institutions in the subspheres of the political economy in the 2010s	30
Fig. 2.3	Institutions in the subspheres of the political economy in the 1990s	31
Fig. 2.4	Institutions in the subspheres of the political economy in the 2010s	31
Fig. 5.1	Model of the GALS: five horizontal axes	58
Fig. 11.1	Participation levels in AET in CE countries as a percentage of EU28 average: 2002–2019. (*Source*: LFS (2022)). *Note*: Data in percent. Participation was measured as involvement of adults (25–64 years) in any AET in 4 weeks prior to survey	135
Fig. 12.1	Selected European ALSs in 1997: Percentage of participation in AET in CE ALSs and average number of hours spent by participants in AET. (*Source*: own calculation based on the data from IALS, 1997; OECD, 2003)	140
Fig. 12.2	Percentage of participation in AET in CE ALS and average number of hours spent by participants in AET: 1997 to 2016. (*Source*: own calculation based on the data from IALS, 1997; AES, 2007, 2011, 2016; OECD, 2003)	140
Fig. 12.3	Trajectories of CE ALSs between 1997 to 2016: From medium-intensive ALSs to highly extensive ALSs. (*Source*: own calculation based on the data from IALS, 1997; AES, 2007, 2011, 2016; OECD, 2003)	141

Fig. 13.1　Selected European ALSs in **2016**: Percentage of participation in AET and the share of FAE on the total participation in AET. (*Source*: own calculation based on the data from AES, 2016) *Note*: The data presented in this figure are reported in percentages. Participation is measured as the involvement of adults aged 25–64 years in AET within the 12 months preceding the survey. Share of DAE measure as a share of participation in FAE on the total participation in AET 146

Fig. 13.2　Trends in share of FAE among selected European ALSs: 2007–2016. Percentage of participation in AET and the share of FAE on the total participation in AET. (*Source*: own calculation based on the data from AES, 2007, 2016) *Note*: The data presented in this figure are reported in percentages. Participation is measured as the involvement of adults aged 25–64 years in AET within the 12 months preceding the survey. Share of FAE measure as share of participation in FAE on the on total participation in AET 147

Fig. 13.3　Trajectories of CE ALSs between 2007 and 2016. (*Source*: own calculation based on the data from AES, 2007, 2016) *Note*: The data presented in this figure are reported in percentages. Participation is measured as the involvement of adults aged 25–64 years in AET within the 12 months preceding the survey. Share of DAE measure as share of participation in FAE on the on total participation in AET 148

Fig. 14.1　Selected European ALSs in 2016: percentage of participation in AET and share of NFE financially supported by employers. (*Source*: own calculation based on the data from AES, 2016). *Note*: The data presented in this figure are reported in percentages. Participation is measured as the involvement of adults aged 25–64 years in AET within the 12 months preceding the survey. Share of employers' financial support of NFE measure as a share of participation in job-related NFE supported by employers on total participation in NFE 152

Fig. 14.2　Formation paths of selected European ALSs based on employers' financial support: 1997 to 2016. (*Source*: own calculation based on the data from IALS, 1997; AES, 2016; OECD, 2003). *Note*: The data presented in this figure are reported in percentages. Participation is measured as the involvement of adults aged 25–64 years in AET within the 12 months preceding the survey. Share of employers' financial support of NFE measure as a share of participation in job-related NFE supported by employers on total participation in NFE 153

Fig. 14.3   Formation paths of CE ALSs based on employers' financial support (1997–2016). (*Source*: own calculation based on the data from IALS, 1997; AES, 2007, 2016; OECD, 2003). *Note*: The data presented in this figure are reported in percentages. Participation is measured as the involvement of adults aged 25–64 years in AET within the 12 months preceding the survey. Share of employers' financial support of NFE measure as a share of participation in job-related NFE supported by employers on total participation in NFE. 154

Fig. 15.1   Selected European countries in 2016: Share of NFE provided by public and private educational institutions. (*Source*: own calculation based on the data from AES, 2007, 2011, 2016) *Note*: The data presented in this figure are reported in percentages. Participation is measured as the involvement of adults aged 25–64 years in AET within the 12 months preceding the survey. NFE public provision is measured as a percentage of all NFE provided by public institutions... 158

Fig. 15.2   Trajectories of CE ALSs between 2007 to 2016: Paths toward ALSs with medium to weak public NFE provision. (*Source*: own calculation based on the data from AES, 2007, 2011, 2016) *Note*: The data presented in this figure are reported in percentages. Participation is measured as the involvement of adults aged 25–64 years in AET within the 12 months preceding the survey. NFE public provision is measured as a percentage of all NFE provided by public institutions... 159

Fig. 16.1   Selected European countries in 2016 based on the variations in demand for AET. (*Source*: own calculation based on the data from AES (2016)) *Note*: The data presented in this figure are reported in percentages. Participation is measured as the involvement of adults aged 25 to 64 years in AET within the 12 months preceding the survey. Demand for AET is measured as percentage of adults who participated in AET and *want to participate* more and those who did not participated and *want to participate* 162

Fig. 16.2   Formation paths of CE ALSs based on demand for AET: 2007 to 2016. (*Source*: own calculation based on the data from AES (2016)) *Note*: The data presented in this figure are reported in percentages. Participation is measured as the involvement of adults aged 25 to 64 years in AET within the 12 months preceding the survey. Demand for AET measured as percentage of adults who participated in AET and *want to participate* more and those who did not participated and *want to participate* 163

Fig. 16.3 Selected European countries in 2016 based on the variations in demand for AET. (*Source*: own calculation based on the data from AES (2016)) *Note*: The data presented in this figure are reported in percentages. Participation is measured as the involvement of adults aged 25 to 64 years in AET within the 12 months preceding the survey. The absence of demand for AET is measured as the percentage of adults who did not want to participate in AET 164

Fig. 16.4 Trajectories of CE ALSs between 2007 and 2016 based on the number of adults with no demand for AET. (*Source*: own calculation based on the data from AES (2007, 2011, 2016)) *Note*: The data presented in this figure are reported in percentages. Participation is measured as the involvement of adults aged 25 to 64 years in AET within the 12 months preceding the survey. The absence of demand for AET is measured as the percentage of adults who did not want to participate in AET 165

List of Tables

Table 1.1	Taxonomy of AET	9
Table 2.1	Typology of formal education systems in advanced industrial democracies	17
Table 2.2	Participation in LME and CME countries: 1997 to 2012	25
Table 2.3	Western European ALS	27
Table 2.4	Eastern European ALSs	28
Table 2.5	Typology of skill formation systems in advanced industrial democracies	34
Table 2.6	Typology of ALSs in advanced industrial democracies	36
Table 2.7	Main characteristics of approaches to constructing ALSs	39
Table 6.1	Sources of data for analysis	71
Table 11.1	Participation levels in AET in 12 months before the survey: 1997–2016	130
Table 11.2	Participation levels in AET in CE countries 4 weeks before the survey: 2002–2019	132
Table 11.3	The average number of hours spent by participants in AET: 1997–2016	136
Table 13.1	Participation levels in formal adult education in 12 months before the survey: 1997–2016	144
Table 13.2	Development of participation levels in formal adult education: 2004–2019 (4-week referential period)	145
Table 14.1	Participation levels in job-related NFE in 12 months before survey: 1997–2016	150
Table 14.2	Participation levels in employer-sponsored job-related NFE in 12 months before survey: 1997–2016	151

Summary of Part V

Table 1	Empirical features of CE ALSs in the late 2010s	168

Table 17.1	Participation in AET among age cohorts over 45 years: 2007–2016	174
Table 17.2	Relative levels of participation in AET among age cohorts over 45 years: 2007–2016	175
Table 17.3	Participation in AET among Men and Women: 2007–2016	176
Table 17.4	Relative levels of participation in AET based on gender: 2007–2016	177
Table 17.5	Participation in AET and NFE based on the highest attained education: 2007–2016	178
Table 17.6	Relative levels of participation in AET based on highest attained education: 2007–2016	179
Table 17.7	Participation in NFE among the employed and unemployed: 2007–2016	180
Table 17.8	Relative levels of participation in AET based on economic status: 2007–2016	181
Table 17.9	Participation in AET among the high-skilled and medium-skilled service workers: 2007–2016	182
Table 17.10	Participation in AET among qualified and unqualified manual workers: 2007–2016	182
Table 17.11	Relative levels of participation in AET among the high-skilled and medium-skilled service workers: 2007–2016	184
Table 17.12	Relative levels of participation in AET among qualified and unqualified manual workers: 2007–2016	185
Table 18.1	Perceived barriers to participation in AET among those who wanted to participate: 2007–2016	188
Table 18.2	Perceived barriers to participation in AET among those who did not want to participate: 2011–2016	191

Summary of Part VI

Table 1	Patterns in participation inequality based on key sociodemographic factors: 2007–2016	194
Table 2	Trends in participation inequality based on key sociodemographic factors: 2007-2016	195
Table 3	The pattern of barriers to participation in CE ALSs	196
Table 19.1	General periodisation of ALSs formation in CE: 1989–2019	206

Part I
Introduction

Chapter 1
The Objective of the Book

This book explores the formation and development of the cross-national patterns of Adult Learning Systems (ALSs) in Central European (CE) countries between 1989 and 2019. My research focuses on four countries that are traditionally considered a core of this region: *the Czech Republic, Slovakia, Hungary* and *Poland*. Besides their geographical proximity, they also share many other commonalities—post-socialist heritage, the timing of the integration into the European Union (EU), the similar nature of the basic education system and, among others, some aspects of the capitalist economy that quickly expanded there after 1989.

Taken together, these characteristics can serve as a good analytical unit for applying the current framework of the *new political economy of adult education*. An ambition of this theoretical approach is to understand a complex system of relations among individuals, governments, employers, and public policies that shape ALSs and impact participation in *Adult Education and Training* (AET) (Desjardins, 2017; Rees, 2013). Based on their more profound understanding, we can better evaluate the quality and effectiveness of lifelong learning policies in selected countries and identify policy mechanisms and instruments for its enhancement.

Drawing on this approach, my work closely examines how the institutional settings in CE countries have formed, evolved and contributed to overall participation in AET, how they have shaped patterns of participation and unequal chances to be involved in this social activity, as well as perceived barriers to access AET and related governmental policies. Such an objective is based on the current empirical evidence on cross-national patterns of AET (Boeren et al., 2017; Ioannidou & Parma, 2022) and adult learning policies (Milana & Vatrella, 2020), which has suggested that existing ALSs typologies are insufficient to explain the cross-national variations. This is especially true for CE countries, which often do not fit the proposed categorisations and are considered a 'nightmare' of comparative research (Verdier, 2018). Similar to some scholars (Eyal et al., 1998; Stark, 1992) from the 1990s, who studied the transformation of societies in this region, this text argues that CE countries can serve as a 'laboratory' for testing various assumptions about ALSs.

This book enhances our knowledge not only about ALSs in the geographical area under investigation but also advances our understanding of the long-term development and change of ALSs—what have been their formation trajectories, how their evolution has been affected by their initial structural setting and how successful they have been in the coordination of organised forms of adult learning. The following findings about ALSs in CE countries will serve scholars in two main research fields.

On the one hand, it is an increasingly growing niche of studies under the umbrella of the political economy of adult education (e.g., Cabus et al., 2020; Desjardins, 2017, 2018, 2023a, b; Desjardins & Ioannidou, 2020; Geiss, 2020; Ioannidou & Parma, 2022; Lee & Desjardins, 2019; Rees, 2013; Regmi, 2020; Schemmann et al., 2020; Walker, 2020) and inquiry focused on cross-national comparative research in AET (Hefler & Markovitch, 2013; Field et al., 2016, 2019; Milana, 2018; Milana et al., 2020).

On the other hand, it is the research concerning adults' participation in organised learning. Although this field of inquiry was established in the 1960s and 1970s (Johnstone & Rivera, 1965; Boshier, 1971; Rubenson, 1975), it has not lost anything from its intensity even in recent years (e.g., Cabus et al., 2020; Hovdhaugen, & Opheim, 2018; Jenkins, 2021; Kalenda et al., 2020; Kalenda & Kočvarová, 2022a; Van Nieuwenhove & De Wever, 2021).

However, we should highlight on this place that the analysis of the impact of institutional settings in shaping participation in AET represents only a minor part of this research niche (Blossfeld et al., 2014, 2020; Dämmrich et al., 2014, 2015; Roosma & Saar, 2010, 2017; Saar et al., 2014, 2023), and thus needs further exploration and elaboration. My research argues that these two fields are two sides of the same coin, and if we really want to deeply understand one of them, we also must explore the other one.

1.1 Content of the Publication

The content of this book is divided into eight parts. The introductory section (Part I) provides a brief overview of key issues related to ALSs and AET and describes their distinctive features in the CE context. The second part (Part II) provides insight into the theoretical framework for analysing the interplay of social institutions and AET. In this regard, it is further divided into three sub-chapters that deal with current typologies of ALSs, theories of participation in AET and barriers related to organised learning. The subsequent part (Part III) looks at the applied analytical framework, methodology and data used for analysis, as well as the primary limits of the proposed analysis based on the available data. At this place, the book introduces a new conception of a *Global Adult Learning Space* (GALS) and a repertoire of sensitive concepts from historical institutionalism for studying the development of

ALSs. The following section (Part IV) turns attention to the formation paths of each of the CE countries. It explores the institutional dynamic that results in the unique construction of ALSs in the Czech Republic, Hungary, Poland and Slovakia. The next part (Part V) provides a detailed examination of the quantitative characteristics of CE ALSs and highlights their distinctions both within the region and in comparison to other European ALSs. Finally, the following section of text (Part VI) sheds light on patterns of adults' involvement in AET and principal constraints to accessing AET. After that follows discussion of the main findings from the previous three parts that links them to key theoretical concepts behind ALSs formation (Part VII). The book's last section summarises the main findings about the evolution of ALSs in CE countries and outlines policy recommendations. Together, the chapters provide a revealing new map of ALSs in CE.

1.2 Significance of AET

According to numerous papers (e.g., Albert et al., 2010; Boeren, 2016; Boeren et al., 2017; Markowitsch & Hefler, 2019) and policy documents (OECD 2019a, b, 2020; UNESCO, 2022), AET is considered both (1) crucial social practice contributing to economic competitiveness and (2) activity that has a vast set of positive non-economic benefits for contemporary societies. For instance, it is crucial for more vital civic society and public engagement (Regmi, 2020). Beyond that, it brings benefits not only to aggregate social bodies—governments, economies and companies but also to individuals (Field, 2012; Schuller & Desjardins, 2010). AET allows people to constantly enhance their skills and qualifications and adapt to labour market changes. Moreover, there is enough evidence that adults who have undergone some form of organised learning have improved their employability (Campbell, 2012; CEDEFOP, 2022; Kureková et al., 2023; OECD, 2019a, b), including the possibility of transitioning from one segment of the labour market to another as well as increasing their earnings and the likelihood of being promoted within an organisation (Jenkins, 2006, 2021). Furthermore, several studies have highlighted that adults can also benefit from participation in AET in areas of life unconnected to the workplace. For example, participants regularly show higher levels of civic engagement (Iñiguez-Berrozpe, 2020) and report better overall quality of life (Field, 2012; Sabates & Hammond, 2008).

For this reason, high and equal participation of adults from all socio-demographic groups is considered a significant policy objective not only for national governments (HUN LLS, 2006; MEYS, 2020) and international political actors such as the EU (EC 2001, 2009, 2021; CEDEFOP, 2018) but also for international organisations such as UNESCO (2019, 2020, 2022) or OECD (2019a, b).

To this topic, ALSs play a unique role. Institutional aspects influence the nature and financing of AET in a particular country and various other (non-financial) political mechanisms implemented to support the provision of organised learning opportunities for adults, like counselling services. For instance, recognition of education outside the formal education system, information campaigns regarding education opportunities or counselling. If they are practical and robust, they could systematically raise participation levels and decrease inequality (Boeren, 2016, 2023; Boeren et al., 2017).

1.3 Adult Learning Systems

ALSs represent structural frameworks in the form of institutional packages related to adult learning. They are defined as a "mass of organised learning opportunities available to adults along with their underlying structures and stakeholders that shape their organisation and governance" (Desjardins & Ioannidou, 2020, p. 145; see also Desjardins, 2017, 2023a). This analytical framework thus includes not only participants (demand side) and providers (supply side) of AET but also institutions, and stakeholders, including for example states, unions, professional associations and firms, as well as policy measures more or less regulating interactions between them. Finally, the framework contains fundamental coordination problems and constraints connected to adults' access to AET opportunities that are responsible for efficacy, efficiency and inequality inside of these systems (for detailed elaboration, see Part III).

In the given form, the ALSs approach provides us with three critical analytical categories that will be utilised across this book: (1) institutions more or less regulating/coordinating AET; (2) the mass of organised learning for adults—i.e., volume and structure of participation in AET; (3) main policies that are aimed to enhance participation in ALSs. Together, they represent the main topics of this text.

1.4 Un-systemic Nature of ALSs

The notion of the 'system' has to be addressed and clarified in this place. The ALSs rarely represent a unified, distinctive 'system' in any country. Instead, they are deeply embedded in clusters of economic, political, educational and cultural institutions like the labour market, the welfare state system, the formal education system, or industrial relations (Desjardins, 2023a, b; Kureková et al., 2023; Saar et al., 2023). More than a system in the structural-functionalist or cybernetic tradition of thinking, they remind an 'ecology' (Abbott, 2016) of loosely connected and overlapping institutions that deal with various forms of AET, emerging and utilising for different aims.

On the one hand, this essence makes them more challenging to capture and typologise. This will be more obvious from the later discussion of theoretical frameworks employed to understand cross-national variations among them. On the other hand, this book argues that it makes them a more valuable object for studying institutional change in late modernity. Contrary to typical institutions of industrial modernity (e.g., the welfare state, higher education system), ALSs, as we know them today, emerged far later, with the 'coming of post-industrial society' (Bell, 1973), as one of the reactions to the 'crisis of Fordism' (Jarvis, 2004); or even later, in the case of CE countries. They have grown up from this background, partially as new institutions rooted in the space among the diverse institutions of industrial modernity, partially within these older institutions themselves, as a shift in their functions and goals. For example, this has been typical for the transformation of the welfare states, which have started implementing more active policy measures, so-called social investment policy (Hemerijck, 2017, 2018) focused on reskilling and upskilling of adults as a part of their new functions (Thelen, 2014) as well as part of the general shift toward 'knowledge-based growth regimes', which should support (Hall, 2022).

From a general perspective, the un-systemic nature is not only present in current ALSs but is also becoming a popular concept for understanding educational governance itself. This is seen as fragmented, decentralised, and characterised by the intersection of private and public providers, as well as various actors responsible for coordination at different levels, from international to regional (Wilkins & Olmedo, 2018).

To map the historical formation and development of ALSs, it is, therefore, necessary to consider the un-systemic nature of ALSs and their heterogeneity. We need to examine the building of new institutions focused directly on AET (e.g., expansion of training provisions in a workplace setting), including their relationships to economic, political and educational institutions, and the transformation of once-established institutions (e.g. universities, unions, employment services) in the form of institutional drift or layering (Hacker et al., 2015) and how they translate the lifelong learning agenda into their everyday practice.

1.5 Adult Education and Training

Through this text, my research understands AET as *organised learning opportunities* undertaken by adults aged *25–64 years* who are not in their regular cycle of education and including non-traditional students in formal education (EC CLA, 2016). Non-traditional students are thought adults who are not in their regular education cycle—i.e., in their initial phase of education but undertake organised and certified learning opportunities, including studying in any national education system.

This approach has an advantage that is closely aligned with the way how EU (EC CLA, 2016) see adult education and training. However, it also has one important disadvantage that must be clarified. It excluded all AET focused on young adults aged 16–24 years that participate in the second chance formal education (ISCED 2–3), so-called Adult General Education (AGE) (Desjardins, 2017, 2023b). This book excludes this segment of adult education from the analysis for two mutually reinforcing reasons. Firstly, there is more available comparative data for adults aged 25–64 years than for younger adults, hence focus on this age group enables reach more analytical depth. Secondly, the participation of young adults in AGE is very low in CE due to a very high completion rate in secondary education that usually reaches more than 90% of the population cohort (WB, 2023).

Organised learning for adults aged 25–64 years is usually divided into two main domains—formal and non-formal education. According to the *International Standard Classification of Education* (ISCED, 2011, p. 11) and the European Commission's *Classification of Learning Activities* (EC CLA, 2016, p. 14), *formal adult education* (FAE) represents:

> [...] institutionalised, intentional and planned [activity] through public organisations and recognised private bodies constitute the formal education system of a country. Formal education programmes are thus recognised as such by the relevant national education or equivalent authorities, e.g. any other institution in cooperation with the national or sub-national education authorities. [...]. Qualifications from formal education are by definition, recognised and, therefore, are within the scope of ISCED. Institutionalised education occurs when an organisation provides structured educational arrangements, such as student-teacher relationships and/or interactions, that are specially designed for education and learning.

Desjardins (2017, 2023b) has identified three relevant subtypes of the FAE that we will follow during subsequent exploration of ALS in CE: (1) *Adult Basic Education* (ABE) and (2) AGE, which contains organised learning activities in primary and secondary levels of education. Most of the time, they represent so-called 'second chance education' for adults who can obtain through them qualifications of the level of ISCED 1–3. According to Boeren et al. (2017), provision from this type of AET is crucial for addressing lack of experience or qualification among adults; (2) *Adult Higher Education* (AHE) that consists of educational programmes for non-traditional students that end up with ISCED 5–6 qualification. Both these subtypes can have strong job orientations, which means that they primarily serve vocational training and professional development.

Non-formal adult education (NFE) can be defined as a wide range of organised learning activities for adults conducted outside the formal educational system:

> [...] it is an addition, alternative and/or complement to formal education within the process of lifelong learning of individuals. It is often provided to guarantee all the right of access to education. It caters to people of all ages but does not necessarily apply a continuous pathway structure; it may be short in duration and/or low intensity; and it is typically provided in the form of short courses, workshops or seminars. Non-formal education mostly leads to qualifications that are not recognised as formal or equivalent to formal qualifications by the relevant national or sub-national education authorities [...]. Nevertheless, formal, recognised qualifications may be obtained through exclusive participation in specific non-formal education programmes (ISCED, 2011, p. 11; EC CLA, 2016, p. 15).

These activities include on-the-job training, workshops, individual lessons, as well as other forms of planned and intentional training (EC CLA, 2016; ISCED, 2011). Although NFE is not always officially certified, many programs are approved by governments and other agencies (Singh, 2015). Also, NFE can be divided into two main domains: (1) *non-formal vocational education* (NFE-Voc) related to the 'formation of human capital' for a particular job market; this comprises learning activities targeting the upskilling and reskilling of the workforce, and (2) a form usually termed 'liberal' or 'popular education'. In contrast to NFE-Voc, this type usually includes leisure-oriented learning activities which take place outside of the work environment; i.e. it is more interlinked with participation in civil society than specifically in the labour market.

In addition to previous definitions, the literature (Desjardins et al., 2016) sometimes distinguishes among (1) *compensatory* and (2) *complementary* types of AET. Compensatory types include mainly publicly founded ABE, AGE, AHE and some forms of ALE, for instance, basic literacy programmes offered by non-governmental organisations (NGOs) for migrants. Contrary, complementary education is based on on-the-job training and continuous vocational and professional training in both secondary and higher education. The taxonomy of various forms of organised learning is summarised in Table 1.1 below.

1.6 Participation Constraints

From overall participation levels in AET across the World (Kaufmann, 2015; Rubenson, 2018), we know that high and equal access to organised learning opportunities is more an exception than regularity. Adults face various constraints in their participation that hinder their chances of entering AET. Therefore, it is crucial to understand key barriers to participation to improve educational policy in this area.

For this reason, perceived barriers to AET have belonged to traditional research subjects of adult education research since their first conceptualisation by Patricia Cross (1981) in the early 1980s. In line with this research tradition (e.g., Darkenwald & Valentine, 1985; Valentine & Darkenwald, 1990; Hovdhaugen & Opheim, 2018; Roosmaa & Saar, 2017; Saar et al., 2023; Van Nieuwenhove & De Wever, 2021, 2023), participation constraints are understood as perceived barriers that include three main types of barriers: (1) *dispositional barriers*, which are related to attitudes and self-efficacy of adults towards AET; (2) *institutional barriers*, covering the educational opportunities and support for potential learner or their lack off; and (3) *situational barriers*. This type includes factors hindering adults' participation that are directly related to their social roles and obligations (e.g., family or civic obligations)

Table 1.1 Taxonomy of AET

Adult education and training (AET)					
Formal adult education (FAE)			Non-formal adult education (NFE)	
Adult basic education (ABE)	Adult general education (AGE)	Adult higher education (AHE)	Adult liberal education (ALE)	Non-formal vocational education (NFE-Voc)
Compensatory adult education	Both compensatory and complementary adult education	Both compensatory and complementary adult education	Both compensatory and complementary adult education	Complementary adult education

or physical state (e.g., health). These barriers have the utmost importance in CE countries because they have had a higher occurrence than in other regions, such as Scandinavia or Western Europe (Roosmaa & Saar, 2017; Saar et al., 2023). For example, according to some analysis (Boeren et al., 2017; CEDEFOP, 2016), provision of ABE and AGE in CE countries is limited and not financially supported. A big part of disadvantaged adults is in a position where they cannot afford to improve their qualifications even to the basic or lower secondary level (ISCED 1–2).

1.7 Central Europe: Spatial-Temporal Framework

The specificity of the following analysis is based on its spatial-temporal framework in the form of CE ALSs and the selected period of 1989–2019. To this framework, this book understands CE as a region located in the central part of the European continent, sometimes called Visegrad countries, including Poland, Czechia, Slovakia and Hungary. One of the critical defining features of CE is its diversity. The region is home to a wide range of cultures and educational traditions and has a unique blend of influences from Western and Eastern Europe. Although some broader definitions (Večerník, 2022) subsume Austria into this region, my research sticks with a narrow delineation (Avlijaš, 2022; Berend, 2009; Magnin & Nenovsky, 2022; Szelewa & Polakowski, 2022) of contemporary CE that highlights shared post-socialist heritage, that has not been typical for Austria. Another defining characteristic of CE is its economic development after 1989. The region has undergone a significant economic transformation in recent decades, with many countries transitioning from socialist economies to market-based systems. This has led to rapid economic and social dynamics and the building of many new institutions, including those responsible for organised learning.

CE region is purposefully chosen for analysis of the interaction between ALS and AET because it can represent a 'negative case study' (Mahoney & Goertz, 2004) when testing the benefits of recent attempts to formulate various typologies of ALSs. Despite fruitful academic interest in the political economy of ALSs, contemporary research elaborates mainly on the development of institutional frameworks in North-West Europe (e.g., UK, Germany, Denmark, Sweden, Switzerland), East Asia (e.g., Japan, Taiwan) and in the USA (see e.g., 2017; Desjardins; & Ioannidou, 2020; Geiss, 2020; Ioannidou & Parma, 2022; Lee & Desjardins, 2019; Schemmann et al., 2020; Walker, 2020). In the same manner, other theoretical approaches to institutional factors influencing one's participation in AET focus on the same geographical regions (Busemeyer, 2015; Busemeyer & Trampusch, 2012; Verdier, 2017, 2018).

To this date, only a few studies (Holford et al., 2008; Riddell et al., 2012; Saar et al., 2013a, b, 2014, 2023; Roosma & Saar, 2017; Boeren et al., 2017) have attempted to catch structural features and functions of institutions that influence AET in CE countries. However, if these works elaborated on this issue, they have only developed essential characteristics of particular countries based on the limited

1.7 Central Europe: Spatial-Temporal Framework

empirical data from one international survey—mainly the *Adult Education Survey* (AES) from 2007 and 2011 or the *Programme for the International Assessment of Adult Competencies (PIAAC) from 2012*. Although these surveys enhance our knowledge of ALSs and their impact on AET, they tend to focus on analysing only one or two CE states or creating a formal/ideal typology of CE ALSs. On the contrary, my work would like to go beyond that and do both, examine ALSs in all CE countries and formulate their empirical grounded historical reconstruction.

Furthermore, previous studies in the field have not mapped the developmental paths of the CE ALSs—their linkages from socialist to post-socialist institutional clusters, as well as their most recent development after 2012. During these latter phases, they have been strongly influenced by the EU's project to construct European educational space by the '*Europeanization*' of policy-making in the sphere of adult education (Milana & Holford, 2014; Holford, 2023; Holford & Milana, 2023) and by new developmental trends inside capitalist economies (Hay, 2020; May et al., 2019; Schedelik et al., 2020). Notably, the process of *liberalisation* (Thelen, 2014), accompanied by a more intense involvement of the private sector in AET (Desjardins & Ioannidou, 2020; Rubenson, 2018) and *deindustrialisation* that has shaped the labour market, required skills and the strength of crucial political actors responsible for ALSs (Boix, 2019; Iversen & Soskice, 2019; Wren, 2013).

To conclude, previous studies have not explored the long-term formation that is immensely important in terms of the development trajectories of social institutions (Hall & Thelen, 2009; Mahoney, 2001; Pierson, 2000) as well as the most recent trends that CE countries have faced. Based on that, the following analysis helps us understand how (1) the combination of unique internal—"divergent"—forces in CE countries after 1989 (e.g., the post-socialist institutional heritage of robust educational systems, semi-skilled production regimes, deconstruction of the welfare state and skill mismatches in the labour market) has intervened into the formation trajectories of local ALSs; (2) these systems were modified by external—"convergent"—factors in the form of liberalisation, Europeanization, expansion of Higher Education (HE) system and deindustrialisation.

In this regard, this book argues that while the first-mentioned set of factors influenced their early formation paths during the 1990s, the latter affected their trajectories after 2000. Nevertheless, it does not mean that the long-lasted consequence of the initial institutional setting disappears, nor that it has lost its effect on AET in CE countries. Both have enormously impacted the supply and demand of organised learning even 20–30 years after they had been established.

Part II
Theory

Chapter 2
Typologies of ALS

This chapter reviews key theories that help us understand ALSs, participation in AET, and perceived barriers to adults' involvement in organised learning activities. My aim here is to develop a theoretical framework around *sensitising theoretical concepts* (Blumer, 1969) that aid in understanding the process of ALSs formation in CE and to identify *mechanisms* (Tilly, 2006, 2008) that can help us explain trends and patterns of participation in AET and related barriers in those countries.

In the first step, the chapter provides a critical review of current approaches to ALSs, as well as their theoretical and empirical relevance and applicability for studying the formation pathways of ALSs in CE countries. Based on that, the following text presents a basic theoretical framework that connects previous work from the *political economy of adult education and historical institutionalism*. After that, the chapter examines key current explanations behind participation levels and patterns in AET, including global trends in the provision of education since the 1990s. The findings from this section will be informative in a later discussion of specific features of organised learning among CE ALSs. Finally, my analysis provides an overview of the current state of the art regarding perceived barriers to AET, including findings from CE countries.

Although current adult education research agrees on the idea that adult participation in AET is bounded by broader structural conditions in which adults live (Boeren, 2016, 2023; Blossfeld et al., 2020; Cabus et al., 2020; Kureková et al., 2023), there is less agreement on the nature of those conditions (Desjardins & Ioannidou, 2020). As was discussed in the previous chapter, AET is *unevenly embedded in various social institutions*, and as a result, they may be influenced by various institutional clusters, namely the configuration of the formal education system, the type of welfare state institutions, or key economic features related to employees' training and workforce preparation.

For these reasons, it has not been easy to answer the crucial question of how and to what extent ALSs differ from one another. In attempting to address this issue, scholarship on ALSs has primarily focused on identifying key institutional

© The Author(s), under exclusive license to Springer Nature Switzerland AG 2024
J. Kalenda, *Formation of Adult Learning Systems in Central Europe*, Lifelong Learning Book Series 32, https://doi.org/10.1007/978-3-031-59827-2_2

conditions that influence the nature of the provision and coordination of organised learning. Identifying these characteristics is seen as an essential prerequisite for any comparative understanding of adult education models around the world.

2.1 Two Theoretical Approaches to ALSs

Since the 2000s, many researchers have investigated institutional aspects and contributed to the field by constructing (1) various typologies of institutions influencing AET (Blossfeld et al., 2020; Boeren, 2016, 2017; Busemeyer & Trampusch, 2012; Roosmaa & Saar, 2012, 2017) or (2) directly constructed typologies of ALSs (Desjardins, 2017; Green, 2006, 2011; Verdier 2017, 2018).

In the following section, my research argues that current theories of ALSs can be distinguished into two theoretical streams based on how they approach the construction of ALSs typologies: (1) *typologies built from above* and (2) *typologies built from below*. These two streams represent different theoretical traditions of understanding ALSs. The first, typologies built from above, tend to concentrate on the institutions within which *ALS is embedded* and draw from theories from other social science disciplines, like sociology, comparative politics and political economy. They tend to understand ALSs as an outcome of the structural characteristics of different institutions and their combination, such as welfare state regimes, types of a capitalist economy, or VET systems. ALSs are generally understood here as a "volume of participation" in AET or the levels of inequality connected to this phenomenon.

On the other hand, typologies built from below focus more directly on the *nature of ALSs themselves* and their internal components and pay less attention to the broader structural conditions. In addition, it also puts more emphasis on the various features of ALSs, such as the power relationships between key stakeholders, modes of provision, and coordination between them, as well as the related volume of AET and their change over time. This does not necessarily mean that the first type completely ignores the (internal) structural features of ALSs or that the second type turns a blind eye to surrounding institutional packages, but rather that they tend to follow the logic described above and treat the other factors as secondary.

The chapter advocates that using this new (alternative) approach to the classification of ALSs theories has several advantages. At least, it allows us to accomplish three things.[1] First, it enables us to show problematic theoretical assumptions and empirical inadequacy of typologies constructed from above as a mode of theorising about ALSs, especially in relation to the temporal domain of these systems. Second, it demonstrates the vast potential of an alternative approach to ALSs theory construction, such as building theories from below using principles of abduction in the

---

[1] Different approaches to classification of ALSs can be found in Desjardins and Ioannidou (2020), Holford and Mleczko (2010), Lee (2017), Saar et al. (2013a, b), Saar et al. (2023).

form of the interaction between sensitive theoretical concepts and available empirical data (Timmermans & Tavory, 2012; Alvesson & Kärvana, 2011), as well as a reorientation toward institutional change rather than institutional equilibrium. Following Mahoney and Thelen (2015), my argumentation highlights that temporal analysis should be at the centre of attention in studying social institutions like ALSs or AET. Third, it assists us in introducing a theoretical model—as a set of sensitive theoretical concepts and mechanisms—that draws from the tradition of typologies built from below, which will be used in our empirical research.

2.1.1 Typologies Built from Above

Formal Education Systems and AET

The first framework that has been frequently utilised for understanding cross-country variations between ALSs is the *formal education approach*. According to Verdier (2018) and Saar et al. (2013a, b), it has been taken from the comparative sociology of education. Behind its employment, we can find an idea that every ALS is deeply rooted in a country's (initial) formal education system. This is due to the fact that the formal education system shapes learners' educational paths from the start and establishes the foundation for their future needs in AET. If the formal education system is not flexible and open to non-traditional students, and does not provide enough 'second chances' for them to supplement their initial education, inequalities in access to AET among adults may increase (e.g., Boeren, 2016; Lee, 2017). Some research has also suggested that characteristics of the formal education system may influence the extent to which employers invest in their employees' NFE, particularly in terms of job-related skills (Brunello et al., 2007).

According to many authors (Green, 2011; Lee, 2017; Saar et al., 2013a, b), we can characterise formal education system in relation to AET by two key dimensions: (1) standardisation of education and (2) stratification of VET, that were first introduced by a German sociologist Allmendinger (1989). Table 2.1 shows the main types of educational regimes regarding adult formal education. *Standardisation*

Table 2.1 Typology of formal education systems in advanced industrial democracies

Standardisation of education	High	School oriented model (FRA, ITA, CE and EE countries)	Dual education model—work-based system during initial education (GER, AUT, DEN)
	Low	On-the-job-oriented model (UK, USA)	Theoretical vocational model—VET training in schools (NED, SWE)
		Low	High
		Stratification of formal education (VET)	

Source: Base on Allmendinger (1989), Blossfeld (1992), Blossfeld and Stockman (1998, 1999), Green (1991)

refers to the extent to which identical standards are applied in a given country or group of countries (e.g., the EU) for accreditation or recognition of educational programs. *Stratification,* on the other hand, refers to the degree to which various parts of secondary education within the formal education system are separated from one another. This includes separating initial basic education, which focuses on developing general skills, from VET, which is dedicated to preparation for a specific profession.

Ellu Saar and Bjørn Ure (2013) argued that standardisation's effect on participation in AET begins to play a significant role if it reaches a high level. In this regard, a certificate of the highest attained education becomes an essential prerequisite for obtaining a job. At the same time, a high degree of standardisation of initial education reduces the need for supplementary NFE in workplace settings, which should balance employees' diverse and potentially unequal entry skills (Kilpi-Jakonen et al., 2015). In contrast, the opposite direction can be observed in countries with a low standardisation level, such as Nederlands. As an outcome, participation in job-oriented NFE should be high in ALSs with a low level of standardisation. However, this does not necessarily mean that the involvement of adults in all types of organised learning should always be elevated. A high degree of standardisation also contributes to the fact that certified outputs of AET, mainly AHE and ABE, have significant social relevance and encourage adults to return to the formal education system.

The *stratification* of the education system is responsible for the extent to which initial and further education complements each other and to what extent they serve as a substitute for each other (Wolbers, 2005). While highly stratified educational systems (e.g. Germany, Switzerland) have strictly separated general education and VET, systems with a low level of stratification (e.g. Sweden, USA and UK) have more permeable boundaries. They assume that the development of specific job-related skills should only take place after the initial, general phase of education (Saar et al., 2013a, b; Kilpi-Jakonen et al., 2015). According to this argumentation, highly stratified educational systems should have lower requirements for AET and contribute to its smaller overall volume. On the other hand, educational systems with opposite characteristics require more AET after the initial formal education in the form of NFE in the workplace. As an effect, they should contribute to more frequent participation in organised learning of adults (Lee & Desjardins, 2021).

In conclusion, the formal education system should shape the landscape of adult learning through the effect of two main institutional arrangements. Firstly, it should directly influence the volume of FAE in a particular country. Countries with more advanced, open, and standardised formal educational systems should tend to have higher volumes and better access to FAE opportunities. This thesis has been supported by previous literature using data from international comparative surveys conducted in the mid-2000s (Kilpi-Jakonen et al., 2015) and mid-2010s (Lee, 2017). From the perspective of ALS, countries that systematically develop their FAE tend to have a higher level of state involvement in AET, including a coordination role and public expenditure on organised learning.

Secondly, the formal education system should indirectly influence the volume of NFE through the stratification of initial education. However, this thesis *has not been empirically validated*. Investigations using data from the 2000s (Dämmrich et al., 2014; Roosmaa & Saar, 2012; Saar et al., 2014) and 2010s (Lee, 2017) did not find support for this thesis. One possible explanation for this finding is that the volume of NFE has grown so much across both stratified and non-stratified formal educational systems that this feature of the institutional package has started to lose its relevance. The rise of job-oriented NFE and employer-sponsored training in most countries (Lee & Desjardins, 2019; Desjardins, 2020; Rubenson, 2018) has diminished its effects on the total volume of AET provision.

Moreover, it is important to note that the formal education approach has limitations in terms of understanding the formation and development of ALSs in CE countries. This is partly because *only a small proportion of participation in these countries depends strictly on the formal education system*, and partly because previous literature wrongly assumed that CE countries, due to their highly standardised and low-stratified education systems, would have low levels of supplementary NFE in the workplace. In fact, NFE is the most common form of organised learning in CE countries (Csanádi et al., 2014; Kalenda et al., 2020; Vaculíková et al., 2021), very similar to countries with low-standardized systems. I believe that this highlights the importance of considering the unique context and characteristics of each country when studying ALSs and the need for a more nuanced and complex approach to understanding the factors that shape them.

Welfare State Regime Typology and AET

The conception of the *Welfare State Regime* (WSR) from the ground-breaking work of Esping-Andersen (1990, 1998) is commonly used in the adult education field as a typology for understanding ALSs. This approach suggests that AET is closely linked to the institutions of the WSR in a particular country. This is because much of the publicly funded organised learning is either part of active labour market policy (ALMP) or a broader strategy of pursuing social peace and cohesion (e.g., provision of second chance ABE, AGE or AHE provided by a formal educational system). In other words, it should be deeply embedded in welfare state institutions and their public goals (Schröder, 2009, 2013).

Based on two crucial features, Esping-Andersen (1998) distinguished between three ideal-typical models of WSR. On the one hand, it is the level of union organisation measured by union density (i.e., percentage of *union members on the total number of employees*). On the other hand, it is a prevalence of social democratic (left-oriented) parties in a government. Both these characteristics predispose a particular country to build distinct settings of welfare policy. This theoretical argumentation is originally borrowed from previous Korpi's (1983) study of industrial relations, which pointed out that the more advanced the organising capacity of the labour movement is, the more developed WSR becomes.

Following these aspects, Esping-Andersen (1990, 1998) created three basic types of WSR:

1. *The social democratic model*, which is characterised by high levels of union organisation (density rates over 60%) and the dominance of social democratic parties. Countries such as Sweden, Denmark, and Finland are typical examples of this model. These countries have highly interventionist and costly social security systems that provide a broad range of de-commodified services to various social groups across the population.
2. *The Christian democratic model* is characterised by lower levels of union organisation (density rates between 20% and 40%) and a lower prevalence of left-oriented parties. Germany and Austria are typical examples of this model, which has an average size and level of spending on welfare systems and provides social services that are not universally available to all members of society but rather based on social status and earnings.
3. *The liberal model*, which is typical of weak unions (density rates under 15%) and a lack of or minor presence of social democratic parties (e.g., UK, USA). This model relies on limited measures to support social policy and depends on individuals' social security and the self-regulating function of the market. Social services are heavily commodified in this model.

Empirical Support

The idea of possible outcomes of national WSRs has formed the foundation of many comparative analyses in the field of adult education. For instance, Rubenson and Desjardins (2009) have used it to explain the different participation rates in AET among EU countries, as well as to understand different types of perceived constraints. Drawing on data from the IALS from the mid-1990s and the AES 2007, they argued that Scandinavian countries with a typical social democratic model of WSR provide their citizens with more support for accessing organised learning opportunities than other types of WSR.

This is because Scandinavian countries have implemented more social policy measures that target the public provision of AET for all social groups, including those at risk (e.g., unemployed, low-educated/low-skilled workers, migrants, and the elderly). Additionally, they have also provided more general support to adults in both the workplace (support of NFE inside companies) and outside the job market, for instance, support for family care (Dieckhoff et al., 2007; Rubenson, 2006; Rubenson & Desjardins, 2009). These policy tools have helped remove barriers to participation in AET in everyday life. Overall, the social democratic model appears to have better-resolved coordination problems related to AET (Desjardins & Rubenson, 2013; Ure & Aaslid, 2013).

The WSR approach to ALSs is particularly effective in explaining the overall level of inequality in AET provision and differences in participation among adults at risk. Empirical research (Dämmrich et al., 2014; Desjardins, 2017, 2020; Lee,

2017; Roosmaa & Saar, 2012, 2017; Rubenson & Desjardins, 2009) strongly supports the notion that the *social democratic model*, with a broad repertoire of social policy measures, *better supports AET than WSRs with less expenditure on ALMPs and less systematic policy targeting potential learners.*

However, the original Esping-Andersen framework is not optimal in answering two related empirical questions that are vital for the investigation of ALSs formation in CE. The first is why the overall volume of AET has grown in all types of ALSs despite vast differences in WSRs. To this question, we have seen a rise in the provision of AET across all types of WSRs. Based on the data from the PIAAC survey or AES 2016, there has been only a small difference between countries with the social democratic and the liberal type of WSR (Saar & Räis, 2017). This empirical trend, visible in international comparative surveys since the 2010s, requires an assessment that goes beyond this framework. The second question is, what is the pattern of WSR in CE countries that have only started building democratic WSRs in the 1990s? According to many authors (Bohle & Geskovirts, 2007, 2012; Cerami & Vanhuysee, 2009; Saar & Ure, 2013; Saar et al., 2013a, b, 2023), their WSRs differ significantly from Esping Andersen's typology. Therefore, they need their own theoretical conceptualisation regarding an impact not only on social cohesion but on AET as well.

To address these questions, scholars have proposed modifications to the original Esping-Andersen framework. For example, Busemeyer and Trampusch (2012) developed a typology of skill formation systems that combines the VoC approach with formal educational approaches, specifically the stratification of VET. Their view provides more insight into the differences between various models of job-oriented NFE and FAE coordination. Roosmaa and Saar (2012, 2017) also expanded upon the VoC and Esping-Andersen's framework by introducing a new type of capitalism (Dependent Market Economy) and three specific modalities of WSRs for CE and EE countries. These types of WSRs offer different approaches to balancing social cohesion and economic liberalisation in conditions of post-socialist societies.

Variety of Capitalism Typology and AET

The third approach to ALSs is based on the neo-institutional economic perspective (Chavance, 2008) that is widely applied in comparative political science and political economy. Its core ideas were outlined by Hall and Soskice (2001) in their seminal work, *"Variety of Capitalism: The institutional foundations of comparative advantage."* In contrast to the WSR approach, the Variety of Capitalism (VoC) theoretical framework shifts the focus from public, social security and protection institutions to the private sector, specifically the interlinkages between companies and other institutional packages. This does not mean that public institutions are ignored in the VoC approach; they still have an important place as one of the crucial institutional domains (Iversen & Soskice, 2019; Iversen & Stephens, 2008; Schröder, 2009). However, the primary ontological and *analytical unit is the company.*

Therefore, the VoC approach may help to understand better phenomena related to AET in the company/work-related setting, particularly NFE and vocationally-oriented HE, than the WSR approach. The same could be said for aspects of ALSs that are directly connected with employer-sponsored or employer-realised training activities.

Hall and Soskice (2001; see also Hall, 2006, 2007) proposed two main types of capitalism: (1) *Liberal Market Economies* (LMEs) and (2) *Coordinated Market Economies* (CMEs). Each of these represents a different institutional configuration that creates specific conditions for companies' strategies and development. Although each type operates on a different logic, Thelen (2014) argued that both are stable, even when facing new challenges and strains. The stability is based on a stable set of institutional configurations across five domains that tend to support one another. This mutual reinforcement is referred to as *"institutional complementarity"* by scholars within the VoC approach (Hall, 2006, 2007; Hall & Soskice, 2001; Hall & Gingerich, 2009; Thelen, 2014). The particular domains include (1) companies needs, (2) a system of corporate governance, (3) industrial relations, (4) a system of inter-company relations, and (5) education and training systems, which is most relevant for understanding the possible effects on cross-national patterns of AET coordination.

Liberal Market Economies and ALS

In LMEs, it is typical for governments and other stakeholders (e.g., trade unions and other intermediate associations) to be minimally involved in the coordination of the economy. Countries such as the USA, Canada, Ireland and the UK are common examples of this economic pattern. Its leading internal logic is based on the so-called *"low road"* of competitiveness (Crouch & Streeck, 1997), which is characterised by low expenditure on the labour force and minimal protection. In this context, pressure for product and service innovation is weak, and the state usually provides public support only for general primary and secondary education. The labour market is highly flexible in LMEs, which prompts individuals to invest in general skills that are easier to transfer across different companies. The education and training system is generally oriented towards the provision of non-specialised skills (Hall & Soskice, 2001).

In the context of lifelong learning, we can see that the institutional characteristics of LMEs should lead to weak requirements for highly-specific job-related skills, which are necessary to enter the labour market. On the other hand, there should also be a low requirement for upgrading these skills—upskilling and reskilling. Therefore, the high volume of intensive AET focused on job-related specific skills does not make sense on the system level of LMEs because the labour force is easily replaceable and the priority is given to minimising expenses for it (Estevez-Abe et al., 2001). There may also be a greater emphasis on individuals taking responsibility for their own learning and development rather than expecting the state or employers to provide learning opportunities. Additionally, there may be less investment in public AET programs, particularly in AHE and BAE, with a greater reliance on private providers and individuals paying for their own education and training. Based on this, we can deduce that LMEs should not only have a higher level of inequality in AET access but also not contribute to high participation rates of adults in organised learning.

Beyond that, the nature of LMEs also provides specific preconditions for the formation of ALSs. In these circumstances, we can expect that the ALSs will be underdeveloped, with minimal involvement from the state, low levels of coordination, and decentralisation of AET providers. Most of the supply of AET will be concentrated in private hands, including professional training agencies and larger companies. In line with this, public expenditure on any type of vocationally oriented, especially FAE will be minimal.

Coordinated Market Economies and ALS

CMEs are characterised by a much higher level of involvement by the state, trade unions, and professional organisations in intra- and inter-company relations. Countries such as Germany, Sweden, and the Netherlands, which belong to CMEs, are typically economically advanced and build their competitiveness strategy based on the so-called *"high-road"* (Crouch & Streeck, 1997) of competitiveness. This strategy focuses on producing technologically demanding products with high added value. However, for its successful implementation, both a higher level of workforce skills and the associated higher labour costs are necessary. In addition to these characteristics, the state and trade unions in CMEs more often intervene in inter-company relations, resulting in a higher level of labour protection. The combination of these factors leads employers in these economies to rely more on their own employees, who are difficult to replace and to invest more in their skills (Estevez-Abe et al., 2001).

In CMEs, AET is often seen as a means not only for promoting economic competitiveness and productivity but also social cohesion and equity. As a result, these systems tend to place a strong emphasis on initial VET, as well as continuous AET for the development of professional skills. The state often plays a central role in coordinating and funding AET initiatives, particularly in the areas of VET and continuing professional development. CMEs also tend to have strong systems of labour market regulation and social protection, which can support the involvement of adults in organised forms of learning (Estevez-Abe et al., 2001). Moreover, workers in these systems are encouraged to invest in sectoral-specific or company-specific skills.

Overall, the key implications of CMEs for AET are a focus on vocational-oriented AET, a strong role for the state in shaping and supporting AET policies, and a commitment to lifelong learning and the development of professional skills. Based on this, we can assume that ALS will have a higher level of centralisation as well as more intensive coordination. Most of the supply of AET will be concentrated in public hands or in institutions, which employer associations, trade unions, and the state jointly manage. Following this argument, public expenditure on enhancement of labour-market-focused skills, especially in FAE, will be high.

As a result, there are should be better structural conditions for participation in AET in CMEs and a lower level of inequality in access to AET provision.

Empirical Support

The empirical research of the last decade has provided only *"weak support"* (Saar & Räis, 2017, p. 541) for some of the theoretical claims of the VoC approach through the publication of a body of evidence. Scholars (Dämmrich et al., 2014, 2015; Lee, 2017; Saar & Räis, 2017; Roosmaa & Saar, 2017) who have used data from AES from 2007 and PIAAC from 2012 have identified minor differences between CMEs and LMEs in terms of overall participation and its patterns (i.e., levels of inequality between various social groups). In this context, CMEs generally have reported slightly higher levels of participation in AET than LMEs, as well as slightly lower levels of inequality.

However, this generalised statement needs three important corrections. First, the differences between them are more significant in the case of FAE than NFE, so it can be argued that this finding is likely due to the influence of the formal education system rather than the logic of the economy and whether FAE is considered as a public good, rather than being purchased as a private good in the market (Bukodi et al., 2018).

Second, the variations between them are more visible when looking over time. Based on data from IALS 1994–1997 or PIAAC, mild differences in overall participation in AET according to the binary logic of VoC can be seen. As a result, there has been a decrease in the disparity in participation between LMEs and CMEs (see Table 2.2). In the 2010s, a difference between CMEs and LMEs was, on average, five percentage points, and both types have similar annual growth.

Third, the differences between LMEs and CMEs vary depending on the countries included in the analysis. For example, if Denmark, Sweden, and Norway are taken as representative examples of CMEs, they may outperform LMEs such as the UK and the US. However, if Germany, Austria, and other "problematic" (Ebenau, 2012, p. 208) and "ambiguous" (Hall & Soskice, 2001, p. 21) representatives of CMEs, like Belgium or France, are included, the results are less conclusive.

These empirical issues within CMEs, we can title *"Iversen and Soskice's problem"* (Iversen & Soskice, 2001; see also Iversen & Stephens, 2008). Authors have spotted that intragroup differences in CME countries are in concern of skill formation or human capital formation too big that only the incorporation of another set of mechanisms—welfare policy and its measures—can explain them. Following the previously discussed Esping-Andersen schema, they divided CMEs into two camps—coordinated economies with Christian democratic WSR (e.g., Austria and Germany) and those who have social democratic WSR (Scandinavian countries). Such a distinction highlights that the lower level of inequality in Northern European countries may be more the result of a specific type of WSR and its ALMPs than an outcome of companies' training and development strategy. As a result, the following scholars (Busemeyer & Trampusch, 2012; Roosmaa & Saar, 2012, 2017) have

2.1 Two Theoretical Approaches to ALSs

Table 2.2 Participation in LME and CME countries: 1997 to 2012

	Countries	IALS 1994–1997	PIAAC 2010–2012	Annual growth
LMEs	UK	48	55	1.1
	IRL	22	50	4.2
	USA	42	59	1.9
	CAN	37	57	3.0
	Average	38	55	1.1
CMEs	NED	36	64	1.9
	DEN	56	56	0
	BEL	21	48	1.8
	NOR	40	64	1.6
	SWE	53	65	0.8
	FIN	58	65	0.6
	Average	44	60	1.1

Note: Data in percent. Participation measured as involvement of adults in any AET in the 12 months prior to survey
Source: IALS (1997), OECD (2000), PIAAC (2012)

proposed an institutional typology incorporating more institutional packages to explain the volume and distribution of organised learning.

Enlarged Model of WSR and VoC

According to Saar et al. (2013a, b), the inclusion of CE and EE countries in the previously discussed typologies is problematic. Due to their institutional features and the massive transformation that occurred after the fall of the Berlin Wall, accompanied by a transition from a state-planned socialist to a free-market capitalist economy, these countries do not perfectly fit the proposed models of capitalism or WSR. Based on this, the authors argue that the nation-specific institutional packages of CE and EE countries that emerged in the 1990s have affected local ALSs differently and led to unexpected outcomes in terms of overall participation in AET and policy-making in the 2010s.

Building on this point, Roosmaa and Saar (2012, 2017, see also Saar & Ure, 2013) developed their own widely used (Boeren et al., 2017; Milana & Vatrella, 2020; Saar et al., 2023) typology of ALSs that combines the VoC approach and classical Esping-Andersen's (1990, 1998) WSR typology. In addition to this theoretical fusion, they enhanced these concepts by introducing a new type of capitalism as well as three novel modalities of WSR.

Specifically, drawing on the popular contribution of Nölke and Vliegenthart (2009) regarding "enlarging the variety of capitalism," the authors added the so-called *dependent market economy* (DME) to the basic typology of market economies. They argue that this unique type of economy better reflects the key institutional features of CE and EE countries than LMEs or CMEs because it emphasises the dependency of these economic systems on foreign enterprises. In addition to a strong dependence on foreign capital as the primary source of investment, DMEs are characterised by corporate governance under the hierarchical control of transnational companies' headquarters, which becomes the central coordination mechanism in DMEs, in contrast to markets and contractual relations in LMEs or networks and associations in CMEs. Additionally, the position of employees in DMEs appears to be weaker than in CMEs, as transnational corporations look for a low-cost but skilled labour force. However, labour legislation is less flexible in DMEs than in LMEs in order to avoid high social inequality and conflicts. Therefore, a decentralised wage bargaining organisation at the firm level is likely to be widespread among DME countries (Magnin & Nenovsky, 2022).

In the educational sector, low taxation to attract foreign capital results in limited government spending on education, which further inhibits the development of a high level of basic skills, as in LMEs. Additionally, according to Nölke and Vliegenthart (2009), transnational organisations are not motivated to invest heavily in enhancing adults' skills due to the industrial specialisation of DMEs. In conclusion, DMEs represent a comparative advantage for CE and EE countries as they can produce relatively complex and durable goods (primarily in the automotive and consumer electronics sectors) for export.

In addition to DMS, Roosmaa and Saar (2012, 2017) also integrated three new types of WSRs that emerged across CE in the first two decades after 1989. Borrowing from the analysis of Bohle and Greskovits (2007, 2012), they distinguished: (1) *post-socialist, neoliberal*; (2) *post-socialist, embedded neoliberal*; and (3) *post-socialist, Balkan* WSR. Each of these shows a different approach to balancing social cohesion and the liberalisation of the economy. Post-socialist, neoliberal WSR (e.g., Baltic countries) typically involve radical liberalisation with minimal investment in social services, while embedded neoliberal regimes (e.g., CE countries) dedicate more resources to welfare state measures. In contrast, Balkan WSRs are underdeveloped due to the weak position of the state and its limited financial resources.

As shown in Tables 2.3 and 2.4, Roosma and Saar's (2012, 2017) enlarged version of the European ALSs typology runs at two institutional levels. The first level is the market economy, which sets a general characteristic of capitalism, including economic and corporate governance, innovation transfer, industrial relations, and general features of education and training systems. Like the VoC approach, this level dictates the broader socio-economic conditions for organised educational activities. The second level is the WSR, which specifies the country-specific approach to mitigating social inequality, including ALMP and the main features of AET. This second level differentiates the structural outcomes of the market economy on AET through governmental interventions and the development of welfare policy measures.

While the categorisation of Western European ALSs more or less corresponds to previous typologies (see Table 2.3) known from VoC approach (Hall & Soskice, 2001; Estevez-Abe et al., 2001; Iversen & Soskice, 2001), ALSs in CE and EE

2.1 Two Theoretical Approaches to ALSs

Table 2.3 Western European ALS

Market economy	Liberal market economy (LME)	Coordinated market economy (CME)		
Economic Governance	Limited business coordination, antitrust laws	Strong business associations, inter-company networks		
Corporate governance	external control/dispersed shareholders	Internal control/concentrated shareholders		
Industrial relations	**Market based** Few collective agreements Decentralised bargaining Trade unions and employer associations are weak; low-cost hiring and firing	**Corporatist** Sector-wide and even national agreements Coordinated bargaining Statutory worker representation Strong trade unions and employer associations; employee cooperation in firms and wage moderation		
Education and training system	General competence			
	Initially employers invest little in human capital	Industry and/or company-specific competences Initially employers invest in human capital		
Transfer of innovations	Based on markets and formal contracts	Important role of joint ventures and business association		
Welfare state	Liberal	Social democratic	Conservative, continental	Southern Europe
Labour market policies	Minimal income protection	Generous income protection; Strongly developed active labour market policy	Good income protection; Medium developed active labour market policy	Medium income protection, less developed active labour market policy
Adult education and training	Relatively widespread, unevenly distributed, mostly in-company training	Prevalent, often subsidised by the state	Education and training provide appropriate skills. Comparatively low participation	Low participation, inequality in participation high
Country	United States, United Kingdom, Ireland, Canada, Australia, New Zealand	Sweden, Norway, Finland, Denmark	Germany, Austria, Belgium, The Netherlands, Switzerland	Greece, Spain, Portugal, Slovenia, Italy

Source: Adapted from Roosmaa and Saar (2012, pp. 481–482; 2017, p. 61; see also: Saar & Ure, 2013, pp. 68–69)

Table 2.4 Eastern European ALSs

Market economy	Dependent market economy (DME)		
Economic governance	Hierarchy within transnational corporations Control by headquarters of transnational enterprises		
Corporate governance	Company-level collective agreements Decentralised bargaining Trade unions and employer associations are weak		
Education and training system	Limited expenditures for further qualification		
Transfer of innovations	Intra-firm transfer within transnational enterprises		
Welfare state	Post-socialist, neoliberal	Post-socialist, embedded neoliberal	Post-socialist, Balkan
Labour market policies	Minimal income protection; less developed active labour market policy	Minimal income protection; less developed active labour market policy	Minimal income protection; less developed active labour market policy
Adult education	Participation on medium level, unevenly distributed	Participation quite low, inequality in participation quite low	Participation very low, inequality in participation quite high
Country	Baltic countries	Hungary, Czech Republic, Poland, Slovakia	Bulgaria, Croatia, Serbia

Source: Adapted from Roosmaa and Saar (2012, pp. 481–482; 2017, p. 61; Saar & Ure, 2013, pp. 68–69)

belong to new types of WSR. In particular, CE ALSs are constituted by post-socialist, embedded neoliberal WSR. Their key characteristics are included in Table 2.4.

Empirical Support

Roosmaa and Saar's (2012, 2017, see also Saar & Ure, 2013) enlarged version of the European typology of ALSs represents the most advanced theoretical conception of the embeddedness of ALSs. While it also covers CE countries and makes detailed distinctions between various ALSs systems, it still has some empirical pitfalls that are common for typologies built from above.

If we compare key theoretical claims (see Tables 2.3 and 2.4) about AET and compare them with the results of the PIAAC or the AES from 2016, we easily find that they are not empirically supported. For example, differences between members of conservative continental WSR (Austria vs. the Netherlands) are much larger than between them and another cluster of countries, such as liberal WSR (for detailed differences see e.g., Desjardins, 2020; Desjardins et al., 2016). Furthermore, participation in CE countries, with the exception of Poland, cannot be considered quite low as it used to be in the 1990s, because it has become as high as in the case of the most conservative continental and liberal WSR (Kalenda et al., 2020; Kalenda & Kočvarová, 2022a).

Also, Milana and Vatrela (2020), as well as Boeren et al. (2017), found *mixed* evidence to support the enlarged typology of WSR in the explanation of variations in policy tools and measures focused on AET of youth adults. For instance, Boren et al. (2017) argued that many countries within the same WSR differ from each other in the financial support of learners, the extent of workplace learning and post-secondary VET provisions accessibility for learners. Not to mention a role of the third sector, which appears to be another area of differentiation both between WSRs and between countries within the same WSR.

2.1.2 Critique of ALSs Typologies Built from Above

Although ALSs typologies built from above provide an exceptional tool for understanding broader structural conditions of AET, they are less persuasive in explanation of the key features of ALSs and their evolution over time. My research argues that it is due to two mutually reinforcing issues that are part of their theoretical logic and dominant heuristics—it is a problem of social change and the analytical unit.

The Problem of Social Change

Witt and Jackson (2016) pointed to the current empirical inadequacies of capitalism typologies, heavily used in adult education research, being partly a result of data utilisation from the mid-1990s or their "lack of" for constructing original models of VoC. According to Isakjee (2017), the same could be addressed to WSRs. Despite ALSs being embedded in the welfare system and country VET approach and companies' training needs, the key characteristics of these institutional clusters have changed over time and may have resulted in different forms of organised learning and their coordination.

As time has passed, it is unclear whether the characteristics that were assumed and measured in VoC and WSR approaches in the past are still applicable to particular countries today. As support for this argument, this part of the book presents a series of figures (Figs. 2.1, 2.2, 2.3 and 2.4) that depict key measurable characteristics of LMEs and CMEs that were originally utilised by Hall and Soskice (2001, pp. 18–21) to delineate both types of capitalism. According to Hall and Soskice (2001), the original VoC thesis posits that levels of paid employment are higher in LMEs and levels of social inequality, as measured by the GINI index, are also high in these economies. Figures 2.1 and 2.2 demonstrate shifts in the GINI index and levels of employment over time. The results show that while differences between CMEs and LMEs in terms of full-time equivalent employment were minor in the late 1990s, the main differences between the two clusters of countries were in terms of social inequality. The data suggests that while this distinction has not

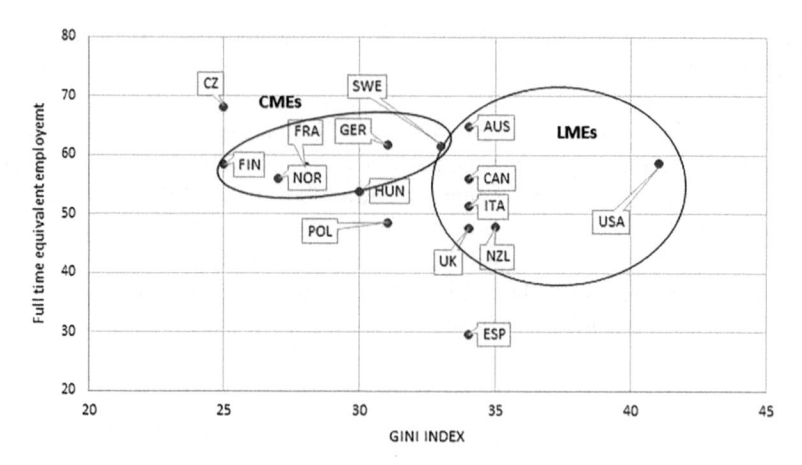

Fig. 2.1 Institutions in the subspheres of the political economy in the 1990s

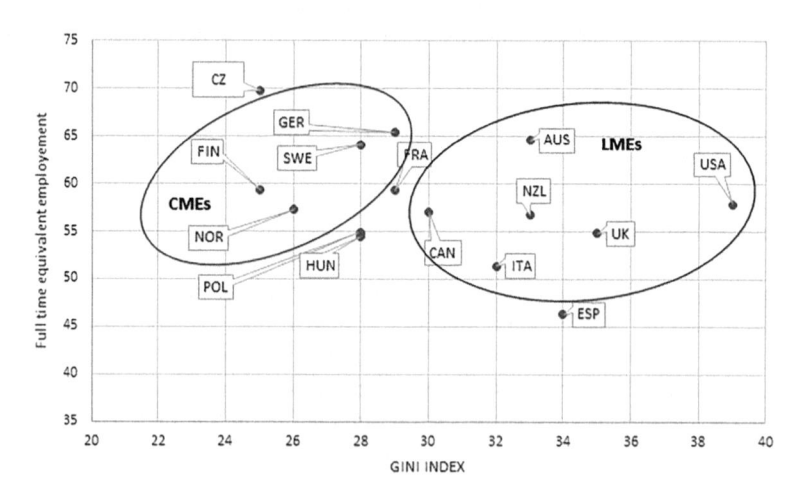

Fig. 2.2 Institutions in the subspheres of the political economy in the 2010s

disappeared, it was lower in the 2010s compared to two decades prior. Additionally, the analysis found that the level of social inequality has declined in LMEs.

In addition, Figs. 2.3 and 2.4 cover changes in indicators of corporate finance and the labour market. According to Hall and Soskice (2001), the first indicator reflects reliance on market modes of coordination in the financial sphere, while the second reflects levels of non-market coordination in the sphere of industrial relations. The data shows that in the 1990s, LMEs had very high market stock capitalisation and low employment protection levels, which significantly differentiated CMEs from LMEs. However, the analysis identified that during the 2010s, both modes of capitalism converged, with CMEs experiencing a decline in non-market coordination and an increase in market stock capitalisation, in many cases reaching the same levels as LMEs.

2.1 Two Theoretical Approaches to ALSs 31

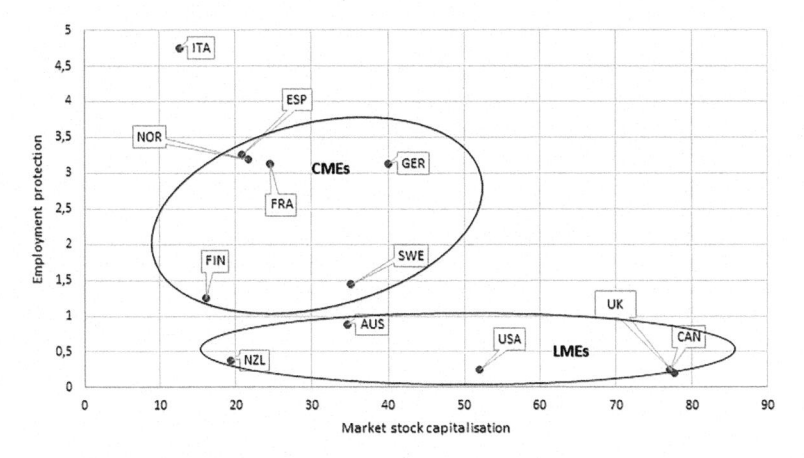

Fig. 2.3 Institutions in the subspheres of the political economy in the 1990s

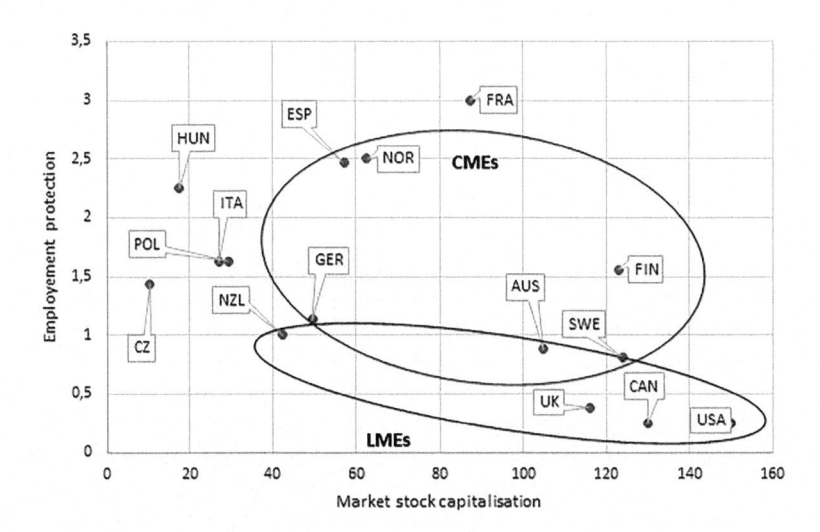

Fig. 2.4 Institutions in the subspheres of the political economy in the 2010s

Beyond that, many critics (Isakjee, 2017; Thelen, 2014) of these approaches have suggested that research should focus more on changes within these institutional domains rather than assuming their unchangeable, functionalist logic. There are two lines of thinking in this argument. One supposes that there are tendencies towards convergence between countries and their institutional packages, known as *institutional isomorphism* (DiMaggio & Powell, 1983), which assumes that all types of WSR and VoC will become more and more homogenous, and as a product, ALSs will also become more homogenous. Expand this argument further that uniformity will lead to similar institutional settings regarding cooperation and provision of AET, as well as similar levels of participation across countries.

The second line of thinking assumes that instead of homogenisation, it is more likely that will occur *hybridisation* (Verdier, 2017; Witt & Jackson, 2016) of institutional packages in the form of an unexpected (re)combination of original institutions with new features created in response to the main social challenges that countries face, including internal conflicts. As a consequence, new forms of institutional complementarities appear. In this regard, institutional complementarities:

> "[…] should be understood as political projects, not equilibrium outcomes. […] new hybrid configurations of institutions are no more stable configuration than more coherent configurations. Rather institutions change dynamically over time. […] These 'success models' of one era eventually run their course, often because the winners and losers of changing institutional arrangements push for further processes of institutional change (Witt & Jackson, 2016, p. 796).

From this point of view, ALSs should also be understood as a political project in the form of dynamically evolving institutions with possible unexpected recombinations. This option has been systematically elaborated by authors (Busemeyer & Trampusch, 2012; Verdier, 2017, 2018), who try to build typologies of education systems and ALSs from a perspective of their change with more attention to the temporal dimension of these systems.

The Problem of the Research Unit

Furthermore, this subchapter argues that the inability of current typologies adopted from comparative sociology, politics, and political economy to capture key empirical variations between ALSs is also due to a focus on factors that are not directly connected with the empirical structure of ALSs in a particular country. It is often observed that initial analytical and independent variables proposed to measure ALS are only loosely related and much broader than the measured aspects of AET—they are distinctive from social relations that directly constitute ALSs. For example, Dämmrich et al. (2014) and Blossfeld et al. (2020) found that various forms of AET are often influenced only by one institutional factor while others are not. In this regard, participation in NFE was positively influenced by public expenditure on education. However, other forms of AET, like surprisingly FAE, were not. As a result, proposed institutional conditions may not be specific enough to explain subtle changes in ALSs. As Desjardins and Ioannidou stated in this context:

> […] empirical cross-national pattern on the level of participation in organised adult learning do not neatly line up with the typologies […] This suggests a need to take account of specific institutional features, that are more proximally related to organised adult learning (Desjardins & Ioannidou 2020, p. 152).

For this reason, even if countries share similar conditions (e.g., welfare state expenditures or company strategies regarding HRD), they may differ significantly in the structure of providers of AET and the demand for organised adult learning that alter causal sequence. These internal characteristics may not only better explain the differences between ALSs themselves and establish their classification, but they may also give a better understanding of the effects of ALSs on participation in AET and related coordination problems. Accordingly, it is crucial to first focus on available data that can be used to construct empirically grounded characteristics of ALSs and their relationships to other institutional domains, specifically their embeddedness—for example, systematically assessing the structure of AET providers in a particular country or the perceived demand for AET from both adult learners and employers' perspectives.

In the following part of the text, my analysis highlights that theories and typologies built from below are able to better cope with these two issues, and therefore they may represent better theoretical apparatus for understanding long-term formation of ALSs.

2.1.3 Typologies Built From Below

The upcoming chapter contains recent scholarly contributions that have dealt primarily with the developmental aspects of ALS or put more emphasis on the internal empirical features of ALS—i.e., two main building blocks of heuristics of theories built from below.

Skill Formation Systems Typology

The first insight of this approach is Busemeyer and Trampusch's (2012) work about skill formation regimes. Contrary to previous attempts from WSR or formal educational approach, they primarily concentrated on elaborating historical development in the construction of skill-formation system. Their perspective employed a *dynamic model of institutional change* inspired by historical institutionalism (Hall & Thelen, 2009; Thelen, 2007, 2014), which emphasises the long-term, contingent transformation in institutional packages, rather than viewing them as static, self-reinforcing, or tending towards equilibrium. Instead, they are seen as "temporary and contested solutions to ongoing conflicts" (Busemeyer & Trumpsch, 2012, p. 4). By focusing on the aspect of social change, this approach helps to understand educational systems not as fixed but rather as ongoing "redesign" (Ibid., 2012, p. 4) of institutional arrangements. This dynamic notion is important in considering the ways in which institutional packages and ALSs may change over time in response to various influences and conflicts. For instance, in countries where there is high structural unemployment and a need to reskill a large portion of the population or when there is a wave of migration that puts pressure on cultural integration and language training for refugees.

Following this analytical framework, they proposed typology of various skill formation systems based on examination of the relationships between VET and the institutional packages of various countries. Their contribution is significant in terms of advancing our thinking about the typology of ALSs. According to them, skill formation systems represent the institutional settings of VET, and can be seen as an extension of certain aspects of the VoC approach to VET (Estevez-Abe et al., 2001; Hall & Soskice, 2001; Hall & Gingerich, 2009).

While Busemeyer and Trampusch's approach still builds upon the company-centred orientation of VoC, they did not use VoC categories as empirical features of various countries but rather as sensitizing concepts for understanding relationships inside investigated countries. In this regard, they specifically addressed *the division of labour between companies, intermediate associations, and the state in providing initial VET*, which allows for the inclusion of intergroup variation among CME countries in their approach to skills development. This focus on the role of different stakeholders of VET helped to shed light on the various ways in which initial VET is provided and the potential impacts on skills development and AET.

Beyond that, Busemeyer and Trampusch also employed the concept of *beneficiary constraints* (Streeck, 1992, 1994a, b). These represent the dense institutional constraints that balance the influence of the market or coordinated exchange between companies and other stakeholders. The creation of these constraints often involves a conflict between different stakeholders, such as companies, intermediary associations representing workers, and the state. In the skill formation system, beneficiary constraints in many countries may encourage companies to invest in skills even when market logic would dictate that it is not rational (Becker, 1993). However, in relation to other social institutions, such as collective wage bargaining, labour protection, and welfare security, such an investment can be rational and help companies' labour force make more loyal and engaged in their work. Therefore, understanding the role of beneficiary constraints in shaping the interactions between stakeholders and influencing investment in skills development that goes beyond the binary logic of VoC tradition is an important aspect of this approach.

Based on the concepts and heuristics outlined above, Busemeyer and Trampusch (2012) created a theoretical model with two main axes: (1) the role of the state and private stakeholders in the provision of initial VET (firms), including the willingness to invest in skill formation, and (2) the degree of public commitment to further VET, including state subsidies and public policies targeting certification and standardisation of VET in both formal and non-formal education settings (see Table 2.5). Using these two axes, they identified four ideal-typical types of skill-formation systems:

Table 2.5 Typology of skill formation systems in advanced industrial democracies

Public commitment to VET	High	Statist skill formation system (e.g., SWE, FRA)	Collective skill formation system (e.g., GER, AUT)
	Low	Liberal skill formation system (e.g., UK, US, IRL)	Segmentalist skill formation system (e.g., JAP)
		Low	High
		Involvement in firms in initial VET	

Source: Adapted from Busemeyer and Trampusch (2012, p. 12)

1. *The liberal skill system* (e.g., UK, US), which is characterised by minimal state coordination and high employer involvement in VET. These systems typically feature frequent NFE with a focus on on-the-job training and no specific vocational track in initial formal education.
2. *The statist skill system* (e.g., Sweden, France), which is typical of high public involvement in VET with only a minor role for employers and is often referred to as "state-run training" (Busemeyer & Trampusch, 2012, p. 12) The integration of VET into the initial formal education system is a typical feature of this system.
3. *The segmentalist skill system* (e.g., Japan), for which is common the provision of general skill training by companies, a weak coordination role for the state, and the delegation of VET to companies that self-regulate skill preparation.
4. *The collective skill system* (e.g., Germany, Austria) represents a model of vocational preparation with high involvement of intermediate associations like unions in its coordination. Public expenditure on skill formation is high, as is the coordination role of intermediating associations.

The proposed typology is understood as a set of ideal types in the Weberian sense, serving as a comparative model for the current empirical characteristics of various national regimes. It is important to note that specific countries are only more or less similar to these types and that they are subject to change over time. For example, two firms may begin to play a smaller role in the public support of VET, as is the case with Germany, resulting in a shift towards a less collectivist system (Trampusch, 2009).

While Busemeyer and Trampusch's typology of skill-formation systems has not been empirically tested in the adult education field, it does provide a useful conceptual framework for understanding the various relationships between stakeholders involved in producing and reproducing alternative ALSs. As this book elaborates further, this typology has many similarities with Desjardins' (2017) typology, which directly focuses on relationships between AET stakeholders and providers.

Desjardin's Typology of ALS

Another approach that emphasises key characteristics and measurable aspects of AET is Richard Desjardins's (2017) conception of ALSs. Similar to Busemeyer and Trampusch's model of VET systems, it operates with two main dimensions that distinguish between the division of labour between companies, intermediate associations, and the state in providing AET on the one hand and the coordination role played by these actors on the other (see Table 2.6). This approach allows for examining the various roles and relationships between different stakeholders in the provision of AET and the ways in which they coordinate their efforts. It can provide insight into the factors that shape the availability and accessibility of AET and the forms in which it is organised and delivered.

Table 2.6 Typology of ALSs in advanced industrial democracies

State support of the supply side of ALS	High	State-led ALSs	State-led ALSs with a high degree of stakeholder involvement
	Low	Market-led ALSs	Stakeholder-led ALSs
		Low	High
		State support of the demand side of ALS	

Source: Based on Desjardins (2017)

Following this logic, we can distinguish two aspects of ALSs: (1) state commitment to AET, i.e. the level of involvement of the state in providing learning opportunities for adults, which separates state (public) and market (private) led models of ALSs. This domain primarily influences the supply side of organised learning opportunities. (2) Involvement of the state and other stakeholders in stimulating the demand side of AET through various forms of coordination and policy tools. This allows to differentiate four ideal types of ALSs (Desjardins, 2017, pp. 25–31) that can be empirically measured by the volume of public provision of education and spending on policy tools to support AET, for instance, ALMPs or private spending on educational activities:

1. *Market-led ALS*, which is characterised by no or minimal state involvement in the coordination of AET, and the provision of further adult education that is largely in the hands of the private sector. Public institutions provide only a minimal volume of AET.
2. *State-led ALS*, which is typical of very high governmental involvement in both the provision of AET, particularly in the form of BAE and FAE and the coordination role in reducing inequality in access to organised learning opportunities.
3. *Stakeholder-led ALS*, for which is common a limited number of learning opportunities for adults provided by the state apparatus, but with an important role for stakeholders such as professional or sectoral associations in regulating VET.
4. *State-led ALS with a high degree of stakeholder involvement*, which combines high state involvement in the provision of AET with an important role for stakeholders in supporting the demand side of ALS. This type of ALS reflects a balance between state and stakeholder involvement, with both playing important roles in the provision and coordination of AET.

Extensive and Intensive ALSs

In addition to the typology of ALSs discussed earlier, Desjardins (2011; Desjardins et al., 2006; see also OECD, 2003) has also identified a distinction between (1) *intensive* and (2) *extensive* ALSs. Extensive ALS refer to the organisation of AET in which a relatively low volume (measured by the number of training hours per participant of AET) is provided to a large number of adults (measured by the number of participants). Intensive ALS, on the other hand, concentrate a higher volume of training hours on fewer people. Using data from the IALS 1994–1997 among OECD countries, Desjardins found that the UK, US, and Sweden belong to countries with intensive models of AET provision, while Ireland and Slovenia were typical examples of extensive ALSs. Given these points, my research considers the differentiation between intensive and extensive ALSs to be helpful in understanding variations in the overall volume of AET within ALS that have the same level of participation. It allows for the identification of internally different ALSs, even when they have the same level of participation, which this book argues is a necessary precondition for a more nuanced classification of ALSs.

Verdier's Lifelong Learning Systems Typology

The last typology, which is discussed in this section, is the conception of "lifelong learning systems" formulated by Éric Verdier (2017, 2018). This approach to adult learning is interesting for two mutually reinforcing reasons. On the one hand, as in Busemeyer and Trampusch's case, it has drawn from the work of historical institutionalism (Thelen, 2004) and highlights the crucial role of gradual institutional change in the development of AET. On the other hand, it sees value in using ideal types in the Weberian sense but puts more emphasis on using them not as classification categories for sets of different countries, but rather as a methodological tool for exploring the differences between ideal types and particular countries. In other words, Verdier uses ideal types only as sensitive concepts that help him gain insights into the data (Alvesson & Kärvana, 2011) regarding the coordination of AET and adults' participation in this activity. The application of this heuristic strategy has helped him uncover a process of gradual transformation of some national lifelong learning systems since the 2000s.

According to his analysis, adult learning always represents "the result of a historically constructed compromise between ideal types of regimes" (Verdier, 2018, p. 478). In constructing these ideal types, he has focused, similar to Busemeyer-Trampusch's and Desjardins' conception, on the institutional network directly providing and coordinating AET. In this context, he has distinguished between the following characteristics of organised adult learning:

1. *The governance aspect of AET*, in the form of the role of private (companies and intermediary associations) and public (governments) actors in funding AET opportunities.
2. *The organisational aspects of AET*, which include not only the provision of training and its content (general versus specific skills) but also the site of the training (school-based versus dual-model of training).
3. *The social aspects of AET*, which encompass policy tools for mitigating social inequality in terms of participation in AET, such as compensation and subsidy schemes for adults.

Based on these categories, Verdier has developed five ideal types of adult learning regimes. Three of them have a high level of de-commodification of AET, while the other two have organised learning for adults that is primarily commodified. To label these ideal types, he has used the overarching category of *justice*, which refers to a form of public justification of the promises and functions of AET used by the institutions responsible for providing and regulating it, for example, by government, universities or employer's associations. The particular types are: (1) academic (meritocracy)-oriented adult learning, (2) corporatist (vocation)-oriented adult learning, (3) universal (solidarity)-oriented adult learning, (4) pure market competition (utility)-oriented adult learning, and (5) organised market (quality-price ratio)-oriented adult learning. As mentioned above, Verdier does not use these types as representatives of particular countries but rather as ideal types to be compared with the developmental paths of particular lifelong learning systems.

Based on the analysis of selected European countries, he has shown that the complexity of ALSs has grown in these countries. For example, while the Swedish ALS had been characterised by universalism for a long period, since the 2000s, its universalist orientation has weakened due to the introduction of many rules belonging to the organised market model of ALS. Similarly, the Danish ALS has undergone many changes after 2000 that has resulted in a situation in which the original corporatist model has increasingly been transformed into a compromise between corporatist and universalism-oriented ALS. Similar changes, which Verdier (2017, 2018) refers to as the *hybridisation* of originally uniform national systems, can be found across Europe.

2.1.4 Two Types of Theorising Regarding ALSs

There are three main take-home messages from the previous chapter. First, typologies built from below represent more empirically oriented and grounded forms of theorising about ALSs, because they directly target some key constitutional parts of these heteronomous institutional systems. Instead of thinking of ALSs as reflections outcomes of the development of WSRs or economic conditions of companies, they directly assess characteristics of national ALSs. Second, they do not focus on confirming assumptions of theories from other social science disciplines concerning the influence of a specific set of institutions on ALSs characteristics (e.g., levels of participation in AET or coordination of organised learning), but rather build their own concepts that enable to explore various dimension of ALSs. Thanks to that, they unpack higher heterogeneity between countries and do not contribute to the over-homogenisation of ALSs. Third, the "bottom-up" approach treats temporal aspects of ALSs more carefully, which are necessary for understanding both their continuity and discontinuity. The following table (Table 2.7) summarises the key differences between both approaches.

2.1 Two Theoretical Approaches to ALSs

Table 2.7 Main characteristics of approaches to constructing ALSs

Typologies of ALSs built from above	Typologies of ALSs built from below
Deductive logic: Typologies are built according to theories from the social science disciplines.	*Abductive logic*: Typologies are built according to the interaction of empirical data and sensitive concepts regarding the main features of ALS
Intellectual resources: comparative sociology of education, institutional economy, comparative politics	*Intellectual resources*: Historical institutionalism, the political economy of adult education
Analytical focus: one or more institutional domains related to some institutional characteristics of ALS, mainly participation levels.	*Analytical focus*: features of the country's institutional system of ALS, main providers of ALS and system of coordination.
Analytical unit: a group of countries with similar institutional conditions in one or more institutional domains.	*Analytical un*it: country case
Mainly synchronic logic—focus on comparison over the space	*Mainly diachronic logic*—focus on comparison over time
Theory driven: Empirical analysis serves to theory testing (corroboration/falsification).	*Empirical driven*: Empirical serves to develop a middle-range theory focusing on variation in ALS between countries, including mechanisms responsible for this variation.
Over-homogenisation of cases Over-generalisation	Multiple approaches to ALS analysis. Focus on heterogeneity.
Simplification desired	Complexity, range of variation and outliners exploration desired

This book follows the approach focusing on the construction of ALS typologies from below and argues that it is worth following in seeking to understand the formation paths of ALSs in CE. In Part III, drawing on the heuristic principles presented above (Table 2.7), the text of the book elucidates more specifically on sensitising concepts and how they are employed in the latter empirical analysis.

Chapter 3
Participation Theories in AET

Participation in AET has been a crucial policy issue for lifelong learning, particularly in the European region (EC, 2012, 2021). It has also been a "strong research programme" in the sense of Imre Lakatos (1978). This means that it involves continuous testing and improvement of theories based primarily on data from international surveys conducted since the 1990s. Richard Desjardins (2011, p. 205) has identified three fundamental questions that this research programme aims to address: (1) What is the extent of participation in AET? (2) Who participates in AET? (3) What are the reasons why some individuals or groups participate more or less, or not at all?

To answer these questions, multiple theories and explanatory models have been developed by scholars (Boeren, 2016, 2017; Desjardins, 2011; Groenez et al., 2008; Kondrup, 2015; Rubenson, 2018; Saar et al., 2013a). Current theories aim to explain participation levels and patterns using the *bounded agency model* (Rubenson & Desjardins, 2009). According to this model, the decision to participate in organised adult learning is influenced by several factors, including the individual's decision-making, their perception of the usefulness and value of AET, and the institutional features of the countries in which they live and work, as well as their life and work conditions.

3.1 Theoretical Approaches to Participation

Theories of participation in AET identify different social mechanisms that shape access to and involvement in AET (Saar et al., 2013b). Mechanisms refer to a specific combination of conditions and processes that usually lead from one set of conditions to outcomes through the properties and forces of events and entities in the given domain (Little, 2006, 2010). This definition is based on the work of McAdam et al. (2001), who describe mechanisms as a limited set of events that change relationships among a group of elements in a similar way across different situations. These mechanisms do not exist in isolation from each other, but rather they build upon each other and create processes, which are usual sequences of mechanisms that produce more complex and random transformations of these elements.

Applying this approach to analysing AET participation means identifying the conditions and processes that lead from a specific set of causes (such as the lack of state financial support, pressure from employers, and growing individualisation in professional and educational careers) to different outcomes (such as sharp increases or decreases in the participation of certain groups of adults in work-oriented NFE, a change in motivation to engage in FAE or in the perception of barriers to AET, or the emergence of new learning opportunities).

Mechanisms operate along a continuum of social reality, from macro-social to micro-social levels (Archer, 1995; Bhaskar, 2008). Macro-social mechanisms are primarily based on institutional factors of countries, such as the skill requirements of the economy and the strength of employee associations. On the other hand, micro-social mechanisms utilise sociodemographic characteristics of adults to explain their participation. For example, age or the highest attained education are factors that can improve or lower the chances of being exposed to workplace training.

To empirically measure these mechanisms, variables (such as attained education and spending on ALMP) or indicators (such as the regional innovativeness index or Gini inequality index) are often used in analyses. Indicators typically represent macro-social mechanisms, while sociodemographic variables are used to measure micro-social factors (see e.g., Cabus et al., 2020; Groenez et al., 2008; Lee, 2017).[1]

Conceptions explaining participation in AET have mainly been constructed as middle-range theories (Merton, 1976), which focus on participation in different forms of AET, such as company-sponsored training, and are grounded in empirical evidence. Instead of building a grand theory that can explain all facets of AET participation, but has weak empirical support due to the complexity of the functions and relationships between NFE, AHE, ABE, and other social institutions. Depending on the level of social reality they focus on (macro/micro), the research can be distinguished into three sets of participation theories: (1) those that target macro social mechanisms, (2) those that are oriented towards meso social mechanisms, and (3) those that deal with micro social mechanisms.

The current theoretical approach also suggests that a nuanced understanding of participation levels and patterns in a specific country or group of countries requires the consideration of multiple mechanisms operating at different levels. Key contributions to the field, such as those by Boeren (2016, 2023), Cabus et al. (2020), and Lee (2017), have emphasised that participation is a complex phenomenon with multiple layers. These mechanisms can either reinforce each other or limit their impact.

---

[1] Of course, such an approach is not without problems, as some scholars point out issue of "operationalisation" of these variables and indexes (Rubenson, 1999, 2011), their cross-country (Desjardins et al., 2006) and time comparison (Widany et al., 2019).

3.1.1 Macro Social Mechanism

Macro social theories of AET participation focus on the broader structural context of ALS, including WSR, VoC, and crucial characteristics of educational system. These theories suggest that key institutional packages are responsible for both the overall level of AET participation and the chances of different social groups being involved in adult education and training activities.

Since Chap. 2 covered these theories extensively, the following part only provides a brief summary of their main idea. The institutional arrangements of a country, such as its educational system, WSR, and VoC, have an impact on the level and pattern of participation in AET by different social groups. For example, certain features, such as the orientation of the economy toward high-skilled work and government support for workplace learning tend to increase participation in NFE, particularly in job-oriented training. On the other hand, state support for secondary and higher education can limit access to FAE and reduce participation in AET.

In addition, the institutional characteristics specific to a country can affect not only the overall participation level in AET, but also the level of inequality in access to organised learning opportunities among social groups who are at risk and those who participate the least. These groups typically include low-educated adults, the elderly, immigrants, people living in rural peripheral regions, and the unemployed. When states implement measures aimed at supporting these groups, the level of inequality is usually lower, as observed in studies conducted by Rubenson and Desjardins (2009), Desjardins and Rubenson (2013), and Lee and Desjardins (2019).

3.1.2 Meso Social Mechanisms

Theories using meso social mechanisms focus on the factors that affect AET participation at the level of organisations, providers, and occupational structure, as opposed to theories using macro-social mechanisms. This includes factors such as the characteristics of organised learning suppliers and the demand for AET by employers' organisations. Recent studies have identified three key mechanisms that influence participation: (1) occupational status, (2) employer size, and (3) the economic sector in which the employer operates (Cabus et al., 2020; Desjardins, 2014; Desjardins & Kim, 2023; Desjardins et al., 2016; Groenez et al., 2008; Saar & Räis, 2017). With the transition to knowledge-based economies, the influence of these mechanisms is expected to increase. Desjardins and Kim (2023) recently supported this thesis empirically, finding that meso-social mechanisms are more important than individual and socio-demographic factors in predicting the probability of receiving employer support for job-related NFE, based on data from the IALS and PIAAC survey.

Occupational Status

Many studies (e.g., Dæhlen & Ure, 2009; Illeris, 2003, 2006; Brunello et al., 2007; Kaufmann, 2015; Ure & Asslid, 2013) have shown that occupation status is a significant factor that affects opportunities for workplace education and training. Therefore, low-skilled workers are more likely to report that they do not require frequent training to keep up with changing work demands, whereas high-skilled professionals and managers indicate the need for longer onboarding training (Wilder, 2023) and more frequent skill development throughout their careers (Decius et al., 2023). As a result of this mechanism, there is a significant inequality in access to AET based on skill level (Lee & Desjardins, 2019; OECD, 2014). This is typical especially for companies that prefer a low-value-added business model depending on low-skill routine work and a low-wage workforce for their employees (Brown et al., 2001). In addition, certain studies have suggested that participation inequality is linked to the distribution of occupations and workplaces with varying skill requirements. Consequently, inequality is influenced by the proportion of low-skilled workers, with countries having higher numbers of them typically displaying lower demand for NFE and lower participation rates (Roosmaa & Saar, 2012; Saar et al., 2023).

Employer Size

According to several researchers (Hefler & Markowitsch, 2008, 2010; Saar & Räis, 2017; Wotschack, 2020), employees in large companies have more opportunities for education and self-development. This is because they often have specialised units such as HRM/HRD or R&D that are responsible for workplace training and include it in their corporate policies and workers' career and development plans. They also have higher requirements for AET participation and offer it as a company benefit to attract and retain top talent. The intensified global competition among large companies, who invest more resources to adjust to technological development and enhance the skills of key workers, further drives this effect (OECD, 2005). Moreover, Wotschack (2020) noticed that large companies have stronger employee representation and bargaining power, which allows them to offer more workplace training to lower-skilled workers. In contrast, workers in small and medium enterprises often have to fulfil multiple roles, leaving them with less time for training and development, and fewer opportunities for support from their companies (OECD, 2021). This situation is exacerbated by their weaker bargaining power and representation. Consequently, countries with a high proportion of workers in small firms tend to have less employee support for AET.

Economic Sector

Lastly, employees in knowledge-based services and economic sectors where is high pressure on innovation, like ICT, finances and telecommunication, are more likely to participate in AET (OECD, 2005). In these fields, there are more professions that require continuous training due to non-routine cognitive work (Wilder, 2023). Individuals working in knowledge-based services also more often consider self-development as part of their job ethos, accept individualisation, and view education as a regular part of their professional growth (Iversen & Soskice, 2019) or as part of their professional identity (Desjardins & Huang, 2023). Conversely, employees in low-skill services and manufacturing sectors have fewer opportunities for continuing training because of lower skill requirements, replaceable workforce, and HR policies focused on minimising employee expenses.

Beyond that, workers in the public sector generally receive more training than those in the private and NGO sector, according to several studies (Lee & Desjardins, 2019; Desjardins & Kim, 2023). The reason for this is that many public sector jobs require specific certifications or qualifications that are regulated by the government. For example, nurses, teachers, and police officers must meet certain educational and training requirements to be eligible for employment. As an outcome, public sector employees receive more training than workers in other sectors who may not be subject to the same regulations. Additionally, public sector jobs tend to offer more job security and long-term stability, which means that public sector employees are more likely to receive ongoing training and development throughout their careers. Finally, public sector organisations generally have a better institutional capacity (due to their size) to provide AET, which allows them to more easily provide development programs for their employees.

3.1.3 Microsocial Factors

To explain participation in AET, microsocial mechanisms rely on sociodemographic variables that predict the likelihood of adults participating in organised learning. In recent years, several studies (Boeren, 2016, 2019; Boudard & Rubenson, 2003; Cabus et al., 2020; Desjardins, 2017, 2020; Desjardins et al., 2016; Kaufmann, 2015; Lee & Desjardins, 2019; Rubenson, 2018) have identified the most significant factors affecting participation as education level, socioeconomic status, age, and gender.

Education

Attained level of education is probably the most corroborated variable determining participation in AET (e.g., Boeren, 2023; Cincinnato et al., 2016; Van Nieuwenhove, & De Wever, 2021, 2023). The higher level of education a person has, the more probable it is that he/she will participate in any form of AET. This is an example of what has been called the "Matthew effect" (Boeren, 2009; Blossfeld et al., 2020; Desjardins & Ioannidou, 2020) and can also be considered as an example of the cumulative advantage principle (DiPrete & Eirich, 2006). For adults who already have a higher level of education, it is easier to find new learning opportunities, since these individuals are better oriented in the educational environment as well as more conscious about the possible benefits of learning (Rubenson, 2018). Furthermore, this population is also superiorly prepared for learning, as their self-efficacy is usually higher (Boeren, 2016). Finally, they are more motivated to further learning because their attitudes toward AET are generally more positive, and they can more easily use newly acquired skills and knowledge in their lives (Kalenda et al., 2023; Kyndt et al., 2013; Yamashita et al., 2015, 2017).

Economic Status

Another key factor found to profoundly affect the inclusion of adults into AET is economic status, in many cases affected by the so-called "long arm of work" (Rubenson, 2018, p. 348). Adults who are employed have more opportunities for education than those who are not, which increases their likelihood of participating in AET. This is due to the emphasis of contemporary lifelong learning on job-related training and the direct application of new skills and knowledge in the workplace (Boeren, 2016; Desjardins & Ioannidou, 2020). Thus, being employed is one of the most critical predictors of AET involvement among sociodemographic factors (Kalenda & Kočvarová, 2022a, b; Kalenda et al., 2020).

Age

In regards to participation in organised learning activities for adults, the situation for older adults is more complex than that of younger populations. Several studies, such as those conducted by Albert et al. (2010) and Desjardins et al. (2019), indicate that as employees age, their employers become less willing to invest in their education and training. For instance, Hämäläinen et al. (2015) found that employers tend to adopt new technologies with younger workers rather than older ones. Additionally, older adults tend to invest less time and money in work-related learning and face more barriers to participation due to health and mobility related issues (Boeren, 2016, 2019). However, it is not just these limitations that impact participation rates among older adults, but also a shift in values, social roles, and expectations about the future. Findsen and Formosa (2011) suggest that older adults tend to prioritise post-materialistic, leisure-time, and family-oriented roles, which may decrease opportunities to be involved in AET. Schmidt-Hertha and Rees (2017) argues that this outcome is more common for job-related education, rather than non-job-related education.

Gender

The role of gender in participation in AET is not yet firmly established as studies have reported mixed findings. Some researchers (Blais et al., 1989; Hansen & Brady, 2016) have found that men are more likely to participate than women, while others (Boeren, 2011; Dämmrich et al., 2015) have not found such gender differences. These inconsistencies can be attributed to the varying focus of studies, including the types of AET being investigated, such as formal versus non-formal education and job-related versus non-job-related training. However, there are two trends that can be observed: women are more likely to participate in formal education and non-job-related training, while men are more likely to participate in NFE and job-related training (Vaculiková et al., 2021). As a result, we can expect women to participate more in AET after retirement when NFE and non-job-related education usually dominates (CEDEFOP, 2012; Findsen, 2018).

3.2 Global Empirical Trends

Research based on data from international surveys such as IALS, PIAAC, and AES since the 1990s has identified two main trends in organised adult learning in advanced industrial and post-industrial countries. Firstly, participation in AET has significantly increased over the last three decades. While countries with high participation rates in the 1990s have experienced modest growth, countries with lower participation rates at the start underwent a much steeper rise (Desjardins, 2020; Desjardins & Ioannidou, 2020; Kaufmann, 2015; Rubenson, 2018). Secondly, there has been a growing emphasis on job-oriented NFE, particularly those financially supported by employers (Boeren, 2016; Desjardins, 2020; Desjardins et al., 2016; Rubenson, 2018). These trends have reinforced each other, with countries with a high vocational orientation of AET tending to have a higher overall share of adults involved in organised learning.

In addition to participation levels, the latest empirical research has identified two key trends related to educational inequality. These are the *Matthew Effect* and the *Partial Democratization thesis* (Blossfeld et al., 2020; Boeren, 2016; Desjardins, 2020; Desjardins & Ioannidou, 2020; Desjardins & Kim, 2023; Kosyakova & Bills, 2021). The Matthew Effect suggests that people with higher education, occupational status, and younger age have an advantage in accessing AET, while those with lower status, lower education, outside of the labour market, and older age face more barriers to participation (Boyadjieva & Ilieva-Trichkova, 2021; Kosyakova & Bills, 2021). On the other hand, the Partial Democratization thesis indicates that the situation of some typically low-participation groups (such as the elderly, unemployed, or low-skill workers) gradually improves over time (Blossfeld et al., 2020; Dämmrich et al., 2014; Lee & Desjardins, 2019). According to Desjardins and Kim (2023), this democratisation may result from the growth of employer-supported adult education, which could mitigate inequality in participation and is part of a broader trend of upskilling across the skill spectrum in a range of advanced economies.

Chapter 4
Barriers to Participation in AET

4.1 Types of Barriers

To develop targeted policies for lifelong learning, it is crucial to identify the barriers that individuals face when participating in AET. Previous research has highlighted that without effective measures in place, overall adult participation rates and social inequalities are likely to be higher (Boeren, 2016, 2023; Boyadjieva & Ilieva-Trichkova, 2021; Ioannidou & Parma, 2022; Rubenson, 2011, 2018). Understanding the perceived barriers that prevent adults from engaging in organised learning and how these barriers change over time can help to determine the reasons for non-participation and how different social groups may experience these constraints differently. It is essential to address these questions, especially in relation to non-participants in AET, to effectively support their participation in AET (UNESCO, 2020, 2022).

In her book *"Adults as Learners: Increasing Participation and Facilitating Learning,"* Patricia K. Cross (1981) developed a theory which specifically focuses on the perception of barriers to AET (Cross, 1981). This forms the basis of the three-factor typology of barriers in AET that has been widely utilised over the years (Darkenwald & Valentine, 1985; Cabus et al., 2020; Hovdhaugen & Opheim, 2018; Ioannidou & Parma, 2022; Karger et al., 2022; Roosmaa & Saar, 2017; Valentine & Darkenwald 1990; Van Nieuwenhove & De Wever, 2021).

According to Cross (1981), barriers can be divided into three types, which simultaneously represent partial phases of an individual's internal thought process regarding their participation in adult education:

1. *Dispositional barriers.* They are related to an individual's perceptions of obstacles based on their educational and life experiences and needs. These barriers may take the form of concerns about the meaningfulness of continuing education, lower levels of self-efficacy, or perceived competence. If someone does not

see the value of organised learning, does not feel prepared for AET, or lacks confidence in their abilities, they may avoid participating.
2. *Institutional barriers.* On the other hand, they are obstacles on the part of education providers. These may include perceptions of the sufficiency or insufficiency of educational opportunities, awareness of the provision in the AET market, and the perceived quality of education. Even if an adult sees their participation as beneficial, these factors may discourage them.
3. *Situational barriers.* Finally, they are directly related to an individual's life situation and may impede their participation in AET, even if they have sufficient opportunities or are well-informed about it. Common situational obstacles include a lack of time for organised adult learning, family obligations, or a lack of support from the employer.

The presented overview of barriers reveals that AET participation levels result from the interaction between three types of barriers. These are dispositional barriers (related to adults' needs for education), institutional barriers (related to educational opportunities), and situational barriers (related to obstacles arising from family life and work position). The absence of barriers in the social environment increases participation, while their presence and accumulation decrease interest and willingness to engage in AET.

Barriers play a crucial role in perpetuating inequality in adult education. According to Kjell Rubenson (2011, 2018), several groups of adults, such as women, older adults, migrants, low-skilled individuals, and those excluded from the labour market, face more barriers to organised learning than the typical participant. These barriers accumulate and significantly reduce opportunities for these groups to participate in educational activities, leading to inequality in adult education.

In addition to Patricia Cross's (1981) basic typology of barriers (Rubenson (2011, 2018) has discussed whether the availability and quality of information about AET represents a separate and specific obstacle. This issue is distinct from institutional barriers, which Cross originally classified. The idea is that information differs significantly from both the perception of educational activities in which adults had the opportunity to participate or heard about, as well as from the actual provision, for example, within their workplace or community.

To further the discussion, there is an ongoing debate among researchers regarding the classification of economic resources in adult education. While Patricia K. Cross identified it as a situational barrier, more recent literature (Desjardins & Rubenson, 2013; Hovdhaugen & Opheim, 2018; Ioannidou & Parma, 2022; Roosmaa & Saar, 2017) suggests that it should be classified as an institutional barrier. The reasoning behind this argument is that an individual's financial resources available for AET mainly depend on the social welfare system and institutional support for organised learning within a given country (and particular workplace), rather than solely on the individual's financial situation (Rubenson & Desjardins, 2009; Rubenson, 2011).

4.2 Current Findings

Previous empirical research has yielded several significant findings. Firstly, situational barriers have the highest frequency of occurrence, which individuals perceive regardless of their class position or institutional characteristics of the country they live in (Desjardins et al., 2006; Ioannidou & Parma, 2022; Roosmaa & Saar, 2017; Rubenson, 2018). Both non-participants and participants in AET report situational barriers. However, participants differ from non-participants in the point that they have more educational opportunities and more positive attitudes towards further education, which leads them to engage in organised learning (Kalenda, 2021; Kalenda et al., 2023).

Institutional barriers are strongly influenced by the type of WSR in the country. As a result, the perception of these barriers among adults varies significantly internationally. While countries with extensive WSR and effective ALMP (e.g., Denmark, the Netherlands, Finland) show a low incidence of this type of barrier, individuals in countries with opposite institutional characteristics (e.g., Eastern European countries and Balkan countries) report them more often (Desjardins & Rubenson, 2013; Rubenson & Desjardins, 2009; Saar et al., 2013a, b).

Regarding dispositional barriers, several studies (Boeren, 2016; Darkenwald & Valentine, 1985; Hovdhaugen & Opheim, 2018; Kalenda & Kočvarová, 2022c; Kalenda et al., 2023) have investigated dispositional barriers and their relationship to various sociodemographic characteristics of adult learners. They are closely related to adults' class position, position in the labour market (occupational status), and the highest level of attained education. These barriers are most frequently perceived by low-skilled workers, individuals with basic education, unemployed, migrants, and retirees. These groups typically have a lower perceived competence level, readiness for learning, and/or more negative attitudes towards further organised learning.

Part III
Analytical Approach and Methodology

Chapter 5
General Analytical Approach

> *The absence of theory leaves the researcher to pray to unexamined, unreflexive preconceptions and dangerously naïve ontological and epistemological a prioris*
>
> (Ball, *1995, pp. 265–266*).

CE countries are often seen as 'nightmare' (Verdier, 2018) for classic comparative approaches in the field of AET. For this reason, they are treated as a specific 'negative case' (Elman, 2005; Mahoney & Goertz, 2004) that represents a problem to current theoretical classifications of ALSs. To overcome this challenge, this book has developed an analytical framework based on the premises that were sketched in Part II—constructing sALSs from below (for details see Table 2.7). This chapter argues that this new framework allows us to capture key *quantitative features* of these systems in order to understand their cross-national differences. In this regard, my research has followed a research tradition of a new political economy of skill formation and adult learning systems (Brown et al., 2001; Busemeyer & Trampusch, 2012; Desjardins, 2017, 2023a, b; Desjardins & Huang, 2023) and have tried to advance this approach by *developing a spatial model of ALSs*—constructing the *Global Adult Learning Space* (GALS). Besides this theoretical apparatus, my examination also employs an analytical framework borrowed from historical institutionalism (Mahoney & Thelen, 2010, 2015; Verdier, 2018) that helps me uncover "qualitative" aspects inside these systems and their transformations over time, including a description of mechanisms and processes that affect participation level and pattern in AET.

Any valid analysis of institutional processes must rest on plausible ontology—the nature of social reality. This study has adopted a perspective called *relational realism* (Bourdieu, 1985, 1990; McAdam et al., 2001; Tilly, 2001, 2008). This doctrine assumes that relations, transactions, social ties and conversations constitute the heart of social life (Tilly, 2008). The reality has a relational nature, and the relations between entities are seen as primary, rather than entities themselves (Abbott, 2016;

Bourdieu & Wacquant, 1992). According to Lybeck (2020, p. 186), "(…) there is no specific reason to put one of these components before the other."

Following this assumption, my research concentrates on connections among people and social ties, which in this case are mainly participants of organised learning, organisations providing AET and various governmental bodies and stakeholders that more or less coordinate and regulate AET practice. Relational realism sees these connections as constituting and aggregating reality but also forming an organisational structure in the form of social institutions that at the same time shape individual behaviour. This ontological perspective aligns with the "bounded agency" model (Rubenson & Desjardins, 2009) that is widely accepted in the field as well as with ontological assumptions of ALSs theories built from below.

While the primary interest of this book lies in exploring what Charles Tilly (1984) calls "big structures, large processes and huge comparisons," its explanation is based on another of Tilly's (2008) concepts—*local theory*. This means that the employed theoretical approach is always grounded in available data and focuses on explaining the variability among related empirical structures and processes, rather than simply identifying similarities across them and generalising them beyond the observation level. To address this topic directly, the book does not only look at the similarities between CE and other ALSs in Europe. Instead, it focuses on the distinctive features and specificities behind the formation path of CE ALSs. The utilised framework combines locally specific mechanisms with transnational societal processes, such as deindustrialisation, Europeanization, and democratisation of higher education access, that put institutional packages responsible for AET under pressure. This approach allows to understand how different social settings and actions of key stakeholders have produced different forms of ALSs and various participation levels and patterns in AET. While differences between CE ALSs and other European ALSs, as well as differences among CE countries, are investigated in Part V, the interaction of locally specific mechanisms of ALSs formation and large-scale societal processes are explored in Part IV.

5.1 Global Adult Learning Space (GALS): Mapping Quantitative Features of ALSs

The conception of the GALS provides an approach to understanding the structure of ALSs and their constitutive parts. Drawing on Pierre Bourdieu's (1985, 1990, 2018) *concept of social space*, this relational spatial model aims to capture the complexity of ALSs as social phenomena. By adopting this model, presented analysis wants to move beyond one-dimensional and one-directional representations of ALSs, which often categorise them based on high/low levels of participation/inequality countries, or their positioning as 'advanced' versus 'developing' or catching up lifelong learning regimes.

5.1 Global Adult Learning Space (GALS): Mapping Quantitative Features of ALSs

My research further argues that ALSs exhibit internal dynamics and changes that extend beyond a unidimensional growth trajectory. The following analysis seeks to incorporate these dynamics by integrating other crucial features of ALSs, such as their orientation toward employers' support or the prevalence of public provision of AET, which are often excluded from singular representations of ALSs. Through this approach, the book uncovers what will be referred to as the *horizontal transformations* occurring within ALSs and explore the multilateral directions of their development. Moreover, in line with the previous critique of typologies of ALSs from above, my analysis is not focus on ALSs as clearly defined groups of countries, but rather a configuration of more or less distant and proximate ALSs, which could be defined only by relations between them.

What is the basis of GALS? Originally, Bourdieu (1985, 1990, 2018) argued that social reality is founded upon *differences* that delineate one actor from another. Consequently, a theoretical *social space* can be constructed to represent these divergences, aligning with the real/empirical social space. Bourdieu posits that the foundational principle of these distinctions lies in the possession of various types of capital. These include: (1) economic capital, which primarily signifies an actor's property and financial resources; (2) cultural capital, encompassing cultural objects, skills, diplomas, certificates and other evidence of cultural competencies (Bourdieu, 1984).

Building on this framework, Bourdieu developed an empirically observable model of social space, which is organised along two primary axes. This topological model, famously depicted in Bourdieu's book *Distinction*, presents a diagram that maps the social positions in French society and their associated lifestyle attributes (Bourdieu, 1984, pp. 128–129). The vertical axis represents the overall volume of capital possessed by a social actor, while the horizontal axis reflects the composition of partial capitals, specifically cultural or economic ones. By positioning actors along these two axes, their location within the social space can be determined, and their proximity or distance to other actors can be established.

GALS, similar to this approach, assumes that the *social reality of ALSs can be conceptualised based on differences that delineate one ALS from another*. Based on these differences we can construct the global adult learning space. Foundational differences here are not different types of capital as in Bourdieu's original theory, but different attributes of ALSs related to variations in the "mass of organised adult learning opportunities available to adults" (Desjardins & Ioannidou, 2020, p. 145) and its coordination, supply and demand side, which represent a statistically observable part of these systems.

Every ALS can be empirically built around several key features. This book proposes six of them. First is the overall volume of participation in AET which defines the size of ALS. This factor represents a *vertical axis* of GALS, and it is the common approach to classification and understanding ALSs. Based on it, we can differentiate between ALSs with low and high participation rates. However, the distinction in the absolute volume of AET simplified differences among ALSs around the world, indeed, when many of them have experienced convergence in this dimension in recent years (for details see Part II, Chap. 3). Therefore, the analysis includes five other measurable dimensions that can represent different *horizontal axes*, that can reveal various differences between ALSs with a similar level of overall participation (see Fig. 5.1 below).

The dimensions are as follows:

1. *The extensification of ALS* (extensive/intensive ALSs): This dimension refers to the number of hours adults spend by training. This aspect complements and clarifies the scope of ALSs. While countries might have more or less similar levels of participation in a number of adults, they can highly differ in the amount of provided training hours for learners. In other words, incorporating this dimension, helps us clarify whether ALS is *extensive* (few training hours per participant) or *intensive* (a high volume of training hours per participant). Although this dimension of ALSs has been studied in the past (Desjardins et al., 2006), it has received less attention in recent years.
2. *The role of FAE* (ALSs with high/low FAE orientation): The second dimension puts attention to participation levels in FAE for adults aged 25–64 years. This aids in determining the position of the formal education system within ALS as

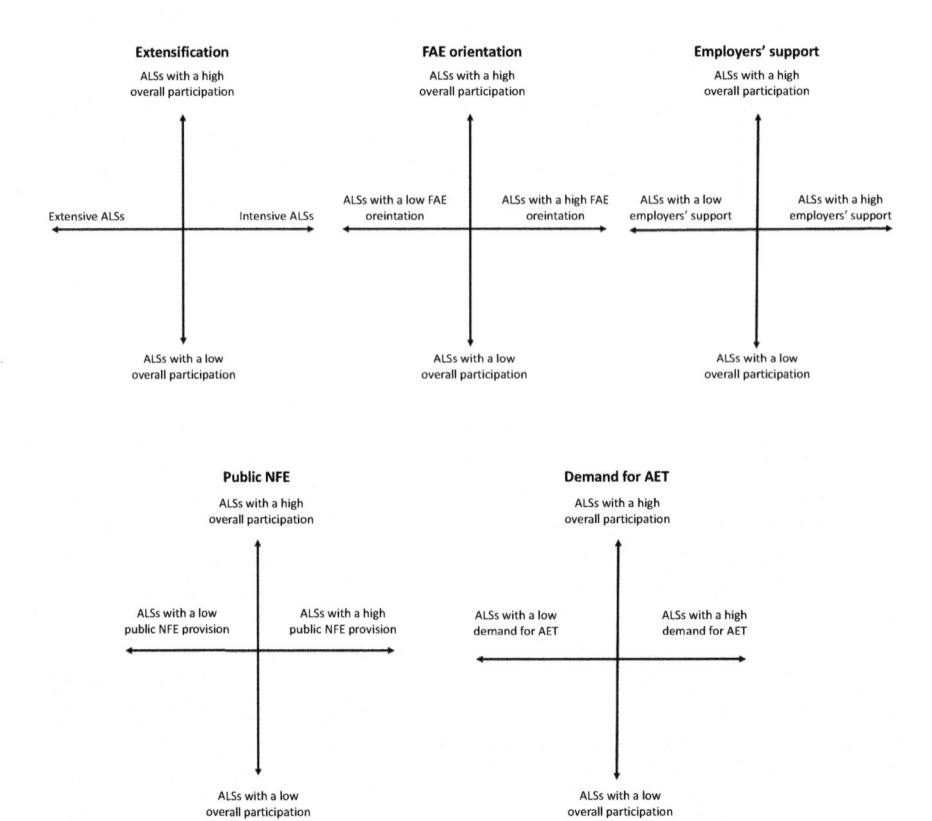

Fig. 5.1 Model of the GALS: five horizontal axes

well as the level of direct government contribution through state-controlled and publicly recognised/certified adult learning. This part of ALS represents a main intersection between the formal educational system of the country and AET. According to some scholars (Boyadjieva & Ilieva-Trichkova, 2021; Kosyakova & Bills, 2021), a proliferation of FAE is one of the main signs of highly inclusive ALS that can offer plenty of second-chance education for potential learners in AGE, ABE or AHE.

3. *Employers' financial support to NFE* (ALSs with high/low employers' financial support): The following dimension focuses on employers' financial support to NFE within the country. By measuring employer involvement in AET provision, we can empirically distinguish ALSs with a high financial contribution from employers from those with a low contribution. As current literature has stated (Busemeyer & Trampusch, 2012; Kureková et al., 2023; Verdier, 2018; Wotschack, 2020), this dimension represents one of the key differences among systems of organised learning. Moreover, also, one of the main observable global trends in AET has been rising participation in the job-oriented NFE financially supported by employers (Desjardins, 2020; Desjardins & Kim, 2023; Rubenson, 2018). Even though, a little attention has been done to variations in this dimension between ALSs.

4. *The public NFE supply* (ALSs with high/low public provision of NFE): Another dimension of ALSs focuses on the share of different NFE providers, which helps to understand the diversity of learning provisions—whether ALS is private provision-oriented or public provision-oriented. The higher the public provision of NFE, the more chances to meet the learning needs of various groups of adults, especially in popular, non-job-related NFE (UNESCO, 2022). Also, this dimension is a strong indicator of how public AET is developed beyond FAE and can serve as a measure for achieving social inclusion through social investment (Hemerijck, 2017).

5. *The demand side of AET* (ALSs with high/low demand for AET), which includes how much individuals perceive they need or do not require additional education and training. This allows us to distinguish between ALSs with high and low perceived demand for AET. Reconstruction of this empirical feature enables measuring the perception of needs for reskilling/upskilling on an individual level, which can influence the willingness of adults to be involved in AET (Kalenda et al., 2023; Kyndt et al., 2013).

By tracing these constituting empirical characteristics, we can construct multilevel and multidimensional models of national ALSs and the differences between them. In this regard, one of the goals of this book is to *expand the descriptive properties of ALSs by adding layers that can help to characterise them.*

Every ALS can be located along these six principal axes—the total volume of participation as a main vertical principle of differentiation and five rest axes that specify its horizontal location (see the model in Fig. 5.1). Together, these positions define the fundamental structure of GALS. Following this argumentation, it should be highlighted, that these positions of ALSs within space are always relative, as can be only high or low, distant or proximate with respect to the positions of other ALSs. The closer the ALSs are situated in this space in one of these six dimensions, the more common properties they share, while the more distant, the fewer they possess.

As my analysis demonstrates in Part V, GALS is not only a metaphor or theoretical model, but it is a model grounded in data and based on numerical elaboration. All differences are constructed based on the available statistical data regarding ALSs.

Furthermore, my research reflects that the model should not be static but change over time. For this reason, the following analysis utilises data from multiple surveys to cover the evolution of CE ALSs over time. On a theoretical level, my examination is primarily interested in two types of movements of CE ALSs in GALS. First, change in the overall volume of participation (*vertical movement*). Second, it is a change in the composition of various aspects of AET inside these systems (*horizontal movement*). Such an approach goes beyond the synchronistic view of ALSs, uncovers their diachronic dimension, and elucidates dynamics in the formation of ALSs in the CE region.

Because one of the leading heuristic principles behind this book is to uncover the complexity and heterogeneity of ALSs (revealing the variability between related empirical structures), this chapter does not claim that these five horizontal axes are indeed only principles of differentiation of ALSs. There can be even more lenses that can be used for constructing juxtaposition between them. However, utilising these five is a very efficient way how to further our understanding of the development of ALSs.

5.2 Institutional History: Mapping Qualitative Features of ALSs

My investigation of the formation paths of ALSs in CE is closely linked to the examination of long-term institutional change and the argument that 'time matters' in this case. Following the current state of the art in historical institutionalism (Hacker et al., 2015; Mahoney & Thelen, 2010, 2015), institutions are viewed as formal or informal rules and procedures that shape social behaviour related to participation in AET and decision-making on AET policy and ALSs structures over time. These institutions can include laws, regulations, customs, and norms that govern social processes, such as legislative procedures regarding FAE, the establishment of new governmental institutions responsible for quality assurance of AET, the application of specific policy instruments like ALMP for the youth, or administrative practices focused on recognition of prior outcomes of learning.

This approach highlights that institutions are not static but rather change and adapt over time in response to societal challenges, as a consequence of past and ongoing interpretations, choices, decisions, and events (Hacker et al., 2015; Thelen, 2004, 2014), while these changes are adaptive responses to challenges faced by society (Culpeper & Thelen, 2008). This means that ALSs are not only made up of formal rules, but also involve the interpretation and adaptive implementation of those rules by actors in response to emerging challenges such as the transition to knowledge-based societies and the effects of demographic changes, e.g., ageing of population. In essence, ALSs are dynamic systems that evolve over time.

To account for the uneven and unsystematic nature of ALSs, the upcoming analysis concentrates on three main clusters of institutions that impact the overall design of a specific system of organised adult learning. These clusters are (1) the coordination side of ALS, (2) the provision side of ALS, and (3) the demand side of ALS. These domains encompass the critical connections between different areas of coordination, delivery, and engagement in AET.

5.2.1 Coordination Side

The coordination side of ALS primarily refers to various stakeholders responsible for the coordination of AET—state, supranational organisations, unions, professional associations, and representatives bodies of various economic sectors or NGOs. In the case of CE countries, the state has a prominent role among them, as primarily creates the legislative and strategic framework of the official AET policy and a broader meaning framework that includes the terminology and philosophy of lifelong learning in a given country. According to Archer (2013), the more centralised the education provision is, the higher the level of direct state control over the educational field. Additionally, the coordination side comprises key ministries, their departments, and organisational units responsible for AET, as well as policy measures such as certification, quality assurance, and financial as well as tax incentives.

Moreover, the coordination side also involves connections with non-governmental entities, such as professional or sectoral associations, which are responsible for coordinating AET. The nature of their relationships with government representatives or the lack thereof determines the level of cooperation between the state and non-public stakeholders—the division of labour in regard to its coordination (Desjardins, 2017). When non-state stakeholders have a greater level of involvement, coordination becomes more multilateral. In general, this notion aligns with the current approach to educational government that emphasises the importance of understanding education as a field of relationships and interactions between different actors, discourses, and resources, both public and private (Ball, 2009).

Contrary to other European regions (Ante, 2016; Busemeyer & Trampusch, 2012, Mayer & Solga, 2008; Thelen, 2014), the level of cooperation between the state and other stakeholders in skill formation has been low in CE. The key reason behind this has been the weak position of unions and other professional associations in the region after 1989 caused by quick liberalisation where professional associations were perceived as constraints of establishing a free capitalist market (Farkas, 2016; Spiecer, 2007).

5.2.2 Supply Side

The supply side of ALS refers to the institutions and organisations where adults receive education and training, as well as the types of skills being trained (Mayer & Solga, 2008). It involves the production and delivery of organised learning opportunities for adults and is typically comprised of a regulated market with both public and private providers offering various forms of AET. The number and structure of these providers have a significant impact on the content of learning and access to it. One critical aspect of the provision is the role of the state, especially in ABE, AGE and AHE, and the role of the private sector, primarily in workplace learning. While the involvement of employers in the initial phase of education has been traditionally discussed in relation to skill-formation regimes (Busemeyer & Trampusch, 2012; Mayer & Solga, 2008), in the case of ALSs, it is more focused on job-related NFE (NFE-Voc).

5.2.3 Demand Side

The institutional features of ALS also include the demand side, which consists of individuals, households, communities, and firms that seek to benefit from organised learning activities. This dimension is crucial because it impacts the state and providers of AET, either positively or negatively. There are two key social factors responsible for significant changes in the demand side of ALS. First, the social structure, specifically the occupational and educational aspects, affects the demand for AET. An increase in the number of adults in high-skilled occupations and with higher levels of attained education usually leads to a higher demand for AET due to the need for workplace learning in high-skilled job positions and the Matthew effect (for detailed discussion, see Part II). Second, firms' strategies in the labour market can also affect demand. If more firms change their business strategies and require more employees with advanced or different skills than they have, the demand for AET increases. Therefore, skill mismatch is a critical issue her not only in the sense of under-skilling but also over-skilling of the workforce (Brown et al., 2001). Finally, the demand side of ALS depends on the financial resources of individuals and firms necessary to pay for AET. This includes tuition fees, educator fees, the purchase of educational resources, and investments in technology or other tools required for learning. If both individual and collective actors face financial shortages, the demand for AET is significantly limited.

5.3 Sensitive Concepts

For exploring these three institutional packages that constitute every ALS, my research does not utilise a deductive or inductive analytic strategy. Instead, it is employing an abductive approach based on theoretical concepts borrowed from historical institutionalism. The theory does not represent a general leading model of my thinking, but rather a group of sensitive concepts that help me gain insight into the data (Alvesson & Kärvana, 2011; Timmermans & Tavory, 2012). To further conceptualise the data, the analysis employs the following concepts regarding institutional change.

5.3.1 Critical Junctures

According to Cappocia's argumentation (2015), the formation of any kind of institution is a two-fold historical process, consisting of shorter periods of fluidity and change followed by longer periods of stability and adaptation. "Settled times" are replaced by "unsettled times" (Swidler, 1986), where institutions are more open to reinterpretation, reimagination, and redirection, and society is more receptive to establishing new institutions. These periods of significant change are referred to as *critical junctures*, which often serve as turning points in institutional development, initiating mechanisms that transform existing institutions or establish new ones (Collier & Collier, 1991). During these critical junctures, key actors' decisions and choices have a more significant influence on institutional development than during periods of stability (Cappocia & Kelemen, 2007).

My research suppose that critical junctures accompany the transformation of ALSs. These junctures occur during significant societal crises such as changes in political regimes, fiscal crises, pandemics, or wars. During these crises, ALSs are more open to change in their direction. However, we must consider the uneven nature of these systems because critical junctures may not affect all sides of ALS simultaneously. Although critical junctures may result in the reconstruction of institutions responsible for coordinating organised learning and crucial policy objectives (coordination side of ALS), their demand side may not be directly impacted by these processes.

5.3.2 Coalitions

Institutions, including those involved in adult learning, are political projects and, as Busemeyer and Trampusch (2012, p. 2) highlight, "represent temporary and contested solutions to ongoing conflicts." Therefore, the following analysis focuses on political coalitions responsible for the framing, management, and proliferation of these institutions, as historical institutionalism views institutions as arenas of conflict rather than equilibria. In other words, not only time but also *politics matters* in ALSs formation. Building on Culpeper and Thelen (2008), this book supposes that political alignments are crucial not only for skill formation but also for AET in a particular country, with various coalitions between firms, the state, and intermediary associations playing a significant role. These coalitions may support or oppose the survival or expansion of AET, as well as its particular organisations. Such coalitions are especially important during critical junctures, when institutional redesign usually occurs. Various beneficiary constraints (Busemeyer & Trampusch, 2012; Streeck, 1992, 1994a, b) are frequent outcomes of these coalitions as they institutionalised at least part of the requirements of winning a coalition. In the case of AET, it could be a higher public investment in job-oriented NFE across companies in a particular sector based on the alliance between the government and leaders of this sector or introducing a legal obligation for continuous training in some professions.

5.3.3 Path Dependency

According to the idea of path dependence, institutions can have lasting effects on future outcomes and limit future choices. This means that the initial design and implementation of institutions, especially during critical junctures, can shape the future in ways that are difficult to change, due to the high costs of institutional change. In this regard, the concept of path dependence is central to historical institutionalism, which suggests that the formation of institutional clusters can create self-reinforcing patterns of behaviour that become difficult to alter (Mahoney, 2000, 2001; Pierson, 2000). For example, even if there are economic or demographic pressures for change in the provision of WSR, this does not necessarily translate into political demands for transformation. This is because the costs of transformation of these institutions are high, and interest groups and electoral coalitions may resist change in order to preserve their current benefits (Huber & Stephens, 2001; Pierson, 2000, 2004). As a result, institutional robustness is an outcome of the cost of institutional change.

Path dependency in the context of CE ALSs can take on different forms. One possibility is that it affected the demand side of ALSs, as a result of capital and managerial skill shortages that were present during the initial economic reforms in those states, as well as the immediate outcomes of those reforms. The coordination side of ALSs could also be impacted by the influence of international organisations such as the EU and OECD (Farkas, 2011, 2016). On the other hand, some scholars (Bohle & Greskovits, 2007, 2012) argue that the perceived inheritance of the communist legacy was the key component of path dependency among CE countries—i.e. the way how political actors interpreted the previous socialist heritage and preserved parts of the robust welfare state structure during the first phase of economic liberalisation.

5.3.4 Diffusion, State Capacity and Weak Institutions

The formation of ALSs involves the concept of diffusion, which represents the spread of ideas in the field (Tilly, 2008). Following this concept, we can emphasise its importance in establishing ALSs in CE countries after 1989, as the agenda of lifelong learning was not developed in these states before. Instead, it was diffused from international organisations such as the OECD, UNESCO, and especially the EU. Therefore, part of the story of ALSs formation is the story of the adoption of concepts, strategies, policy aims, and measures from abroad and their local application.

To understand the role of the state in coordinating ALSs, it is important to recognise that not all states are equal. They vary in their *governmental capacity* and infrastructure strength, which refers to the degree to which government action affects the distribution of populations, activities, and resources within the government jurisdiction. As noted by Mann (1986) and Tilly (2006), we can categorise states into those with high and low infrastructure power. States with low infrastructure power have less capacity to coordinate various spheres of social life, including AET, and to implement policy measures in this field.

Path dependence, which we discussed earlier, assumes some kind of institutional strength, i.e., consistent enforcement and a high degree of persistence of formal rules in the society, which engenders expectation in actors that the investment in skills, technologies and organisations will not go to waste (Levitsky & Murillo, 2009, 2015). However, in many low-income, semi-industrial as well as early post-socialist countries, it is more common that institutions are for some time in the process of creation, and they possess a less institutional impact on actors. Drahokoupil and Myant (2011) call such institutions *"transitive"* and argue that in post-socialist countries they are especially common for spheres of law, corporate governance, financial system and state administrative apparatus. As a result, institutional path dependence may be inhibited in CE countries, and these weak institutions may have less of an impact on AET compared to countries with longer-established institutions focused on organised adult learning. According to Saar et al. (2023), the institutional systems of post-socialist countries have exhibited a high level of variety and inconsistency, as well as lacked stability, which has made it challenging to predict the impact of these systems on lifelong learning opportunities in comparison to other European nations.

5.3.5 Pace and Sequencing of ALSs Formation

The *pace, duration* and *sequencing* of institutional change are important characteristics to consider when studying a process, such as the formation of ALSs (Bonoli, 2007; Falleti, 2010; Falleti & Mahoney, 2015; Pierson, 2004). The following data analysis rargets two aspects related to the temporal dimension of social change.

First, the research examines the timing and speed of ALS formation in selected countries, including when it started and how fast it progressed. It also considers whether it was a quick process of establishing key institutions and introducing AET policy (mainly during critical junctures) or a slower, continuous process of cooperation with various stakeholders and building of AET institutions. Second, the analyis examines the sequencing of various processes of ALSs formation, such as the timing of the diffusion of the EU lifelong learning policy framework or the introduction of measures to support job-oriented NFE. According to representatives of historical institutionalism (Falleti, 2010; Falleti & Mahoney, 2015), the position of such a process in the chain of the other transformation processes can substantially differentiate the final outcome. Therefore, the findfings from the reseach also reconstruct the sequence of all processes responsible for ALSs formation in studied countries.

5.3.6 Drift and Conversion

Institutional change can take many forms, including *drift* (Hacker et al., 2015). Drift occurs when political or institutional efforts are intentionally maintained despite changes in the broader political and economic context. For instance, technological advancements may render existing regulatory regimes ineffective. In the case of AET institutions, drift can manifest as a focus on delivering traditional, school-based curricula in formal settings that do not meet the needs of adult learners or incorporate new educational technologies to improve learning flexibility and availability.

Another version of institutional change is conversion. Mahoney and Thelen (2010) and Streeck and Thelen (2005) characterise this type of change by goals that are radically different from those that led to their creation. An example of conversion in the context of adult education and training is the slow, gradual shift in CE and EE provision of BAE for the Roma minority, which is used more as a tool for disciplining this minority than for enhancing their literacy (Albert, 2019).

5.3.7 External Pressure on Institutions

To better understand how institutions adapt to societal challenges (Culpeper & Thelen, 2008), it is important to identify the main external pressures that affect CE ALSs during the analysed period. In this regard, this book proposes four key processes that have had a significant impact on state policy, firms' strategies, and social structures across post-socialist countries since 1989:

1. *The "Europeanization" of policy-making* in the field of adult education (Holford, 2023; Holford & Milana, 2023; Milana & Holford, 2014) has particularly affected the coordination aspect of ALSs by adopting the EU policy framework

for AET. This framework not only served as a precondition for CE countries' accession to the EU but also introduced concepts related to the roles and functions of AET.
2. *Liberalisation* of the economies, which has challenged newly established institutions related to the labour market—transition from socialist planned economies to market economies, characterised by free enterprise and the emergence of private firms and the inflow of Foreign Direct Investment (FDI), including its influence on the economies (Eyal et al., 1998; Kornái, 2008; Stark, 1992). This transformation has changed not only the position and strategy of firms, including their relationships to skillformation and workplace learning, but also the state approach toward various domains of welfare (Bohle & Greskovits, 2007, 2012; Cook, 2007; Cook & Inglot, 2022; Szelenyi & Wilk, 2010).
3. *Deindustrialisation* of the economies accompanied by a decline in the importance of the manufacturing sector and a shift toward the service and information technology sectors, altering the occupational structure of CE societies and the composition of key economic sectors (Boix, 2019; Iversen & Soskice, 2019). The growth of the service sector has resulted in significant challenges as the productivity of the tertiary sector is lower than that of the manufacturing sector. Consequently, the economy's growth rate and wages have decreased, leading to adverse impacts on public revenues (Wren, 2013).
4. *The democratisation of access to higher education*, which started later in CE countries compared to other European countries, after 2000, resulted in a significant increase in the number of higher education graduates concentrated within a particular age cohort (Garritzmann, 2016; Garritzmann et al., 2022; Jungblut et al., 2023). This process has created challenges for skill matching in the labour market, which was oversupplied by graduates with higher-level skills, leading to a shift in educational policy focus toward higher education and away from building tools to enhance further AET.

Chapter 6
Methodology

From a methodological standpoint, this book is based on a purposeful comparative analysis that employs a mixed-method methodological design. Following the principles of Even Lieberman's (2005a, b, 2015) *Nested analysis*, the methodology combines cross-country macro quantitative analysis, including time series analysis, with qualitative case studies with small-N cases. The nested analysis is a sort of multilevel analysis, that combines different measurement strategies as well as levels of analysis. It starts with a preliminary *large-N analysis* using available quantitative data with a sufficient number of observations for constructing key empirical features of CE ALSs—their distinctiveness or lack of. Using these data, the upcoming parts of the book analyses the *positions of various countries in GALS* (see Part V). The purpose of this analysis is not to identify causation or formulate a theory of ALSs development but to reveal differences and institutional characteristics which are relevant to the coordination and the level and distribution of organised adult learning in the Visegrad countries. Simultaneously, quantitative data have been employed for identifying patterns of inequality in participation in AET, perception of barriers and their change over time, as these phenomena are closely related to the formation of ALSs—they co-evolve with them (see Part VI).

Beyond providing insights into the range of variation, this book also focuses on an explanation of these variations or their lack of in the case of both characteristics of ALSs, participation in AET as well as perceived barriers to organised learning. For this purpose, a series of case studies is applied (see Part IV). The main heuristic goal here is to present a *within-case analysis* tracking mechanisms, processes and their variations inside a particular country. Using case studies and understanding the specifics of national ALSs represents a process of their *contextualisation* (Mahoney & Goertz, 2006). Based on Abbott (1997) and Tilly (1984), this book argues that this helps identify crucial mechanisms and processes that are necessary for explaining the formation path of CE ALSs.

The combination of both analytical levels provides distinctive and synergetic insights for the analysis of change both within and between institutions responsible for AET.

6.1 Large-N Quantitative Analysis

To successfully map the unsystematic nature of ALS and the multilayer network of mechanisms responsible for variation in participation levels and perceived barriers to AET, a diverse range of data is required. This is not only due to the complexity of the studied phenomena and numerous intervening institutions but also the selected time frame that I am intended to cover. Its length led to the utilisation of a wide scope of available quantitative data related to AET in CE countries.

A significant advantage in achieving this task is that since the early 1990s, international organisations like the OECD and EU realised several surveys dedicated to lifelong learning, skill formation or workplace learning. Data from them can be used for both cross-country comparison and tracking ALSs formation over time. Originally, they were intended to inform relevant stakeholders, as detailed in Tuijnman (1999), Schuller (1999), and Elfert and Rubenson (2023). However, after 2000, data from them have become one of the tools of governance through numbers, based on which political agendas of certain states and international organisations are governed, and prescribe politically binding norms for participation in AET (Grek, 2008). Despite this policy utilisation and sometimes limited scope, the presented analysis employs them as the best source of information regarding key features and international patterns of ALSs and inequality in AET participation.

6.1.1 Available Data

My research is mainly based on the data from the following international surveys: (1) OECD's IALS conducted in CE countries between 1994 and 1997; (2) data from three waves of AES for 2007, 2011, and 2016 realised by Eurostat; and (3) OECD's survey PIAAC conducted in the CE countries between 2011 and 2012. In most cases, the data were collected by national statistical offices. All of these surveys primarily targeted the topic of adult education or, alternatively, skill formation in medium and high-income countries. Beyond that, my analysis also works with data from the *Labour Force Survey* (LFS), which is an annual household survey that is used by the EC to monitor AET participation rates. A basic description of these data sources is provided in Table 6.1 below.

6.1 Large-N Quantitative Analysis

Table 6.1 Sources of data for analysis

Survey	Data Collection	Conducting Organisation	Basic descriptive information
International Adult Literacy Survey	1994–1997	OECD	Cross-sectional, individual-level microdata, nationally representative of adults aged 6–65, large sample sizes (3000–6000 per country). Included data for Poland, Hungary and the Czech Republic.
Adult Education Survey	2007	European Commission (Eurostat)	Cross-sectional, individual-level microdata, nationally, representative of adult populations aged 25–64. Included data for Poland, Hungary, Slovakia and the Czech Republic.
Adult Education Survey	2011	European Commission (Eurostat)	Cross-sectional, individual-level microdata, nationally, representative of adult populations aged 18–69, large sample sizes (5000–10,000 per country). Included data for Poland, Hungary, Slovakia and the Czech Republic.
Programme for the international assessment of adult competencies	2011–2012	OECD	Cross-sectional, individual-level microdata, nationally representative of adults aged 16–65, large sample sizes (5000–6000 per country). Included data for Poland, Hungary and the Czech Republic.
Adult Education Survey	2016	European Commission (Eurostat)	Cross-sectional, individual-level microdata, nationally, representative of adult populations aged 18–66, large sample sizes (7000–12,000 per country). Included data for Poland, Hungary, Slovakia and the Czech Republic.
Labour Force Survey	Continuously from 2004 to 2019	European Commission (Eurostat)	Annual/quarterly. Cross-sectional household survey. Individual-level microdata, nationally, representative of adult populations aged 18–64. Included data for Poland, Hungary, Slovakia and the Czech Republic.

6.1.2 Measuring Adult Participation

In line with the operationalisation used in the international surveys AES and PIAAC, participation in AET is understood as the involvement of adults (aged 25–64 years) in any FAE and NFE education activity in the 12 months prior to the survey administration. Although these data samples contain data from younger (16/18–24 years) as well as older (65–69 years) adults, the analysis primarily works only with the data for our target population of adults of 25–64 years of age. These data were also used for measuring the overall level of participation in AET as well as in other types of analysis focused on participation patterns.

However, there are other ways to analyse the participation issue. The involvement of adults in AET can be measured by a shorter time duration frame or by the number of hours spent in organised training activities. The first mentioned approach is used by LFS, which maps participation rates in both FAE and NFE education and training in the preceding 4 weeks before the survey among adults aged 25–64 years.

Although, according to Boeren (2016), statistics from the LFS can provide a good source of general trends related to participation in AET through Europe, data from the LFS cover a shorter time frame in comparison to other international surveys measuring participation in AET and not include crucial variables necessary to construct principal characteristics of GALS. Furthermore, they have been available for CE countries only since 2004 and hence cannot be used for understanding of development of ALSs since the 1990s. Therefore, the following anylsis combines both data sources for a more nuanced analysis of AET trends.

6.1.3 Limits of Secondary Data and their Availability

Utilised data do not represent longitudinal panel datasets with the same methodology and exact same wording of questions. In line with the current methodological critique (Boeren, 2016; Widany et al., 2019) in the field, this represents the central limit of the following analysis. Although participation in AET and various features of ALSs have been measured in all previously mentioned surveys, they slightly differ in their definition of various forms of AET and formulation of items in the questionnaires. For example, the IALS survey excluded those who obtained less than 6 h of training among all participants. Moreover, AES 2007, 2011 and 2016 differ in an important note regarding the item measuring participation in NFE. While in AES 2011 and 2016, an item regarding participation in NFE states that short mandatory occupational safety and health training in the workplace should not be considered participation, the item from the 2007 questionnaire missed this information. This could lead to a minor overestimation of participants in 2007. The smallest differences could be found between the AES 2011/2016 and LFS, which used the exact wording and operationalisation of all measured items.

6.2 Small-N Qualitative Analysis

The second level of my analysis is more related to the reconstruction of ALSs in CE countries between 1989 to 2019. The analytical approach adopted here is broadly informed by historical institutionalism (Thelen, 1991, 2014). Like other scholars within this tradition, this book is concerned with illuminating how institutions regarding AET coordination emerged and transformed over time. This analytical level draws more on qualitative data that have been used for a series of four within-case national case studies (see the following Part IV). They reconstruct their formation path in relation to three key components of ALSs that were distinguished in the previous chapter: (1) the coordination side, (2) the supply side and (3) the demand side of ALS. All three crucial aspects of ALSs are analysed with the help of sensitive concepts related to institutional changes: critical junctures, path dependency, institutional complementarities, external pressure and others explained earlier.

6.2.1 Data Used

As other scholars (Boeren et al., 2017; Desjardins, 2017; Geiss, 2020; Lee, 2017) that have conducted case studies of ALSs, utilised qualitative research strategy is primarily based on available documents related to the issue of ALSs in the investigated countries. The document analysis follows the principles of the small-N comparative method (Elman, 2005; Mahoney & Goertz, 2004). Documents includeds: government reports, national strategies, legal documents, thematic brochures, publication of associations, historical magazines and journal articles by national and international scholars regarding AET. Moreover, the research also utilises OECD and UNESCO reports concerning education in CE countries, as well as reports published by Eurydice, CEDEFOP and the EC.

Part IV
Formation Paths of ALSs in CE

> The world of processual approach is a world of events. Individuals and social entities are not elements, but patterns and regularities defined on lineages of successive events (…) Their stability is something to be explained not presumed. (Abbott, 2016, pp. ix–x)

The following section examines the formation pathways of all four CE countries. Each subsequent chapter provides a narrative description of the national ALS's evolution after the fall of 'Iron Curtain', covering the period from 1989 to 2019. To facilitate comparison, their development is divided into three distinct periods—the 1990s, the 2000s, and the 2010s. Applying this temporal breakdown allows me to understand the sequence of the formation process, including potential path dependencies, institutional complementarities, and critical junctures in their evolution.

The analytical narrative primarily focuses on three components of ALSs, as discussed in Part III—(1) coordination, (2) supply, and (3) demand sides. While these dimensions collectively form the structure of every ALS, they are embedded within different institutions of the labour market, welfare state or educational system, encounter diverse challenges, and develop unevenly over time. Following Abbott (2016), this book argues that all these three constitutive elements have emerged as outcomes of specific events and their lineages that only subsequently form their (temporary) institutional pattern and regularity. Therefore, the primary objective of this part of the book is to depict intricate interconnections between historical events and processes and these institutional clusters, as well as show sometimes unexpected impacts on the organisation and provision of organised learning.

Before delving into the analysis of national cases, it is important to emphasise the key commonalities among them. Firstly, prior to 1989, these countries were on a trajectory of convergence and followed a 'Soviet model' of educational system organisation, which was characterised by high centralisation, the absence of private provision, and a *very strong ideological component* (Jelenc, 2001; Kozma & Polonyi, 2004; Saar et al., 2023). Adult education in them did not serve only vocational goals but always ideological aims—i.e., dissemination of ideas related to communism and their internalisation (Maliszewski & Solarczyk-Szwec, 2013; Li & Wei, 2019; Šimek, 1996). While there were some variations between countries during the four decades of socialism, the differences between them were significantly reduced, and the overall trend towards centralisation remained (Szelenyi & Wilk, 2010). Another shared feature of CE ALSs has been a very strong system of secondary education with a very high completion that usually reaches more than 90% of the population cohort in Czechia, Poland and Hungary, and around 80% in Slovakia, which is much higher than is OCED countries average (WB, 2023).

Furthermore, the CE countries collectively faced four transformative processes that posed challenges to both the competitiveness of national economies and social inclusion in them. These processes have played a significant role in the development of ALSs in the region, as policymakers consider AET to be a solution to address issues in the economy and social integration. The four processes are as follows:

1. *Democratisation*: This involved a shift from autocratic to democratic policy regimes, which had a profound impact on the coordination of ALSs in CE. The transition to democracy led to less centralised decision-making regarding organised learning and reduced direct control over the provision of (public) learning. Additionally, as governments became dependent on open elections every four years, political parties had to strategies whether policy measures in the field of AET would garner them new votes.
2. *Development of market economies*: The revolution of 1989 not only brought about political changes but also marked the birth of a new economic regime. CE economies transitioned from socialist planned economies to capitalist market economies, characterised by free enterprise and the emergence of private firms and the inflow of FDI, including its influence on the labour market.
3. *Expansion of higher education*: In addition to the aforementioned processes, CE countries undertook a significant expansion of formal education, particularly in terms of higher education graduates. This expansion had a substantial impact on the social structure of these countries, resulting in a twofold increase in the proportion of working adults with tertiary education compared to the socialist era.
4. *Deindustrialization:* Alongside changes in the market and educational structure, CE countries experienced a process known as deindustrialisation/post-industrialisation. This involved a shift from a manufacturing-oriented economy to one that prioritised the service sector. Consequently, there was a decline in the proportion of adults worked in 'blue-collar' occupations, while the number of individuals in 'white-collar' occupations increased.

These four processes have influenced the trajectory of ALSs development in CE countries, shaping their institutions and patterns of participation in AET.

References

Abbott, A. (1997). Of time and space. *Social Forces, 75*(4), 1149–1182.

Jelenc, Z. (2001). Lifelong learning policies in transition countries. In D. Aspin, J. Chapman, M. Hatton, & Y. Sawano (Eds.), *International handbook of lifelong learning* (pp. 259–284). Kluwer Academic.

Kozma, T., & Polonyi, T. (2004). Understanding education in Europe-East: Frames of interpretation and comparison. *International Journal of Educational Development, 24*(5), 467–477. https://doi.org/10.1016/j.ijedudev.2004.06.011

Li, J., & Wei, K. J. (2019). Polish vocational and adult education: Status Quo, Dilemma and Way O. In *Advances in social science, education and humanities research,* 341. 5th International Conference on Arts, Design and Contemporary Education.

Maliszewski, T., & Solarczyk-Szwec, H. (2013). How? Where to? About the changes and challenges of adult education in Poland in the years 1989-2013. *Universal Journal of Educational Research, 2*(3), 256–261.

Saar, E., Roosalu, T., & Roosmaa, E. L. (2023). Lifelong learning for economy or for society: Policy issues in post-socialist countries in Europe. In K. Evans, J. Markowitsch, W. O. Lee, & M. Zukas (Eds.), *Third international handbook of lifelong learning. Springer international handbooks of education* (pp. 353–374). Springer. https://doi.org/10.1007/978-3-031-19592-1_28

Szelenyi, I., & Wilk, K. (2010). Institutional transformation in European post-communist regimes. In G. Morgan et al. (Eds.), *The Oxford handbook of comparative institutional analysis* (pp. 698–712). Oxford University Press.

Šimek, D. (1996). *Andragogika.* UP Olomouc.

WB. (2023). UNESCO (2023). *Lower secondary completion rate* (indicator). World Bank. https://data.worldbank.org/indicator/SE.SEC.CMPT.LO.ZS

Chapter 7
Hungary

7.1 Early Formation Period: The 1990s

Hungary was not the most typical socialist country. Long before the fall of Communism, it underwent gradual democratisation and liberalisation of the economy and political life under Kadár's regime, making it the most open country of the former socialist block, referred to as *'reformed socialism'* (Kornái, 2008). Consequently, its transition from socialism to capitalism was the fastest among countries from the CE camp and was characterised by a higher level of continuity between the old and new social order (Hahn, 2019). However, this does not imply that the transformation of the Hungarian economy and society was smooth and without accompanying problems. Berend (2009) explained that due to higher openness and deregulation in the early 1990s, Hungary faced issues related to the establishment of a capitalist economy and the decentralisation of state power much earlier than other successors of the Eastern bloc. As a result, the new democratic state had to grapple with a decline in employment participation rates and low tax revenues, as well as a decrease in economic performance and a rise in national debt already in the first years after the end of the socialist period. These factors significantly influenced the first years of ALS formation here. The government's approach to AET was highly uncoordinated and favoured deregulation and decentralisation of education provision, with a primary focus on re-training the unemployed in the newly established network of public institutions targeting NFE-VoC.

7.1.1 The Coordination Side of ALS: Toward the Withdrawal of the State

Similar to other CE countries, most of AET before 1989 was under direct state control and was highly regulated (Jelenc, 2001; Neméth, 2013). The socialist ALS in Hungary was largely based around a network of *'Workers Schools'* established already during the 1960s, which provided VET primarily to young, low-skilled manual workers aged between 16 and 24 years. These schools were located within large public companies or integrated into other formal educational institutions and delivered part-time VET at the secondary level of education which should primarily serve as 'second chance' education. This training model was widely used especially during the 1960s and 1970s, with an annual enrolment of between 170,000 and 175,000 young workers. However, interest in this form of organised learning had already begun to decline in the 1980s, with the number of trainees decreasing by half. This trend was further reinforced during the transitional years of the early 1990s, with over 60% of these centres reporting zero participation (OECD, 1999).

Before 1989, Hungary also had less direct regulation of civic society than other socialist countries, which allowed non-public institutions to organise AET. One such example was the *'Folk schools'*, which gained popularity during the 1980s. These schools provided civic NFE in the form of lectures, cultural events, and courses focused on non-job-oriented topics for their communities (Hordósy & Szanyi-F., 2021; Jelenc, 2001).

After 1990, the development of ALS in Hungary was characterised by the end of the state monopoly over the education sector. This was a *critical juncture* in the evolution of lifelong learning. While state and local governmental authorities remained important providers of ABE and AGE, the new political climate allowed for the formation of a private market for NFE outside of state control. As a result, FAE and NFE have been separate since the early 1990s, with minimum interrelations and overlapping between them (EAEA, 2011).

During the early post-socialist era, AET had a low policy priority. According to the OECD's (1999) report on the state of lifelong learning in Hungary, representatives of the Ministry of Education at the time stated that: "(…) adult learning is not yet among the areas considered of sufficient importance to enjoy general state support in present-day Hungary" (1999, p. 25). As a byproduct, no policy or strategic framework specifically focused on AET was elaborated or formulated, and significant governmental coordination of AET did not exist until the beginning of the 2000s (Jelenc, 2001). This lack of coordination was further exacerbated by existing regional disparities, and a lack of coordination between ministries and agencies responsible for education and training as well as insufficient financial resources, that state apparatus faced during the 1990s (OECD, 1999).

In retrospect, the responsibility for partial areas of the existing AET lay with two state bodies—the *Ministry of Labour* (MLA) and the *Ministry of Education* (MED). Although they did not cooperate or introduce a conceptual framework for organised adult learning, they represented the first state bodies that provided public AET for specific target groups after 1989.

In regard to the MLA, Hungary significantly downsized its inherited socialist welfare state from the period of Communism (Bukodi & Robért, 2007), and quickly started to liberalise and introduced its first employment-sustaining measures, including re-training and training courses for the unemployed. However, these restrictions only partially hit the core of socialist welfare state: a free formal educational system, public healthcare and pensions (Cook, 2007; Cook & Inglot, 2022; Szélenyi & Wilk, 2010). For new ALMPs, the Ministry set up a national network of nine regional Labour Development and Training Centres and 20 Labour Offices that offered courses to the unemployed based on the Act 4/1991 of Unemployment. Although this public NFE system was financed by the Labour Market Fund and was without fees for its participants, it suffered from a lack of funds since the beginning (Csanádi et al., 2014). The volume of public provision was therefore limited.

The MED was mainly responsible for the provision of AGE at the secondary level, which was on the decline, and AHE at the tertiary level, which expanded after 1989, contrary to the previous type of organised learning (Csanádi et al., 2014). A couple of acts from the early 1990s regulated this provision. Act 9/1993 on Public Education introduced ABE, AGE and AHE into the structure of the formal educational system, while Act 76/1993 on Vocational Education specified the conditions of implementation of part-time and distance VET, which could be considered as the main FAE focused on non-traditional students. Although this type of training was public, all variants of FAE (part-time and distance study programs) charged fees for students, with study fees among the highest in Europe since the 1990s (Hordósy & Szanyi-F., 2021). Therefore, the state-provided FAE was not easily accessible for most of the population.

7.1.2 The Supply Side of ALS: Birth of Deregulated AET Market

After 1989, the supply of AET was left solely to market forces. 'Second chance education' in the form of ABE and AGE fell back and almost faded away during this period (OECD, 1999). The former state system of NFE, which focused on VET for manual workers, was privatised. As Fodor (2015) noted, many of the first private training organisations of this time were actually successors of the large socialist training centres that formerly operated under the authority of the government. The remaining state centres were closed due to low demand for their services (Németh, 2013). However, hand in hand with the deregulation and privatisation of AET, many new providers emerged. From 1992 to 1995, the range of actors in the AET market increased. Most of them offered NFE courses that targeted job-related skills, mainly for business and enterprise (Farkas, 2015).

Part of the AET field that remained very active under the new social order was Folk Schools. These non-profit organisations established a network of ten regional centres that represented over 130 learning organisations and continued to provide civic education for local communities across Hungary (OECD, 1999).

The state provision of AET in Hungary included courses related to ALMP and FAE by secondary VET schools and universities as well as NFE provided by regional cultural centres. The most visible part of the system was a new ALMP provision by the Labour Development and Training Centres and Labour Offices that offered a total of 3000 training and re-training courses to the unemployed, in which participated between 26,000 and 35,000 persons per year for most of the 1990s. FAE provided by universities quickly expanded during this period, as the number of students in part-time and distance study programmes rose from 21,000 to 51,000 students at the end of the decade (OECD, 1999).

Another aspect of state-funded and supported provision was represented by cultural centres. Act 140/1997 on Public Community Education confirmed their position and emphasised the importance of community education for the cultural life of the Hungarian population, mandating local municipalities to establish and maintain cultural centres in every town with over 1000 inhabitants (Hinzen et al., 2022). As an outcome of this policy measure, 2674 such centres were established across Hungary, organising public lectures and leisure-oriented education (Harangy & Toth, 1996). However, these centres were underfunded, and their activities were more spontaneous than systematic (OECD, 1999).

7.1.3 The Demand Side of ALS: Inherited Social Structure

Similar to the rest of the post-socialist countries, in Hungary, the demand for AET from both firms and individuals was very low during the 1990s. Although thousands of small and medium enterprises were established at the beginning of the 1990s and many state companies were sold to foreign investors (Kornái, 2008), interest in the development of a professional system of HRM and HRD among the companies was minimal. This was partly because foreign enterprises were interested in recruiting cheap, low to medium-level skilled workers, and partly because new emerging companies did not require intensive innovation and investment in R&D (Berend, 2009; Magnin & Nenovsky, 2022). For example, a national survey conducted by the Ministry of Labour in 1996 found that only 13% of companies considered on-the-job training as an essential practice, confirming this approach (OECD, 1999).

Despite the existence of reform socialism and a comparatively smoother transition, Hungary inherited a pre-capitalist social structure with a high occurrence of 'blue-collar' occupations and a high share of adults working in agriculture (Kornái, 2008). In 1993, 48% of the Hungarian labour force was employed as skilled and unskilled manual workers, and although this proportion decreased to 38% 10 years later (OECD, 2023a), it still represented a significant portion of labour market positions that typically have low demand for AET.

Beyond the unfavourable occupational structure, Hungary also had a high share of the adult population with only elementary education (39%). Furthermore, 30–40% of the population lived below the poverty line, mainly including the unemployed and almost half of the Roma minority in rural areas (OECD, 1999). These structural features hindered both the readiness of adults to participate in organised learning and the financial resources that they could invest in their education.

As an outcome of these structural forces, early demand for AET was very low during the 1990s.

7.2 Development Phase: The 2000s

In the early 2000s, the Hungarian ALS underwent significant changes as the state sought to regulate the AET field, particularly the deregulated market with NFE that was inherited from the 1990s. This policy shift was driven by the implementation of the EU framework of lifelong learning policy, which was part of the recommendations made to the Hungarian government regarding accession to the EU. Therefore, this initial diffusion of concepts and vocabulary from Brussels to Budapest had a significant impact on the national policy discourse regarding AET. In response to the EU guidelines, Hungary developed a strategic and legislative framework for the initial delineation and development of AET. Moreover, it also built institutional infrastructure in the form of an accreditation board and national register of training providers that enabled to the state control part of the NFE provision. In this regard, the EU was a main driver of policy innovation in the sphere of AET during the 2000s.

7.2.1 The Coordination Side of ALS: Introducing a Legislative and Regulative Framework

Unlike other CE countries, Hungary implemented stricter legislative regulations for AET. In 2001, the MED published Act 101/2001 on Adult Education, which established a basic framework for quality assurance and rules regarding financial support for AET providers (Csanádi et al., 2014; Fodor, 2015; HU DLL, 2008). This legislation primarily focused on NFE and expanded state capacity over this part of ALS by regulating services. It aimed to ensure transparency and accountability of educational institutions. The legislation led to the establishment of the *National Adult Training Council* and the *Adult Training Accreditation* body, responsible for accrediting NFE providers and their courses. Two years after that, two other acts followed: Act 83/2003 on Vocational Education Providers, which specified accreditation requirements for VET for adults of secondary level, and Act 139/2005 on Higher Education, which specified conditions for provision and access to FAE at the tertiary level of education (HUN DLL, 2008). As an outcome, by the mid-2000s,

Hungary had the most developed legislative framework for AET among CE countries.

In addition to the legislative framework, Hungary adopted a new policy strategy. The country integrated the EU's concept of lifelong learning, including terminology, general philosophy and aims as well as indicators into its strategic documents, following the results of the Lisbon Summit (Nastase, 2018). The *Hungary Lifelong Learning Strategy* and the *Vocational Training Development Strategy 2005–2013* were both published in 2005 to support this integration.

The fundamental premise of the adopted legislative framework was to use AET to enhance competitiveness and employability of the population. According to the *Hungary Lifelong Learning Strategy,* there was a growing need for institutional systems that can adjust to individual and community expectations for learning and knowledge dissemination in a competitive, knowledge-based society and economy. The strategy also identified weaknesses in the Hungarian ALS at that time, including the absence of a coherent institutional system to monitor AET implementation (overallapin coordination framework) and the lack of stability of legal and financial conditions for AET provision (HUN LLS, 2006).

Building on this strategy, the state formulated critical policy measures to coordinate and support participation in AET. These measures included not only the establishment of higher education-based regional knowledge centres, the development of school-based FAE at the secondary and tertiary level, but also the introduction of financial incentives for employers to support AET at the workplace based on Western European models of on-the-job training, and the creation of a single system for AET validation. The implementation of these measures was to be supported by financial resources from EU funds (HUN LLS, 2006).

To implement this strategy, two ministries took responsibility for AET: *The Ministry of Education* (MED) and the *Ministry of Employment and Labour* (MEAL). In contrast to other CE countries, Hungary's MEAL had greater responsibilities and coordinated not only the typical sphere of ALMP measures, but also NFE and VET (Fodor, 2015). In a more detailed way, the MED was responsible for the compulsory educational system, including AGE and AHE, while MEAL was responsible for all VET and non-school provision of organised learning. The MEAL acquired this dominant responsibility for NFE in 2001, based on The Adult Education Act. Moreover, it also supported the unemployed through a decentralised system of regional Labour Offices and training centres built in the previous decade. For the purpose of systematic monitoring and evaluation of NFE, the National Institute of Vocational and Adult Education was established in 2002. This organisation was responsible for the research and strategic development of AET in Hungary. Since 2004, it has also included the National Accreditation Board for NFE providers and was responsible for the development of the National Qualification Register (NQR). Beyond these two institutions, The Ministry of National Cultural Heritages (MNCH) was newly responsible for the coordination of NFE organised by regional cultural centres and folk schools (EAEA, 2011).

The state coordination efforts were not only present in the sphere of the legislation regulation and policy outline but also in the set of measures that the state implemented after developing an institutional core of ALS. First, the National Qualification Register (NQR) was established, which served as a source of requirements for NFE programmes that were recognised and acknowledged by the state. Soon after its establishment, the supply of NFE recognised by the state began to quickly mimic NQR requirements and dominate the offer of certified NFE. As an outcome, the provision of AET strongly turns to job-oriented education (Fodor, 2015).

Simultaneously with realising the Adult Education Act, the National Training Register was established. The register newly listened to all courses and programmes that meet the state requirements for recognised NFE (Nastase, 2018). As a consequence, the AET market segmented to NFE recognised by the state on the one hand and NFE realised by employers and civic organisations without state recognition on the other.

In addition to the regulatory measures, the state provided limited financial incentives to support both the supply and demand sides of AET. Although training and re-training of the unemployed and public employees were still subsidised from the public budget, mainly by the Labour Fund, other public NFE and FAE activities were not supported by the state, except for support for regional cultural centres by local municipalities (Csanádi et al., 2014).

The sources from EU funds were primarily used for building the institutional framework of AET, such as the National Qualification Register, and National Training Register, and preparation of accredited courses. Additionally, the funds were used to support civic NFE (e.g., Folk schools) and development of lifelong learning at the university level. However, the amount of resources dedicated to their activities was small (Németh, 2014).

7.2.2 The Supply Side of ALS: From Free to Segmented Market

The Hungarian supply side of adult learning experienced a significant shift during the 2000s, from a free, deregulated market to a partially regulated and more segmented one. Providers included not only the state and its provision and unregulated private companies but also new private providers accredited by the MEAL. This new branch of provision quickly expanded, with 7987 state-registered providers, including 1469 accredited organisations and 6365 accredited adult education and training programmes, offering 39,406 courses by 2010 (Csanádi et al., 2014). The majority of these provisions were aimed at adults with higher levels of education (ISCED 4 and higher), and courses were mainly oriented towards job-related skills (Fodor, 2015).

In the mid-2000s, the unemployment rate in Hungary decreased to 5% from 10% in the mid-1990s. As a result, public provision of NFE for the unemployed decreased while tertiary education provision expanded, leading to an increase in the number of students in AHE. This expansion not only influenced the educational structure of

Hungarian society but also resulted in a growth of non-traditional students and diversity among higher education students. As a solution, 12 Hungarian universities established the *Hungarian University Lifelong Learning Network* (MELLearN) in 2002 to promote cooperation in the field of lifelong learning and cope with growing number of untraditional adult learners (Németh, 2010).

Other than universities, various organisations began to cooperate more closely in the field of AET. One of these was the *Association of Lifelong Learning*, established in 2006 as a non-governmental and non-profit organisation, which aimed to protect the interests of its 20-member organisations. The association facilitated fundraising and effective resource allocation, advocated on behalf of its members, provided a database of results and activities, organised conferences, and helped disseminate best practices. In addition, Folk schools created the *Hungarian Folk High School Society*, which had over 100 members and focused primarily on supporting community learning and promoting active citizenship (EAEA, 2011).

7.2.3 The Demand Side of ALS: Increasing Demand among High-Skilled Adults

After 2000, the economic and social conditions in Hungary improved significantly, which led to an increase in demand for AET. Hungary recovered from the economic shock of the early transformation years and experienced remarkable employment growth in the service sector. The percentage of highly qualified workers in the labour force was the highest among post-socialist countries, accounting for more than 30% by the turn of the 2010s (Večerník, 2022). Furthermore, FDI in Hungary increased, with foreign companies employing 47% of the workforce and contributing to 82% of investment in the mid-2000s (Berend, 2009). Their growing presence inside the national economy meant a higher diffusion rate of corporate practice from abroad, including the establishment of modern HRM and HRD practice across medium and large enterprises (Misiak-Kwit et al., 2023). Also, the positive economic growth after 2000 led to more available funds for spending on AET by both individuals and companies.

The transformation of the occupational structure, economic growth, and higher diffusion of on-the-job-training models into Hungary from Western Europe were accompanied by another factor positively influencing demand for AET—expansion of tertiary education. OECD (2023e) reported that by the end of the decade, 26% of 30–34-year-olds had attained ISCED 5–8 qualifications, which further supported the rise of the service economy in Hungary mentioned above. The number that was 16 percent points higher than in the previous decade.

Although these structural changes increased the demand for participation among high-skill and educated workers, many adults still had an insufficient level of basic and labour-market skills and did not show intention to participate in

AET. Additionally, most employers across Hungary were still reluctant to finance AET for their employees (HU LLS, 2006).

7.3 Late Phase: The 2010s

The political situation in Hungary profoundly changed after 2010 when a newly elected government led by Prime Minister Viktor Orbán began to introduce measures focused on centralisation in all areas of public policy, including AET. Facing the adverse effects of the economic crisis of 2008, rising unemployment (up to 11%), and slowing economic growth, the state applied austerity measures on the one hand and re-oriented the labour policy toward the mobilisation of labour power for key industrial, financial and business sectors on the other hand. These policy measures should lead to the idea of a "work-based society" (Szikra, 2014), where all segments of society are fully integrated into the labour market, including a big part of the Roma minority living mainly in the eastern part of the country (Szelewa & Polakowski, 2022).

Due to a tight political coalition with key industrial and financial sectors, politically represented by the *Chamber of Industry and Commerce*, the government lowered the level of taxation and decided to increase the competitiveness of the Hungarian economy by a strong focus on the supply of low to medium-skill low-cost labour power in automotive and electronics manufacturing sectors (Nahalka, 2018). The labour market policy led to both strong and very fast liberalisation of Hungarian ALS and the profound vocationalisation of NFE. From this point of view, we can even consider this new policy approach to AET as a *second institutional juncture* in the development of ALS, because it completely changed the target groups of lifelong learning policy, solely focused on low- to medium-skilled workers for a selected segment of the national economy that was in close alliance with the government. However, these reforms have not been aimed at providing social protection to the most vulnerable groups of society, rather they focused on maximally mobilise all available labour force in Hungary in order to lower unemployment and improved competitiveness of national economy (Szikra, 2014).

7.3.1 ALS Coordination Side: Turn to Centralisation and Specialisation

By the beginning of the 2010s, AET was considered a crucial policy tool to fulfil the needs of major economic players after a change in political direction. To align with this new policy doctrine, the state enacted a law between 2011 and 2013 that restructured the education system, consolidated decision-making power, curbed university autonomy, and emphasised vocational training over general education. However, these changes coincided with a reduction in state spending on education, which made AET financing even more reliant on the EU funds that were utilised in the narrowest way to support preferred target groups.

The state released three acts that profoundly impacted the direction of AET during the rest of the 2010s. First, it was Act 204/2011 on National Higher Education that modified the provision of FAE. Based on this act, the universities started to be directly regulated by the state, which introduced restrictions on the number of students for study programs that were not a priority of the national economy (mainly social sciences and arts) and introduced extra fees for these programs. As a result of the new narrow vocational orientation, the universities began to offer less FAE across a smaller number of programs (Kleisz, 2015).

The second act was Act 187/2011 on Vocational Education and Training which introduced a new model of provision of secondary VET (ISCED 03), as well as put the national VET system under the responsibility of a new ministry—the *Ministry of Innovation and Technology* (MIAT). This step tightly interlinked VET provision with the requirement of the main employers.

Finally, the Adult Education Act of 2013 (Act 77/2013) replaced the previous Act on Adult Education of 2001, which had significant implications for state-funded or state-recognised training that was subsidised by the EU funds. The law established new requirements for the organisation, content, quality assurance, implementation, monitoring, and accreditation of NFE recognised by the state. As a direct consequence, the National Labour Office, in partnership with the Chamber of Commerce and Industry, was granted more authority to control all AET and VET strictly. Only forms of AET that were relevant to the labour market were entitled to be funded by the state budget. The reform also resulted in new public actors responsible for coordinating organised learning for adults. AET measures related to social inclusion, public education, and higher education were the responsibility of the *Ministry of Human Resources* (MHUR), while policies related to employment, enterprise, information and communication sectors, VET, and NFE were the responsibility of the MIAT (Eurydice HU, 2022; Ricardo et al., 2016).

All core principles of the new AET policy line were also translated into a strategic framework—the *Lifelong Learning Strategy, 2014 to 2020,* and the *Hungarian National Social Inclusion Strategy II.* The EU approach to AET increasingly supported the notion of organised learning as a crucial tool for securing individuals' employability and enhancing the competitiveness of the national economy. The Hungarian educational policy was heavily influenced by the EU's lifelong learning agenda, and the government emphasised parts of the agenda that supported its labour market doctrine. However, some commentators (Flick-Takács, 2021; Nastase, 2018) noted that while Hungarian strategies differed from other EU countries only in minor details, no policy action was taken to implement key inclusive measures targeted groups facing the highest inequality in access to AET, and not enough resources were allocated for their success. In other words, the EU agenda was implemented very selectively.

7.3.2 The Supply Side of ALS: From Segmented to Directly Regulated Market

All measures introduced by the state since 2011 have had a significant impact on AET provision in Hungary. The new Act on Adult Education narrowed down the scope of organised learning activities that could receive financial support from the state. The fields that were supported were financed by the state or EU funds. According to Farkas (2015), in 2013, between 20% and 25% of NFE in the National Register of Training were supported by the EU funds, while 4% by the state's Labour Fund, and 15% from the state budget. The rest was financed from private resources.

As an effect, most adults participated in training that provided vocational qualifications based on the National Qualification Register. The number of participants in such courses grew to 140,000 persons per year in 2013, which represented 22% of registered NFE provisions. In contrast, training that led to qualifications for specific jobs not recognised by the National Qualification Register included only 33,000 persons. Other frequently used forms of state-recognised NFE were further VET for non-traditional students (112,000 persons/year), courses for foreign languages (118,000 participants/year), and general job-oriented NFE with 73,000 participants per year (Farkas, 2015).

Moreover, the state continued to support the network of cultural centres across the country (Tóth et al., 2021) and directed the provision of AHE in universities. However, the activities of cultural centres were underfinanced, and the provision of AHE was heavily regulated by the state. Consequently, the number of AHE participants declined significantly during the 2010s (Nastase, 2018). The rest of the AET provision was carried out by non-registered educational organisations or by employers (Eurydice HU, 2022).

7.3.3 The Demand Side of ALS: Slowdown of Social Transformation with High Demand for Low-Skilled Work

According to Farkas (2015), the transformation of the occupational and educational structure of Hungarian society slowed down after the introduction of new policy reforms. As a result of the regulation of higher education students and graduates, the number of adults with tertiary education stopped growing shortly after 2014 and remained at the same level for the rest of the decade (Eurostat, 2023). Additionally, while employment in the high-skilled service sector had risen before, the renewed orientation on cheap, lower-skilled workers led to the stabilisation of their proportion in the labour market. As of 2018, 38% of the labour force was still employed in skilled and unskilled manual worker positions, a number that was only eight percentage points lower than in 1989 (OECD, 2023a).

However, this semi-industrial and semi-knowledge workers-oriented occupation structure did not contribute to dividing the demand for AET in Hungary. Instead, high demand for low-skilled work led to more frequent training among adults with lower levels of education (ISCED 0-3) and occupations (ISCO 8-9). As firms in some sectors faced a shortage of workers, they started pressuring the government to provide training for workers with lower levels of education (pressure on upskilling) or those who wanted to transfer from other sectors with lower demand and lower wages (pressure on reskilling), as well as train them at their workplace in order cope with this need. Furthermore, the inclination for training among individuals with lower skill levels stemmed from the implementation of a 'workfare strategy' under the leadership of Orbán's administration. This strategic approach was geared towards alleviating unemployment through the creation of approximately 200,000 fresh job opportunities for those without work by 2016 (Albert, 2019). To be eligible for these positions, the majority of workers necessitated fundamental on-the-job training, given their limited familiarity with the specific labour market domains in which these jobs were established, along with their generally modest levels of education.

***

In general, Hungary has established a highly liberalised lifelong learning system in its adult learning sector, which stands out as the most neoliberal among CE countries. The orientation of AET has primarily been on job-related NFE in select areas of the labour market. However, it is important to note that this orientation did not result from a laissez-faire approach to organised learning, but rather it was shaped by significant state interventions implemented after 2010. From a development point of view, Hungary experienced *two significant institutional junctures* that influenced its AET landscape. The first juncture was associated with the fall of communism in the country and the state-centric model of adult learning. Remarkably, Hungary demonstrated more continuity between the old and new regimes compared to other CE countries which contributed to the existence of a developed system of civic NFE across the country during the 1990s. The second institutional juncture occurred following the change in AET policy after 2010, which led to increased participation, especially among lower-skilled adults, and the reduction of related inequalities. This shift was achieved by narrowing the focus of AET to vocational training in specific sectors and targeting workers in key segments of the national economy, and even mobilising the unemployed for partially forced work. Consequently, Hungary's development in AET diverged significantly from other CE countries after 2010.

Chapter 8
The Czech Republic

8.1 Early Formation Period: The 1990s

The change of political regime in the Czech Republic in 1989 led to a profound transformation in the main features of ALS. The highly centralised and state-controlled system of organised learning was quickly decentralised and left to market forces, as well as experienced a decline in both supply and demand for AET. As a consequence, during the 1990s, the formation of ALS in Czechia was accompanied by minimal state involvement and the emergence of new private forms of AET provision on a large scale.

8.1.1 The Coordination Side of ALS: The Transition from Socialism to Capitalism

Before the so-called "Velvet Revolution" of 1989, adult learning in former Czechoslovakia was overseen by a committee within the *Ministry of Education and Culture* that was created in 1951. This committee was responsible for coordinating all organised adult learning activities in the country. The state heavily regulated the adult learning system and incorporated strong ideological elements into all educational activities (Šimek, 1996). Despite this, the adult learning system in Czechoslovakia was highly developed in comparison to other countries (Jelenc, 2001). The state provided organised learning that covered all dimensions of adult learning: (1) ABE, AGE and AHE, which served as a means for individuals to acquire specific working qualifications that met the requirements of the socialist economy; (2) job-related NFE, which was regulated by two crucial Acts—Act 264/1966 and Act 42/1972—emphasising that corporate education should primarily serve as a complement and extension of work qualifications, and that cyclic executive education should be regulated in all types of managerial positions. Moreover, executives were educated in Marxist-Leninist philosophy in order to disseminate among their subordinates; and (3) non-job-oriented NFE, which aimed at individual self-fulfilment in accordance with the principles and ideals of the communist society (Kalenda, 2015).

Following the collapse of the socialist regime, the centralised system of AET quickly disintegrated, and all state-provided organised learning activities were either shut down or redirected to commercial activities by new providers (Kopecký, 2014). The state intentionally withdrew from the adult education field, leading to significant decentralisation, deregulation, differentiation and marketisation of AET.

The state involvement in AET after 1989 was characterised by minimal intervention. There was no government organisation responsible for AET as a whole, only partial ministries were responsible for small fragments of the previously well-developed ALS. These ministries did not attempt to introduce any conceptual or strategic framework for AET. The *Ministry of Education, Youth and Sport* (MEYS) focused solely on providing ABE, AGE and AHE in state-funded schools, but the volume of these programs was small for most of the 1990s. Apart from the Maastricht Treaty signed by the Czech government in 1993, which delineated basic terms regarding AET, there was no other legislative framework in place (Kalenda, 2015, 2021; Karger, 2021; Pól & Hloušková, 2008). Another ministry partially responsible for AET was the *Ministry of Labour and Social Affairs* (MLSA), which coordinated the preparation of training and retraining programs for unemployed adults. However, similar to other CE countries, welfare policy primarily targeted passive labour market measures like subsidies for the unemployed or favoured other areas of welfare—massive pension system, free healthcare and initial formal education for everyone (Cook, 2007; Szelenyi & Wilk, 2010).

The state's approach to AET was marked by a prevailing liberal policy. This policy was influenced by the zeitgeist of the time when both the state and public discourse favoured deregulation, privatisation, and marketisation in all areas of life (Kopecký, 2014). According to some commentators (Szelenyi & Wilk, 2010), the first Czech democratic government was even more neo-liberal than the cabinet of Margret Thatcher or Ronal Regan during the 1980s. As a result, the preferred model of AET was private NFE coordinated solely by market principles. Public institutions emphasised that AET should be de-ideologised. Any aspects of learning related to communist ideology were removed, as well as any content of learning that did not primarily target skills but rather ideological indoctrination. For instance, university study programs focused on the professional education of adult education lecturers and educators were renamed from "Adult Education and Enculturation" to "Andragogy" because the former title was considered ideologically contaminated by many people (Šimek, 1996).

8.1.2 The Supply Side of ALS: Quick Birth of Free Market

After 1989, the Czech Republic experienced a rapid expansion of the liberal market with organised learning for adults. This led to the emergence of many new private education companies and agencies as well as individual providers—lecturers, educators and tutors. The majority of the provision focused on NFE for both job-related and non-job-related activities such as foreign language courses, entrepreneurship, ICT, and management (Koubek & Brewster, 1995; Kopecký & Šerák, 2015). Due to the absence of any regulatory or coordination mechanism, some private providers established a representative organisation called *The Association of Adult Education Institutions* (AIVD) in 1990 that played a crucial role as an organisation securing the interests of mainly specialised private providers of AET (AIVD, 2023). For the majority of the 1990s, the state had little involvement in the field, limiting its efforts to offering BAE and FAE through part-time study programs or training and retraining opportunities for the unemployed. As a result, private NFE became the dominant orientation of AET provision in the Czech Republic.

8.1.3 The Demand Side of ALS: Structural Constraints

During the early formation period, social and economic conditions in Czechia did not favour a high demand for AET. This was typical of other post-socialist states where the majority of the population held low-skilled positions. In fact, 46% of adults in the early 1990s were employed as manual workers (Večerník, 2022), resulting in a lower demand for continuous enhancement of work-related skills.

Following the "shock transformation" of the Czech economy implemented by the first democratic government of prime minister Václav Klaus, there was a significant economic downturn characterised by high inflation and low GDP growth (Berend, 2009). This caused a decline in relative wages and personal consumption (Večerník & Matějů, 1998), making it difficult for households to participate in AET.

During this time, a large segment of the adult population was preoccupied with job changes or starting their own businesses, with approximately one-third of the economically active population doing so. However, despite this wide social change, job requirements for the labour market remained low, and reskilling on a large scale did not occur. Furthermore, starting entrepreneurial activities required more disposable capital than the actual know-how and skills of the new company founders (Večerník, 1999).

In addition to this, during the transformation period, most large companies were mainly concentrated on their own transition from being state-led organisations to private entities, and did not prioritise upskilling their employees or establishing departments for this purpose (Mlčoch et al., 2000). Although some of them, especially large companies, had HRM/HRD units, most of the training was devoted to managers and high-skilled professionals (Koubek & Brewster, 1995). Additionally, the level of unemployment in Czechia during the early years of the transition was relatively low compared to other CE countries, with a rate of only 2.5% in 1993 (ČSÚ, 2013), which reduced the demand for retraining and reskilling programs.

8.2 Development Phase: The 2000s

During the 2000s, ALS in the Czech Republic underwent significant changes in its development. Firstly, it introduced new policy measures and tools for regulation of AET in response to negative side effects of economic transitions from socialism to capitalism, specifically the rise in unemployment that crossed the 10% level at the turn of the century (ČSÚ, 2013). Secondly, in line with the EU's approach to lifelong learning, the state adopted a new policy framework and started to use EU structural funds to stimulate the supply side of AET. As an outcome, AET policy significantly focused on job-oriented NFE. Thirdly, the state expanded the provision of mandatory training for public employees, as well as AHE, to support the competitiveness of the labour force. To this end, part-time tertiary education was made available to all adults with completed secondary education without any tuition fees. Overall, these processes led to re-centralization tendencies in AET coordination, including the introduction of measures aimed at the standardisation of organised learning.

8.2.1 The Coordination Side of ALS: Attempts to Regulate AET Field

In the 2000s, about 12 years after communism fell in the Czech Republic, the state began to take a more active role in regulating AET, in response to new challenges and adopting a lifelong learning framework from the EU and OECD (Kopecký, 2014). The state saw AET as a tool to support both the economy's competitiveness and individuals' employability. This neoliberal approach became a leading philosophy behind organised adult learning.

To define the field of AET and its societal functions, the state published several strategies between 2001 and 2010. These strategies included key AET definitions and policy aims, such as the *White Paper on Adult Education* (MEYS, 2001), *Strategy of Human Resources Development* (MEYS, 2003), *Strategy of Lifelong Learning* (MEYS, 2007), *Guide to Further Education* (MEYS, 2009), and *Analysis and Implementation of White Paper* (MEYS, 2010). While the state completely employed terminology from the EU and OECD, it emphasised job-oriented forms of AET rather than organised learning focused on leisure time and civic education (Pól & Hloušková, 2008; Karger, 2021; Kopecký & Šerák, 2015).

8.2 Development Phase: The 2000s

To establish a framework for AET provision in Czechia, the government introduced several laws between 2001 and 2010. They included Act 435/2004 on accreditation of adult education and training, Act 197/2006 on workers' rights and obligations regarding job-related non-formal education, Act 561/2004 on education, and Act 179/2006 on verification and recognition of further education results. These laws aimed to regulate and verify knowledge and skills acquired from formal adult education.

A key state institution behind this new strategic and legislative framework was MEYS, which established the *Division of Further Education* that was responsible for both the coordination and development of AET. The MEYS at that time clearly emphasised the requirements for the development of tertiary education and FAE, based on the Lisbon Strategy (2000–2010), rather than NFE. The EU's modernisation perspective prioritised the preparation of a new highly qualified workforce in the age cohort of 25–35 years, or the part-time study programs for the older adults that were to become the main bearer of deindustrialisation of economies in the newly acceding countries, as an incentive for establishing knowledge-oriented economies. Due to the higher proportion of the population with tertiary education, there should be an improvement in skills, innovation, and the expansion of the service sector (Kadeřábková, 2005). As a result, higher education became a significant political priority, while AET and particularly NFE were not a top priority for the state apparatus.

The second reason for overlooking AET as a key policy issue after 2000 was that the characteristics of a dependent market economy (Magnin & Nenovsky, 2022; Nolke & Vligenthart, 2009) with a high proportion of positions in the manufacturing industry did not require such an extensive level of continuous development of job-related skills through workplace training, especially when it was saturated with a higher inflow of university-educated graduates in technically oriented fields.

This created the basic conditions for a *two-way system of AET*, emphasising the education of young adults (Hamplová & Simonová, 2014; Simonová & Hamplová, 2016). The outputs of formal education gained much greater recognition in the labour market thanks to state guarantee, while the majority of NFE outputs were still uncertified. If NFE in the Czech Republic was extensively certified, it was usually only in the area of public administration (healthcare, social services, and police forces), which mandatory requires it (NSC, 2020).

Legislative consolidation of the entire AET system came with a significant delay compared to the everyday practice, which had been developing since the 1990s (Šerák, 2012). There is nothing unusual about this, as according to some authors (Burns & Köster, 2016; Veselý, 2017), the development and implementation of educational policy happen at different speeds. The decision-making of the state apparatus is always at least a step behind the demands of practice because it is based on the principles of bureaucracy, where established procedures are more strictly adhered to than current problems are pragmatically solved.

Moreover, the described period was characterised by substantial inconsistency in the aims and measures of the local education policy, which manifested in the inconsistent implementation of strategic plans by the MEYS, non-functioning communication between actors in education policy, and insufficient use of available knowledge (MEYS, 2020; Prokop & Dvořák, 2019; Veselý, 2013).

The *Division of Further Education* introduced two policy measures aimed at improving participation in organised learning in line with national and EU strategy, with a focus on AET. The first measure was the development of the National Qualification System (NQS), which aimed to standardise AET. The second measure involved investment from the EU funds to support job-related NFE among employers.

The NQS was established in 2007 and aimed to unify the fragmented system of VET by introducing a nationally recognised qualification system that is compatible with the European Qualification Framework (EQF). The NQS consisted of eight levels and covered all types of education and training, including FAE and NFE. The system also includes a National Register of Qualifications, which lists all recognised qualifications. In relation to AET, the intention behind NQS was to establish a connection between education and work and serve as a model for preparing job-oriented organised learning for adults. The system was partially developed based on the needs and requirements of employers that began to press on the government regarding the rising skill mismatch in the biggest industrial sectors. According to Kopecký (2014), key stakeholders involved in creating the system included employers' representatives, such as the Chamber of Commerce and various employers' associations.

The investment from the EU funds to support job-related NFE among employers was introduced in 2007 and aimed to increase employees' participation in organised learning. The programme provided funding for training courses, educational materials, and trainers. It also supported the development of human resource departments in companies and the establishment of networks of training providers. The program was implemented through the Operational Programme Human Resources and Employment and was co-funded by the European Social Fund (Kalenda, 2021).

Apart from MEYS, also MLSA held a more profound position in coordinating AET. Specifically, it expanded the repertoire of training and retraining courses for the unemployed and individuals seeking employment. Additionally, MLSA formulated a new policy agenda focused on the employability of graduates and ALMP (Rabušic & Rabušicová, 2006; Simonová & Hamplová, 2016). However, the state expenses on this sphere of welfare policy have never been high, totalled between 0.5% and 0.6% of GDP. The number three times lower than is the EU average (OECD, 2023b).

8.2.2 The Supply Side of ALS: Expansion and Regulation of the Supply

Two trends were crucial for the evolution of the market with organised adult learning in Czechia in the first decade of the new millennium—(1) state enhancement of AET provision and (2) consequently profound increase in the supply of education and training. After 2000, the Czech government intervened in market mechanisms by subsidising AET supply. This involved several policy measures. First of them was standardisation, democratisation, and universalisation of access to tertiary education, with a significant increase in the number of non-traditional students in AHE from 42,000 to 102,000 annually between 1999 and 2012 (Koucký et al., 2014; Prudký et al., 2010; Šmídová et al., 2017). As a result, AHE became the primary domain of direct public adult education during the 2000s.

Apart from the growth of AHE, a systematic model of VET was also introduced for state employees in the healthcare, social services, and public administration sectors (Kopecký & Šerák, 2015; Rabušicová & Rabušic, 2008). Specific ministries were responsible for organising, regulating, and providing NFE-Voc for their personnel, resulting in a continuous stream of adults who underwent further AET due to obligatory job requirements. Beyond that, the state also widened public training and re-training opportunities for the unemployed and other groups at risk. As an outcome, 50–70,000 adults participated in this ALMP measure every year (LMP, 2019).

The provision of NFE was substantially supported by the operational programme Education for Competitiveness (2.15 billion euros) and the operational programme Human Resources and Employment (1.88 billion euros). These supply-side incentives started in 2004 and led to the training of 187,000 persons in job-related NFE per year between 2004 and 2006, respectively 97,000 individuals annually in a period from 2007 to 2013 (Kalenda, 2021).

While these resources improved access to AET, they had a mixed impact on organised learning, as noted by Janoušková et al. (2008) and Palán (2013a). On the one hand, the programmes were accompanied by excessive administrative burden and problematic cooperation with awarding institutions, mainly the Ministry of Regional Development and regional authorities. On the other hand, they transformed the competitive environment in the AET market and put pressure on providers by inflating quality standards and increasing the supply of AET (Kopecký & Šerák, 2015; Langer, 2009). Beyond that, employers in many cases only provided formal training "on paper" and used financial resources to co-finance their HRM/HRD staff instead of investing in skill enhancement. These practices have damaged the reputation of AET in many companies (Palán, 2013a, b). The implementation of this policy measure exemplifies phenomenon of *institutional conversion*, where the resources and practices related to the provision of AET are repurposed to align with the goals of the participating organisation that are far from their original policy intention.

8.2.3 The Demand Side of ALS: Remaining Structural Constraints

Unlike the intensive development of state policy on lifelong learning between 2005 and 2011, the socio-economic conditions for the implementation of AET were less favourable. In the initial phase between 2005 and 2008, there was a short noticeable drop in unemployment from 9% to 5%, but it was accompanied by significant inflation. By 2009, unemployment was rising again due to the economic crisis, which peaked in Czechia between 2010 and 2011, when unemployment reached the rate of 9% (ČSÚ, 2013). At the same time, there was a general slowdown in the performance of the economy and a reduction in investment in human resources by employers.

Occupational structure in the Czech Republic has undergone significant changes since 1989, with manual workers being the most affected by the transformation. Their proportion in the labour force decreased from 46% in 1988 to 32% in 2005 (Večerník, 2022). However, this significant de-industrialisation did not lead to a proportional growth of high-skill service workers. Their share grew by only two percentage points during the same period (OECD, 2023a). While the number of adults without profound training requirements decreased, the number of positions requiring frequent AET remained almost unchanged.

Another critical factor that worked against the high demand for AET after 2000 was FDI and inclusion into the world economy in a dependent position (Holubec, 2009; Nolke & Vligenthart, 2009). In the mid-1990s, only 5% of companies had foreign owners, but by the 2000s, that number had risen to over 30% (ČSÚ, 2013). By the end of the decade, FDI was responsible for half of domestic employment (NTF, 2017). Many of these foreign companies were interested in low-cost labour as the average monthly wage in the Czech Republic was only one-quarter to one-fifth of the wages in Western Europe (Berend, 2009). Moreover, they did not prioritise training their workforce due to the nature of the skills required for the work. In this regard, Kadeřábková (2005), based on a national representative survey of companies in 2004, found that only 10% of firms considered employees' skills as a source of their competitive advantage. The combination of these social and economic mechanisms resulted in limited demand for AET among Czech adults for most of the 2000s (Rabušicová et al., 2008).

8.3 Late Formation Phase: The 2010s

In contrast to the period before it, the formation of ALS after 2010 was characterised by the state's reduced role in coordinating AET. Instead of centralisation, there were tendencies towards decentralisation. Additionally, the state withdrew support for both tertiary-level FAE and job-related NFE that employers provided. The amount of financial support from the EU funds for enhancing AET supply decreased significantly. On the other hand, since 2011, there have been significant improvements in general socioeconomic conditions, including a decrease in unemployment, economic growth, and in the financial situations of firms and households that led to a rise in demand for organised learning in some economic sectors and among service workers.

8.3.1 The Coordination Side of ALS: Step Back to Deregulation

From the perspective of the state's role, the government did not issue any new laws to regulate further or adjust AET, nor did it create any strategic documents targeting solely organised learning for adults. Based on interviews with key policy stakeholders, Karger (2021) found that the government had lost interest in the topic of AET by this time and included it in the agenda only in a formal way. Instead of introducing new policy tools for coordination and AET development, the state policy focused only on completing the national qualifications system and implementing projects in the field of ALMP supported by the EU funds. Therefore, the dominant AET orientation after 2010 was typical of renewing neoliberalism and NFE-Voc (Kopecký, 2014; Kalenda, 2021).

Although the state included the topic of AET in four various national strategies between 2010 and 2019, it devoted only a little attention to organised learning and systematic policy measures for its enhancement and development. Namely, they were: (1) the *International Strategy of Competitiveness: 2012–2020*; (2) the *Strategy of Education Policy Toward 2020*; (3) the *Impact of Digitization*; (4) the *Impact of Industry 4.0*. In line with the EU agenda, their common denominator was the orientation towards employability and competitiveness of the national economy (Karger, 2021). Nevertheless, because economic growth in the Czech Republic was comparatively high not only among CE countries but also the rest of the EU countries and unemployment was the lowest in the whole of Europe since 2015 (OECD, 2023d), the government was not under any pressure to translate political goals into concrete measures.

Similar to the previous decade, AET coordination remained shared by two key ministries—MEYS and MLSA. However, the activities of both ministries were coordinated only to a certain degree (Karger, 2021; Kopecký, 2014; Palán, 2013a, b). From a legislative point of view, there was no single public administration body which was competent to cover AET as a whole. The field was fragmented into many small segments (Kopecký & Šerák, 2015).

Since 2010, MLSA has directed state employment policy and related training and retraining courses. Further, this ministry also monitored current and future demands for qualification in the labour market and was responsible for developing a national occupation system, as well as was responsible for carrier guidance. For this aim, it established the National guidance *forum* as a crucial advising body in 2010 (Eurydice CZ, 2022).

Contrary, MEYS was responsible for the preparation of policies and strategies concerning AET, mainly the regulatory framework for participation in organised learning—NQF. In this regard, MEYS established the *National Institute for Education* in 2011, which was newly responsible for the authorisation of the NQF built during the previous period. However, the authorisation process of new qualifications was slow and cumbersome, with the approval of new qualification standards taking 1–2 years. By 2015, the development of NQF had slowed down, and the whole system was primarily used in cases where some parts of the state administration required it, rather than as a tool that would be widely adopted among adults across the country. Moreover, the political support for this policy measure waned, leading to understaffing of MEYS, with systemic measures remaining largely unimplemented (Karger, 2021). From the perspective of historical institutionalism, we can observe a notable institutional drift in the case of this policy measure, indicating its diminished relevance in the altered social context.

After 2013, the *Ministry of Industry and Trade* (MIAT) entered the field of AET and became responsible for providing support through the operational programme Enterprise and Innovations for Competitiveness that financially supported on-site training in the workplace. Other ministries were still responsible for VET of employees in regulated professions within their sectors, serving as authorising bodies, as well as preparing qualifications and assessments in their sectors (Eurydice CZ, 2022).

8.3.2 The Supply Side of ALS: Toward Highly Differentiated and Employers-Oriented Market

Rather than an increase in the supply of AET opportunities, further differentiation of AET provision was typical for the Czech AET market. The expansion of the number of providers was slowed not only by the economic crisis, which negatively affected many providers (Palán, 2013b), but also by weakening the flow of resources from the EU funds for NFE support. Their financial allocation significantly declined in the period of 2014 to 2020, while bureaucracy with their utilisation went up as well as competitiveness in applications for this funding scheme (Kalenda, 2021).

By a combination of these processes, the volume of supply of AET opportunities remained approximately the same as used to be during the 2000s. Palán (2013b) reported that there were approximately 4000 adult education and training institutions. A similar number that reported by Zounek et al. (2006) in the first half of the 2000s. These institutions were primarily commercial training institutions, private schools, and employers. Other types of providers, like public schools and higher education institutions, NGOs, sectoral educational institutions, foundations, and trade unions, constituted a minor part of the educational supply.

But employers began offering more NFE for their employees than ever before, establishing themselves as crucial AET providers. As the capacity of many companies to realise workplace training has improved since the 2000s, they were able to deliver more on-the-job training for their employees. For example, the proportion of companies with a person responsible for HRD strategy of workplace training among small and medium enterprises has grown (Łobos et al., 2020; Smerek et al., 2021).

On the other hand, the reverse trend was characteristic of the public provision of AET. Both volume of FAE and AHE substantially declined as the state started to limit its previous support to wide access to tertiary education, worrying about growing skill mismatch (Koucký et al., 2014; MEYS, 2017). Also, the provision of public training and retraining under the umbrella of ALMP measures decreased. After a period of economic crisis with a peak in 2011, participation in this public NFE went down to 20 to 30,000 persons a year, one-half of the volume that was common for the previous decade (LMP, 2019).

As an outcome of these shifts in the AET market, employers became the leading providers of organised learning for adults and the position of state significantly weakened.

8.3.3 The Demand Side of ALS: Limited Acceleration in Demand

As I mentioned earlier, contrary to previous phases of ALS formation, the socioeconomic conditions for AET demand were favourable after 2011. Unemployment decreased significantly during this period, from almost 9% in 2011 to less than 3% in 2019. Simultaneously, the GDP growth and economic dynamics of most companies resumed, which led to an increase in investment in employees. A profound shortage in labour power even exacerbated this firm strategy, as Czechia had the highest employment rate among EU countries in the period 2015 and 2019 (OECD, 2023a) and could hardly mobilise more workers.

As an outcome, many organisations, especially large companies but also public sector organisations, had to develop their HRM/HRD departments and substantially professionalise their on-the-job training services, including also the public sector, to cope with these conditions. In this regard, they widened training opportunities for their employees focused on (1) enquiring skills that were the most needed by companies (Kalenda, 2023) or (2) developing their talents for positions that were the most difficult to hire on the job market.

Furthermore, the occupation structure of the Czech Republic has undergone significant changes in the past decade. The transformation dynamic between low-skill and high-skill occupations has shifted, with a rise in the proportion of white-collar professionals from 28% to 38% between 2005 and 2018 (Večerník, 2022). Additionally, the decline of 'blue-collar' occupations has slowed, with the total share of manual workers declining by only four percentage points during the same period. The proportion of unskilled manual workers has even increased by a small margin (OECD, 2023a). This transformation resulted in an increase in the number of individuals in the labour market and their occupations that had a *higher demand for AET*. Conversely, the decline in positions with low training requirements has stabilised.

***

In conclusion, the development of the Czech ALS can be characterised by a three-phase institutional trajectory. In the first phase, there was a significant decentralisation of the ALS, with the elimination of centralised provision of AET and previous ideological component. During this institutional juncture, the ALS established strong path dependency toward liberal model of AET provision. The second phase, particularly between 2004 and 2009, witnessed the implementation of comprehensive lifelong learning policies, which included various measures aimed at enhancing the supply side of organised learning. Although these policy measures were aimed to regulate market with organised learning, it did not lead to creation of more chances for groups in need. Instead, they oversupply opportunities for those who had xcess to them through the labour market. However, this approach did not change the overall high market orientation of organised learning in Czechia. During the last phase, following the year 2010, the state involvement in AET began to decline once again, with reduced priority and limited financial support, which again strengthened the liberal pathway. The growth of the national economy after 2012, coupled with changing policy preferences, shifted the lifelong learning agenda to a lower priority. Nevertheless, the favourable economic conditions, combined with the new strategies of firms within the rapidly growing dependent market economy and significant changes in the occupational structure, created a more conducive environment for participation in AET, even in the absence of state supportive initiatives, compared to the 2000s.

Chapter 9
Slovakia

9.1 Early Formation Period: The 1990s

Slovakia used to be part of Czechoslovakia until January 1, 1993, when the state peacefully split into Slovakia and the Czech Republic following negotiations between new Slovakian political leaders and the Czechoslovakian government. As a result, the early development of ALS in Slovakia between 1989 and 1992 and the nature of AET during the socialist regime shared many similarities with the Czech ALS. Like in the Czech Republic, AET in Slovakia was tightly controlled by the state apparatus and infused with communist ideology since the establishment of ALS in 1951 (for details see the introduction of the previous chapter). Besides a high level of AET centralisation, state-directed ALS was typical by the provision of all forms of organised learning for adults, i.e., both job- and non-job related as well as FAE and NFE.

9.1.1 The Coordination Side of ALS: Decentralisation of AET

In the years following the fall of communism, ALS underwent significant decentralisation and a decline in publicly-provided NFE and VET. As a consequence of this new institutional juncture, the state intentionally removed itself from the sphere of organised learning. Similar to other post-socialist countries, adult education was not supported by the government, as it was seen as "a child and relict of communism" (Jelenc, 2001, p. 259) and did not have the same social relevance as other public redistributive institutions as healthcare, pension system and formal education (Cook & Inglot, 2022; Szelenyi & Wilk, 2010). However, Jelenc (2001) noted that the situation of organised learning for adults in Slovakia was better than in the Czech Republic in the second half of the 1990s as *The Ministry of Education,*

Science, Research, and Sport (MESRS) established the *Department of Further Education* in 1995, which was responsible for the coordination and development of adult education. The department subsequently issued Act 368/1997 on further adult education, the first legislative document to lay out AET. In this initial phase, AET was defined as organised learning that extended the formal education system and offered adults a second chance to upgrade their skills or help them cope with crises during their life path (Šimek, 1996).

The second organisation responsible for a new part of the public AET was *National Labour Office*. It is worth noting that this unit was an autonomous public organisation without direct subordination to the *Ministry of Labour and Social Affairs* (MLSA), which significantly restricted both its funding and competency (Štefánik, 2018). Despite the National Labour Office introducing the first ALMPs in Slovakia, training and retraining activities contained only a minor part of the policy measures. Instead, most of ALMPs were designed to enhance direct employment in the private or public sector (van Ours & Lubyová, 1999).

Although AET was initially defined and implemented into the structure of the public apparatus, the state provided minimal financial and methodical support for this activity. This lack of assistance was due to several factors, including the challenging economic conditions of the newly formed state, limited revenues, and the prioritisation of other policy issues—especially economic transformation (Cook, 2007; Szelenyi & Wilk, 2010). In other words, both (1) the insufficient infrastructural capacity of the state and (2) the level of institutional development (e.g., lack of know-how and experience in both the sphere of lifelong learning policy setting and effective coordination of various stakeholders). Additionally, there was a strong focus on (3) liberalisation in job-related and VET-related policies (Cook, 2007; Cook & Inglot, 2022; Domonkos, 2016; Trajlinková, 2001), which further restricted state support for AET and legitimised the market orientation of the provision of learning opportunities.

9.1.2 The Supply Side of ALS: Emergence of a Deregulated Market

A free market with AET emerged in Slovakia at a similar pace to that of Czechia. As the provision of organised learning for adults was not legally regulated, a diverse range of providers swiftly emerged, offering adult education courses and programs to anyone. Due to this unregulated nature, offerings of organised learning were highly varied, including educators offering private lessons as well as the first enterprises specialised in both job-related and civic NFE. The most active branch of AET during this period was job-related NFE in the form of foreign language courses, programs regarding entrepreneurship skills, and business and management training (Jelenc, 2001). As the number of providers rose, they started to organise collectively. The most important product of this cooperation was the *Association of Institutions of Adult Education in the Slovak Republic*, which was established as the leading representative body for AET providers, with over 60 members (Šilhár, 2013).

The public provision played a minor role in the supply of educational opportunities. On the one hand, this provision included training for the unemployed that the National Labour Office organised. However, participation in this form of NFE never exceeded 2000 persons/per year (van Ours & Lubyová, 1999), which sharply contrasted with almost 500,000 unemployed in the country by that time (Lichner, 2022). On the other hand, state schools provided limited ABE and AHE in part-time study programs along with regular study programs (Jelenc, 2001).

9.1.3 The Demand Side of ALS: Socioeconomic Constraints

The transformation of Slovakia's social and economic systems had an ambiguous impact on demand for AET. The shift from socialism to capitalism over the course of a decade resulted in economic decline and a rise in unemployment. While not as severe as in Poland, the effects were more significant than in the Czech Republic as unemployment quickly grew to 10% and lasted longer than in other CE countries (Lichner, 2022). This was accompanied by a quick fall in economic growth in 1993, causing Slovakia's estimated GDP per capita relative to Western European countries to drop from 55% in the final years of socialism to 29% in 1999 (Berend, 2009). These factors significantly reduced not only the financial resources available for public forms of organised learning but also limited households' ability to participate in private forms of AET.

Despite high unemployment rates, public policy focused on passive labour market measures such as financial compensation to employers and early retirement of workers instead of promoting re-training and re-skilling (Domonkos, 2016; Hidas et al., 2016; van Ours & Lubyová, 1999). As we showed above, the state introduced ALMP only to a limited extent. Half of the unemployed had only primary education (Lichner, 2022) and were not prepared to undergo systematic long-term reskilling in available part-time study programs. Although the unemployed received some compensation from the state, this financial support was time-restricted and not high enough to enable them to participate fully in formal educational programs like AGE. Furthermore, due to the concentration of unemployment in eastern regions of the country, which faced a decline in the heavy industrial sector and demand for labour force (Gerbery & Džambazovič, 2018), simply improving the level of education or enhancing job skills may not be enough to get a new job position in the local job market. A job-seeking strategy that involves upgrading skills may also require migration to the western part of the country, which was not financially affordable for many adults with a low-income background.

Beyond the economic dynamic, another two robust mechanisms limited an upward trend in demand for organised learning among adults. First, it was the composition of the Slovakian labour force. In 1993, a large proportion of adults (around 45%) worked in manual labour positions, whereas only 12% held high-skill service jobs (Gerbery & Džambazovič, 2018; Večerník, 2022), that require frequent and systematic skill development. Additionally, Slovakia faced significant regional disparities, where eastern regions had a much higher proportion of not only unemployment but also a less favourable occupational structure that hindered demand for AET. The especially difficult position, in this case, had marginalised Roma communities who experienced a cumulation of disadvantages (Studená & Polačková, 2020).

The second mechanism, we can identify at the company level. Many newly established enterprises were not equipped to implement HRM/HRD practices, including workplace education and training (Smerek et al., 2021). According to a national survey that was conducted in 1998, only 36% of Slovakian companies had implemented some form of training and development activities, while the majority of them were concentrated around the capital city—Bratislava (Stachová & Smerek, 2023). This issue was exacerbated by the structure of the country's enterprises, with 60% of employment in small and medium-sized enterprises that usually have underdeveloped HRM/HRD systems and company training (Smerek et al., 2021). In combination with these factors, demand for on-the-job training among companies remained low.

9.2 Development Period: The 2000s

Although Slovakia was an "early adopter" of institutions and legislation related to AET in comparison to other countries behind the former ' Iron Curtain ', this momentum was not sustained during the 2000s as the state renewed its coordination activity only by the end of this decade. A crucial role was played by the Slovakia's government between 1999 and 2006 with Mikuláš Dzurinda in the lead. The conservative government focused on passive labour market policy (mainly subsidising jobs) a prioritised other agenda related to Slovakia's accession to the EU (Domonkos, 2016). Therefore, the state's general approach to organised learning for adults was *highly liberal*, lacking significant coordination and support mechanisms for enhancing both the supply and demand sides of organised learning. This approach was in line with the overall national policy at this time—widespread liberalisation (Berend, 2009; Trajlinková, 2001). Contrary to the other CE countries, who slight retreat from previous neo-liberal policy, Slovakia remained highly neoliberal during the 2000s (Cook, 2007; Szelenyi & Wilk, 2010).

9.2.1 The Coordination Side of ALS: Introducing a Weak Form of Regulation

MESRS continued to be the primary institution responsible for coordinating AET in Slovakia. The ministry only slowly introduced new legislation concerning AET and published the country's first lifelong learning strategy with a significant time gap to other CE countries. As in the rest of CE ALS, the strategic framework for AET was also developed due to Slovakia's accession to the EU. The European Commission insisted on the adoption of the Lisbon Strategy, which led to the publication of Government Note 140/2005—*Slovakia's Strategy of Competitiveness* (also known as the National Lisbon Strategy). This document outlined key developmental areas, including spheres of education, employment, and the building of a knowledge society. Two years later, Slovakia published the *Strategy of Lifelong Learning,* which fully adopted the EU's framework for AET. However, despite the diffusion of policy aims and terminology from the EU, some commentators (MPP, 2020) argued that the strategy was a rather formal document and lacked not only direct responsibility for specific aims and measures but also the necessary resources for their implementation.

For this reason, the only substantial policy measure introduced in fact by the state was a new Act 268/2009 on lifelong education. The act focused mainly on new rules for the accreditation of study programs recognised by the state. In most cases, these programs targeted professions connected with public service or other highly regulated professions. Although the act defined the basic forms of AET, like NFE, FAE and IFL, and their societal functions, it still regarded them as an extension and complement of the state's formal education system and not an independent field. According to Habodászová and Studená (2020), the reason for such a persistent notion of AET was based on the premise that all skill formation for the labour market should be done before entering it and not later.

Following Act 268/2009, the MESRS remained responsible for coordinating AET at the national level. It established the Commission for Accreditation of Further Education Programs, as well as the State Institute for Vocational Education. While the former unit was responsible for accrediting institutions that could provide AET with state certification, the latter began coordinating EU operational programs related to adult education (Eurydice SK, 2022). However, unlike other CE countries, these financial supporting tools for AET were introduced much later, after 2014 (MPP, 2020).

The second important state institution related to AET began to be *the Ministry of Labour, Social Affairs, and Family* (MLSAF), which was newly responsible for ALMP. In 2004, National Labour Office was transformed into the *Central Office of Labour, Social Affairs and Family* (COLSAF), which started implementing the agenda of ALMP under direct subordination of MLSAF (Štefánik, 2018). In this regard, training programs by MLSAF mainly targeted registered job seekers and no other social groups at risk (Studená & Polačková, 2020). Furthermore, the state expenditure on ALMP was one of the lowest among European countries, around 0.2% of GDP, which was six or seven times lower than in Scandinavia (OECD, 2023b). To make things even more financially constrained, only 4% of ALMPs expenditures were directly designated to training activities (Štefánik, 2018). As a result, public NFE focused on reskilling was still heavily underdeveloped in the 2000s.

In addition to the activities of MLSAF, other ministries also became responsible for their own professional staff development during this period, such as for the organised learning of police forces or healthcare professionals (Eurydice SK, 2022).

In summary, besides the introduction of a strategic framework, initiated by the EU, and a system for accreditation and recognition of AET providers in some professions, the state's approach became highly neoliberal and did not focus on the direct support of AET, nor improving coordination between key stakeholders responsible for organised learning of adults. This led the *Association of Institutions of Adult Education* to persuade state representatives to introduce much stricter legislative regulations regarding the adult education profession and quality standards in AET provision. However, these claims did not succeed in this period (Šilhár, 2013).

9.2.2 The Supply Side of ALS: Growth of the Uncoordinated Market

After 2000, ALS in Slovakia continued to be predominantly oriented to the private provision of AET, especially to job-related NFE. The public provision was limited to a basic model of ALMP for the unemployed (retraining courses for registered job seekers) and a limited amount of FAE. According to Štefánik (2018), the accessibility of public training activities for jobseekers was low, with around 1500–9000 annual participants.

Contrary to that, the availability of private provision expanded as the number of private providers has continuously increased since the 1990s and was estimated to be around 4000 during this period (EPP, 2020). This growth continued until 2009 when the new legislative act on lifelong learning allowed AET providers to accredit their programs focused on regulated professions. This motivated many organisations in the field, especially those running AET for professions recognised by the state, to seek accreditation. As a result, around 2000 organisations were accredited based on Act 268/2009 (Šilhár, 2013). A key output of this process was not only the substantial extension of the supply with NFE but also specialisation of the part of providers toward a particular niche of accredited courses.

At the same time, the supply of workplace learning for adults has expanded. Since 2000, many companies in Slovakia have adopted Western models of HRM/

HRD practices, including workplace training of employees, as they have become part of global supply chains (Misiak-Kwit et al., 2023). This adoption led to an increase in NFE provision among employers, particularly in large companies in the western part of the country that was targeted by FDI and had the most advanced systems of HRM/HRD.

However, the provision of popular NFE was not as strong in Slovakia as in other countries because the state did not support this area of adult education, and there were not enough specialised organisations in civic education. Instead, some community and voluntary organisations partially provided this type of organised learning but with very limited human and financial resources (Sládkayová & Krystoň, 2019).

9.2.3 The Demand Side of ALS: Stagnated Demand

Slovakia's economy recovered from the transition to capitalism soon after 2000, becoming one of the fastest-growing European economies (Kornái, 2008; OECD, 2020). However, improvement in general economic conditions did not directly translate into high demand for AET among adults and firms. Like other CE countries, Slovakia followed a dependent capitalism model (Magnin & Nenovsky, 2022) that attracted FDI through low taxation and wages. Such a "low path of economic competitiveness" (Crouch & Streeck, 1997) substantially restricted a large-scale need for updating and upgrading job-related skills of the labour force, which subsequently translated to low demand for AET.

Furthermore, most of the foreign investment was concentrated in the western part of the country, particularly in the Bratislava region, which even deepened economic disparities between western and eastern Slovakia that emerged during the 1990s (OECD, 2021). In relation to AET demand, it led to cementing occupational and educational inequalities in the eastern part of the country where the concentration of low-educated and low-skilled adults was comparatively higher (Studená & Polačková, 2020).

Beyond that, in comparison to other CE countries, the increase of higher-educated adults and high-skilled workers was much slower, and there were no significant changes until the 2010s. For example, the proportion of high-skill occupational positions even decrease a little bit between 2000 and 2008, and the proportion of medium-skill service workers rose only by 0.5% point in the same period. Furthermore, the share of skilled and unskilled manual workers even slightly grew (Gerbery & Džambazovič, 2018). As is evident from these numbers, the transition of social structure to a knowledge-based society in Slovakia froze during the 2000s.

9.3 Late Formation Phase: The 2010s

After a brief economic downturn in the early 2010s, Slovakia's economy experienced positive development (OECD, 2020; Studená, 2018). From 2015 onwards, unemployment has been decreasing and reached its lowest level in 2019, with a rate of 5% (Lichner, 2022). Nevertheless, the country also faced a negative demographic trend and high replacement demand, resulting in extremely high demand for labour power, which was one of the highest in Europe from 2012 to 2019 (OECD, 2022). Although the state approach to AET remained highly neoliberal, it made its first attempts to intervene in the uncoordinated market for adult learning, introducing new measures for the enhancement of the supply of educational opportunities.

9.3.1 The Coordination Side of ALS: Attempts in an Extension of Regulation

The MESRS continued to lead the coordination efforts in Slovakia's AET sector, overseeing national-level coordination and relevant legislation. In 2010, Slovakia released its second AET strategy, the *Strategy of Lifelong Learning toward 2020*, which aimed to establish a functional ALS and identified key stakeholders and forms of provision. The strategy aligned with the EU framework and emphasised the importance of AET for VET, economic competitiveness, and employability. It also aimed to introduce new measures to support participation in AET, such as financial incentives for providers and the system of recognition and validation of prior learning. To implement the new policy direction, the government amended Act 568/2009 on Lifelong Learning in 2012, setting new quality standards for lecturers and guarantors of accredited programs. However, these quality standards applied only to NFE education programs recognised by the state, which represented a minority of the overall education supply (Eurydice SK, 2022).

To improve the accessibility of AET, the state introduced financial incentives from the EU funds. The Institute for Vocational Education under MESRS coordinated the operational programme *Human Resources 2014–2020*, which should enhance the availability of educational opportunities and quality of AET supply through activities like training for educators, and co-financing organised learning in public and private organisations that received the projects.

The state also tried to establish a system of recognition and validation of NFE and IFL, which ultimately failed. Despite being a part of the national strategy until 2020, Slovakia was unable to introduce a law, methodical procedure, or a national qualification framework for this purpose. The Institute for Vocational Education's effort resulted only in the preparation of a set of 30 qualifications without any obligatory requirements (MPP, 2020).

9.3 Late Formation Phase: The 2010s   111

Only in the last few years, has the state begun to implement a new model of ALMP policy measures that directly targeted the social groups facing the most profound level of inequality. The key measure in this regard was the programme REPAS aimed at upskilling low-skilled workers and the unemployed and through consulting navigating them in their careers (Studená, 2018). The programme removed part of the previous constraints that were related to access to this education modality and the low quality of the training (Bondom & Nemec, 2015). As a result, the implementation of this measure triggered a significant increase in the number of participants among the unemployed as their participation rose more than twofold after the launch of the programme (Štefánik, 2018).

To summarise, despite the existence of a lifelong learning discourse and strategy, the implementation of the new AET policy measures mostly failed due to ineffective coordination on national, regional, and local levels, as well as state inefficiency and weak infrastructural power. Although the state improved ALMPs concerning education of the unemployed and job-seekers, involvement of other social groups at risk in public training continued to be low (EPP, 2020; MPP, 2020; Studená, 2018; Studená & Habodászová, 2020).

9.3.2 The Supply Side of ALS: Growth of Employers' Supply of AET

As a consequence of economic crisis, many educational providers went bankrupt (Šilhár, 2013), which negatively affected supply of NFE during the first half of the decade. However, this trend was overcome in the second half as the Report regarding the evaluation of public adult education policy in Slovakia estimated the number of providers higher than the decade before, between 4 and 5000 (EPP, 2020). The primary orientation of these organisations was job-oriented NFE, including courses on managerial skills, languages, self-development, and ICT skills. Consequently, private providers dominated the AET market, while public institutions offered only a small portion of FAE and BAE.

In regard to the supply of job-related NFE, workplace training became not only more common, as was realised by 80% of medium and large companies during the 2010s (Stachová & Smerek, 2023), but also became more specialised and professionalised. According to Stachová et al. (2020), 72% of workplace NFE in Slovakia was outsourced by companies in 2018, compared to 35% in 2010. Nevertheless, the supply of on-the-job training was primarily concentrated on employees in medium and large companies and focused on a narrow set of skills. AET provision in small enterprises remained rare. For instance, OECD's (2022) report on ICT access and usage by businesses found that only 8% of Slovak small companies provided any type of ICT training for their employees—only one-third of the volume that large firms offered.

The provision of AET was highly deregulated until 2015, when the state implemented financial incentives from the EU funds to support the supply of organised learning. However, the results of this financial instrument were at least mixed. On the one hand, accessing these resources was accompanied by a rising bureaucratisation, financial fraud, and non-existent outputs of the projects. On the other hand, the financial efficacy of the measure was questioned due to its high estimated cost of 11,000 euros per training person (Chovanculiak, 2021). Contrary to this expenditure, the average annual spending on the training of one employee in Slovakia's private sphere was usually between 51 and 100 euros. Only a minority (13%) of companies spent over 250 euros annually per employee, according to a national survey of HRD practice (Misiak-Kwit et al., 2023).

Similar to the previous two formation phases, the public provision of AET played a minor role in organised learning opportunities, which led to a low proportion of non-traditional students in FAE (Habodászová & Studená, 2020). Only developed areas of public AET represented new training programs under the umbrella of ALPM, which increased the participation of some social groups at risk that were previously almost excluded from any type of involvement in organised learning.

9.3.3 The Demand Side of ALS: Improving Conditions for AET Demand

Compared to the previous period, Slovakia's population had a higher demand for AET. Positive economic development and changing patterns of occupational and educational structure were behind this change. The percentage of employed individuals with a tertiary level of education has increased from 12% in 2000 to 28% in 2019 (Lichner, 2022; Večerník, 2022). Simultaneously, the proportion of low-skilled and semi-skilled manual workers declined from 45% in 2000 to 30% in the late 2010s. However, the share of high-skilled occupations remained at the same level as in the 1990s (Gerbery & Džambazovič, 2018). The reason behind this apparent mismatch between the rise of higher education graduates and the persistent level of high-skilled workers lay in two factors. First, overall focus on low-skilled and middle-skilled economic sectors (OECD, 2020, 2022) pushed demand for high-skilled occupations down and resulted in a partial skill mismatch in Slovakia's labour market (CEDEFOP, 2022). Second, very high migration trend of tertiary graduates to neighbourhood countries like Austria and Czechia that have proposed better work conditions for them (Haluš et al., 2017). In this case, outward migration caused a decrease in the overall skill mismatch.

However, it was not only a transformation of social and educational structure that influenced demand for organised learning among adults in Slovakia. Another critical mechanism was a strategy of firms that were facing shortages in both higher and lower-skilled workers (OECD, 2020, 2021; Misiak-Kwit et al., 2023; Studená, 2018; Škerháková et al., 2022). In 2018, the number of employers reporting issues with the number and quality of job applicants almost doubled compared to 2002

9.3 Late Formation Phase: The 2010s

(Stachová & Smerek, 2023). To cope with this issue, many companies have begun to train more frequently their employees and prepared them for new working roles that they were not able to fill by external job candidates (Studená, 2018). In this regard, the development of HRM/HRD played a crucial role in the execution of this strategy because only one-fourth of organisations had a position in management responsible for HRM in 2010, but by 2019, it had increased to over half (Stachová et al., 2020).

Despite some positive trends, there were still several factors in Slovakia that limited the demand for AET. Firstly, the economy relied heavily on FDI and low-cost labour in the automotive and electrical engineering sectors (OECD, 2022; Studená & Polačková, 2020). Although Slovakia experienced rising demand in AET, it was mainly concentrated among higher educated and higher skilled adults in the service sector, as well as those who work for large foreign firms, and not across all occupational categories and economic sectors. Moreover, the huge wage differential between foreign companies operating in Slovakia and domestic small and medium enterprises tend to discourage labour mobility towards domestic firms, reducing upskilling and exacerbating the limited training opportunities for workplace learning (OECD, 2022).

Secondly, the share of occupations with low-skilled requirements (Studená & Habodászová, 2020) remained high, and the financial situation of low-qualified workers as well as the unemployed have not changed too much during the 2010s (Studená, 2018). Therefore, financial barriers represented one of the main obstacles to participation among adults from these social groups (Studená & Habodászová, 2020; Studená & Polačková, 2020).

***

The development of the Slovak ALS exhibits various ambivalences. On the one hand, Slovakia introduced numerous institutional innovations in AET policies shortly after gaining independence in 1993, surpassing the pace of other post-socialist countries. On the other hand, the country experienced a more significant form of liberalisation in the late 1990s and refrained from intervening in the field of lifelong learning for almost a decade. This produced a specific policy vacuum where AET were developing without any coordination for much longer period of time than anywhere else in CE. As a consequence, many policy measures that were introduced in Hungary or Czechia were either delayed by a decade here or not fully implemented during the 2010s. Consequently, the lack of policy initiatives in the field of lifelong learning coincided with minimal horizontal changes in the structural features of ALS during the analysed period (see Part V). Nevertheless, similar to the situations in Hungary and Czechia, the gradual evolution of the occupational structure and the upward dynamics of the national economy after 2012 led to an increase in participation rates and improved access to educational opportunities for many social groups, especially those highly represented in the labour market.

Chapter 10
Poland

10.1 Early Formation Period: The 1990s

As in other post-socialist CE countries, the formation of ALS in Poland after 1989 was not a new beginning but was closely related to the restructuring of AET institutions established during the communist era. This process involved the decentralisation of state control over the adult education sector, as well as the differentiation and privatisation of organised learning provision. These changes were accompanied by a shift in the framing of AET, including its new role in a democratic capitalist society, and the redistribution of responsibility for adult education within the state apparatus. Contrary to the rest of the Visegrad countries, focus was done more on FAE system, especially the system of AGE.

10.1.1 The Coordination Side of ALS: The Transition from Socialism to Capitalism

Li and Wei (2019) observed that prior to 1989, ALS in Poland was highly centralised, with unified provision and political dominance of the communist party. All organised learning was part of a state educational system and was strictly VET-oriented. However, participation in AET was restricted to employed adults and members of the communist party, resulting in limited access to others (Dacko-Pikiewicz, 2013). In summary, besides the high level of centralisation and specialisation of AET, the socialist ALS also had a low level of differentiation and was characterised by significant inequality in access.

During the early 1980s, this form of ALS underwent a new reform, which further reinforced its existing features. The primary objective of the reform was to address the shortage of skilled workers in the main industrial sectors (heavy machinery and mining) by expanding workplace learning. This initiative resulted in the establishment of new educational centres that provided on-the-job training in major state-owned enterprises, as well as training for line managerial staff outside of the workplace. The blue-collar-oriented system of upskilling helped many low-skilled workers of this era enhance their professional skills and increased their social mobility. On the other hand, the system did not focus on the development of a broader skill set beyond the immediate learning needs of the heavy industrial sector. Additionally, the outcomes of education were not recognised as an achievement of FAE, and the entire system remained job-oriented and excluded many adult population segments until the 1990s (Dacko-Pikiewicz, 2013).

Following the downfall of the communist regime in 1989, ALS was completely abolished and was largely excluded from the major education reforms that followed (Eurydice PL, 2022). The issue of organised learning for adults was not a political priority at the time, and as a result, the first crucial legislative document of this period, The School Education Act of 1991, only briefly mentioned AET. Specifically, it defined the *Ministry of National Education* (MNAE) and the *Ministry of Labour and Social Affairs* (MLSA) as responsible for coordinating the FAE system and regulating vocational qualifications and ABE/AGE, respectively. Both these state actors became the main public institutions responsible for the coordination of AET.

Significant implications for organised learning of adults were introduced with the amendment of The School Education Act of 1991 in 1995. The amendment included the term "continuing education" in the legislative discourse, along with an outline of its principal social functions and the tools for its implementation. Furthermore, the amendment further specified the roles of the MNAE and the MLSA in the coordination of AET. The MNAE was assigned a leading role in providing training for adults in public schools, while the MLSA was instructed to focus on unemployment and related training (Eurydice, 1999).

Furthermore, the legislation introduced in 1995 brought about a new approach to AET, which diverged from the previous emphasis on on-the-job training in the state's industrial companies. With the MNAE possessing a dominant responsibility, AET was primarily viewed as a *school-based form of learning*, which the state should organise and provide as a *supplement to initial school education*, particularly for young adults with only basic education. This made it an extension of the formal education system, as evident from later developments in Poland's ALS, where there was a strong focus on FAE (Li & Wei, 2019; OECD, 2005).

I contend that the initial emphasis on the formal educational system for adult training in Poland has significantly shaped the development of ALS and operates as an institutional *path dependency*. The decision by the state to rely heavily on the formal educational system has created a strong inclination to maintain this orientation (institutional feedback loop), making it increasingly challenging to deviate from it. In fact, the state's subsequent decisions and policy measures have only further reinforced this "institutional lock" over time.

10.1.2 The Supply Side of ALS: Formation of State-Dominant AET Market

Compared to other countries in Central and Eastern Europe, the development of a non-regulated market with a wide range of AET provisions was slower in Poland. Although the state ended central coordination and support for regional NFE centres, some public companies kept them, albeit in a reduced form and on the periphery of their own interest (Eurydice, 1999). Because job-related NFE was not widely recognised practice across most firms and was believed that education belongs to schools (Dacko-Pikiewicz, 2013; Matysiak, 2003), the state provision of AET began to dominate again. However, it was not in the sphere of large industrial companies but in FAE.

According to the amendment made to the School Education Act in 1995, the state initiated the provision of BAE and FAE at the secondary level (ISCED 3–4) in various types of schools throughout the country. As a result, many state schools, originally established for initial education, began to provide AET, primarily for individuals who needed to enhance their qualifications. As of the late 1990s, about 420,000 adult students were enrolled in 109 adult elementary schools, 765 adult secondary comprehensive schools, and 1829 secondary vocational and technical schools (Eurydice, 1999). It is worth noting that most of these part-time students were young adults aged between 19 and 25 that were working along their studies (OECD PL, 2005). Therefore, the provision of AET in Poland after 1989 favoured FAE orientation.

10.1.3 The Demand Side of ALS: Structural Constraints and Slow Transformation

Structural characteristics of Polish society and economy in the 1990s and their transformation represent two crucial mechanisms that worked against a high demand for any form of AET. Its national economy experienced the highest drop in productivity during the 1990s among CE countries, as it went down from 53% in 1989 to 25% GDP per capita relative to Western European states (Berend, 2009). Furthermore, Poland had the least favourable occupational structure for the transition from industrial to post-industrial society. In this regard, several structural features reduced the demand for AET. First, a large portion (almost 40%) of the population lived in rural areas with limited provision of governmental services, including AET services by the state (OECD PL, 2005). Second, Poland had the highest share of employment (18% of employees) in agriculture among OECD countries (OECD, 2005). The employees in this occupation generally have low requirements for upskilling and also fewer chances to receive training from their employers (Illeris, 2006). Not to mention that they usually have a much lower level of initial education and literacy than workers in other occupations, which further restricts their involvement in organised forms of adult learning (Boeren, 2016). Third, most of the workers (three-quarters of them) were employed in small and medium enterprises (OECD, 2005) that usually have a minimal provision of AET for their staff (Brunello, 2001). Fourth, Poland had significant regional disparities between regions that had a high and low level of economic development (Cook, 2007). Underdeveloped regions usually combine all three previously mentioned factors together. Therefore, adults who lived in them faced a cumulation of structural forces that made their demand for AET at a minimum level.

Poland's transition to a liberal market economy did not trigger a significant demand for training within firms or professional associations. Unlike other CE economies, the shift from a planned to a market economy in Poland was slow and gradual. As an outcome, the state still owned over 3000 firms in the late 1990s (OECD, 2005). The favourable perception of late socialist reforms during the 1980s hindered a drastic break from the past and large-scale privatisation (Bohle & Greskovits, 2012). The slow economic transition also led to lower integration in the global economy and FDI compared to other countries in the region (Berend, 2009; Magnin & Nenovsky, 2022). Consequently, firms in Poland gave a low priority to training employees in the competitive strategies of the capitalist economy during this period.

10.2 Development Phase: The 2000s

After the Millennium, ALS in Poland turned into a new phase that was typical of both the new framing of AET and the first state attempts to regulate organised learning. During this period, two key social processes had a significant impact on the formation of ALS. Firstly, the response to the side effects of the economy and society's transition from socialism to capitalism, which resulted in soaring unemployment rates, up to 20% of the working population (OECD, 2023a), among the highest in post-socialist countries, and slow economic growth that exacerbated living conditions throughout Poland. Secondly, the process of Europeanisation of the public system was initiated when Poland joined the EU, and the government started to implement European Commission requirements, including the adoption of the EU lifelong learning framework. To address these two processes, the state introduced the first coordination mechanisms regarding AET, not only on the strategic, legislative, and policy levels but also through the introduction of a new public AET network.

However, the implementation of these measures was limited in scope. Most public institutions, including those responsible for AET, were still in the early formative stage after 2000, lacking the know-how to approach key social issues and qualified human resources (OECD, 2005). Poland's financial and social system, especially compared to Western European countries, was notably underdeveloped, and the state was only able to provide a weak form of coordination (Mykhnenko, 2007a, b). Furthermore, the political scene was particularly unsettled between 2000 and 2006, resulting in frequent changes not only to ministers responsible for the AET area but also to the title and organisational structure of the ministries. Finally, the state lacked sufficient financial resources for investment in education due to slow economic growth and a public finance crisis that led to austerity policies for much of the 2000s. The situation only began to improve by the end of the decade when Poland began to draw subsidies from EU funds and was more integrated into the world economy and international division of labour (Berend, 2009).

10.2.1 The Coordination Side of ALS: Differentiation and Specialisation

In order to prepare for accession to the EU, Poland initiated close collaboration with the European Commission in 2000. In relation to AET, this cooperation aimed at incorporating EU guidelines for organised lifelong learning into the Polish system. Following the EU principles, two key policy strategies were formulated. First, the *National Strategy for Employment* and *Human Resource Development, 2000–2006* was published by the MLSA in 2001. These strategies aimed at addressing the dominant problems of Polish society at that time, such as employability, labour market participation, and individual adaptation to large-scale market changes. It aimed at adapting the education and training system to labour market needs and implementing ALMP in line with EU recommendations.

Second, the MNAE published a *Strategy for the Development of Continuing Education until the year 2010* in 2005. This strategy introduced the concepts of lifelong learning and AET as regularly utilised by the EU policy, including key indicators of lifelong learning policy and an orientation towards VET for adults. Both strategies aimed at directing Polish organised learning towards a higher level of specialisation in job-related training, differentiating it from FAE provided by the state schools system and NFE by a network of Labour Offices (OECD, 2005; Wiśniewski, 2008).

Despite the establishment of key public institutions responsible for coordinating AET in the previous period, coordination activities were rare and rather formal. According to the OECD's report (OECD PL, 2005) on the state of AET in Poland, there was an obvious lack of horizontal and vertical integration of policy. Different ministries hardly collaborated with each other, although such cooperation is considered necessary for effective governmental action. Moreover, the state had insufficient financial resources for AET coordination and the development of new measures that could effectively increase participation in organised learning (OECD PL, 2005). Therefore, Poland showed one of the lowest levels of education spending among OECD countries during the 2000s (OECD, 2023d).

During this period, the core state institution responsible for AET remained the MNAE. However, the ministry experienced profound instability, as it was renamed four times between 2001 and 2006. It changed its title from MNAE to the Ministry of Education and Sport, then back to the Ministry of National Education in 2005. The following year, it was renamed again to the Ministry of Education and Learning, before switching back to the Ministry of National Education in the second half of 2006. These frequent changes reflect the unsettled nature of the Polish governmental apparatus during this period.

Regardless of these organisational issues, Poland launched an educational reform in 1999, culminating in the new School Education Act, and a new Act on Adult Education in 2003. The reform aimed to raise education levels and adapt the educational system to labour market requirements, following EU recommendations (OECD, 2005). Especially, the new Act on Adult Education brought significant changes to the provision of FAE, separating *Continuing Education Centers* (Centra Kzstalcenia Ustavicnego) and *Vocational Education Centers* (Centra Kzstalcenia Prakzycznego) from traditional schools dedicated to students of initial education. This change helped widen the national networks of AET public providers. Additionally, the act modified the rules for financing private organisations of AET from the state budget, shifting the core responsibility for financing to students (OECD, 2013). Despite organisational issues, the MNAE remained the critical state institution responsible for AET, establishing the Department of Vocational and Continuing Education in 2001 to coordinate and develop AET, including education centres (EAEA PL, 2011; Wiśniewski, 2008).

The system of FAE provision was strengthened by the "Law on Higher Education" in 2005, which introduced new legal regulations regarding post-graduate studies and FAE provision by universities for adults with completed tertiary education. This measure aimed to open universities to adult students who already had a higher level of education but needed to enhance it (OECD, 2013).

The second core institution of early Poland's ALS was the MLSA. The ministry began to have an increasingly important position as the level of unemployment rose to almost 20% at the beginning of the 2000s and remained high until 2007 (OECD, 2023a). Additionally, its role was even more enhanced when the government slowly shifted from a passive to the ALMP (Spieser, 2007).

A key milestone in the formation of AET-related social policy was the Act on Promotion of Employment and Institutions of the Labour Market in 2004. The aim behind this law was to increase the number and variability of retraining and training providers for the unemployed and individuals seeking a job. According to this act, all public and non-public organisations providing NFE for the unemployed or jobseekers must be registered by regional authorities. Only in this case, they were eligible to provide training and have governmental compensation for it (Act on Promotion, 2004). This type of AET was organised and partially provided by a decentralised network of Labour Offices that were established in the 1990s (Rashid et al., 2005). Nevertheless, ALMP ended up receiving very little funding, and most of the training schemes were reactive, rather than proactive investments into enhancing adults' skills (OECD PL, 2005). Furthermore, a big part of these measures was aimed at young people (16–24 years) rather than older adults who were targeted by the early retirement policy, especially in former key industrial sectors (Spieser, 2007). Instead, Poland chose to improve the situation of working women in the

2000s by expanding family policies, rather than implementing large-scale public training programs based on the social investment model (Hemerijck & Rondini, 2022).

Besides MNAE and MLSA, also other Polish ministries entered the field of AET in the 2000s. However, it was not in the sphere of national coordination, but on the provision side. Both the *Ministry of Culture, National Heritage and Sport* and *The Ministry of Health* built their own systems of professional VET training, including requirements for continuing education. These ministries' systems served to educate and develop workers according to their organisational needs. For this purpose, they established their network of school-based training institutions at the secondary and post-secondary level (EAEA PL, 2011).

10.2.2 The Supply Side of ALS: Strengthening of FAE Provision

During this period, the provision of AET in Poland gradually diversified, but it remained heavily focused on FAE. This emphasis was the result of the government's deliberate support of VET at the secondary level through state-run training centres and the expansion of higher education throughout the country. However, the expansion of tertiary FAE was not led by public universities, but by private tertiary institutions. This factor resulted in the intense marketisation of FAE and a fixation on AET's emphasis on job-oriented education.

In 2003, MNAE introduced a new structure of AET providers, which differentiated between Continual and Vocational Training centres. All of these school-based centres were coordinated by regional governments. The number of adult students enrolled in this network continued to grow to more than 350,000 annually, with the main participants being largely from the age group of 19–25 (Maliszewski & Solarczyk-Szwec, 2013).

Hand in hand with this new type of provision, Poland experienced a significant expansion of higher education during the 2000s, which led to a rise in the number of students from 400,000 to 1.8 million by 2011. More than 40% of them were non-traditional students, enrolled in part-time and distance study programmes, which represented a significant portion of FAE participants. However, the overall number of students peaked in 2012 and then declined due to a demographic drop (Kwiek, 2014; OECD, 2013). Unlike other CE countries, the rise in higher education students in Poland relied on the extension of private institutions instead of public ones. The higher education law of 1990 allowed tuition fees for students in part-time and distance study programmes and enabled the creation of private higher education institutions that began to specialise in FAE provision. Consequently, between 1991 and 2011, 350 private institutions were established, while the number of state universities only grew from 96 to 135 (OECD, 2013). This type of FAE was legislatively regulated by the state but became highly commercialised by both public and private universities, leading to high inequality due to tuition fees. However, the demand for higher education diplomas remained high as the relative financial return from obtaining such diplomas continued to be one of the highest among OECD countries (Kwiek, 2014).

Beyond that, universities also expanded their non-job-related AET and started providing education for the elderly (U3A), mainly due to short-term projects financed by EU funds (Maliszewski & Solarczyk-Szwec, 2013).

The second side of the state public provision represented training institutions that cooperated with regional Labour Offices and provided training and retraining for social groups at risk. All these institutions had to be accredited by a local governmental authority. The OECD report (OECD PL, 2005) estimated the number of these state direct or indirect providers in the mid-2000s around 2000.

Only at the beginning of the 2000s did opportunities for AET out-of-school increase, and the structure of private providers widened. Most of these new AET providers focused on NFE for employed, highly qualified individuals who aimed to improve their qualifications and skills to advance their careers (Li & Wei, 2019; OECD, 2005). Despite this new differentiation of the AET market, the offer of organised learning was dominated by FAE providers. This orientation, established already in the previous decade, was only fixed during this period. More emphasis was put on the outputs of formal education and access to it was both highly widened and commodified.

10.2.3 The Demand Side of ALS: Strong Constraints

According to Berend (2009), despite the large-scale shift of Polish society and economy from an industrial-agrarian to a post-industrial society, this transformation was still an unfinished project in the 2000s. Although the occupational structure transformed since the 1990s, employment in agriculture and industry remained high. Moreover, other structural characteristics, such as the proportion of the population living in rural regions, a high proportion of adults with a low-level of literacy, as well as people employed in small and medium enterprises still operated against a significant increase in demand for AET. In fact, these factors were even more pronounced in some regions that experienced de-industrialisation in the form of closing companies specialised in the mining and heavy metal industry, where unemployment rates were as high as 40% (Newell & Pastore, 2000).

Theoretically, the high levels of unemployment and significant changes in occupational structure that Poland experienced should increase the demand for AET due to the need for reskilling (OECD, 2019a, b). However, this phenomenon did not occur here, as only a small proportion of unemployed adults participated in AET. The persistent low demand for AET, despite societal challenges, was attributed to a specific state passive labour market policy with early retirement for workers in high-risk labour sectors, which facilitated the exit of older workers with long experience under the communist regime and inadequate skills for the capitalist labour market (Spieser, 2007). This policy was in line with the core of the post-socialist welfare states: a wide pension system, mostly free healthcare, and free tertiary education for young adults (Szelenyi & Wilk, 2010). Such an approach had side effects as caused a profound increase in state budget expenditure on the one hand, which significantly constrained a state's capacity to invest in both ALMP and quality of education institutions. On the other hand, it resulted in one of the lowest labour force participation rates among OECD countries, which further limited state tax revenue and economic growth (OECD, 2023a).

Following Berend (2009) and Nanovsky and Magnin (2022), another factor that worked against the demand for AET in Poland was a dominant firm strategy. Due to the prevalence of small companies and lower levels of FDI in large companies, on-the-job training was often seen as unnecessary or unimportant. An OECD report (OECD PL, 2005) found that most companies believed that their current staff was already adequately qualified for their jobs. Additionally, companies often perceived training costs as too high and preferred to recruit new workers with the required skills rather than invest in their current employees. Finally, they were concerned about the "poaching of employees" by other companies if they invest in their employees (Report Ministry of Economy and Labor 2004, cited in OECD PL, 2005).

10.3 Late Formation Phase: The 2010s

The development of ALS in Poland after 2010 did not turn in any abrupt modifications in the nature of the coordination or provision of AET. Adult education was still viewed as an extension of school education and retained a strong focus on VET (AET PL, 2020). Nevertheless, Poland's economic and social transformation brought it closer to the features of post-industrial societies, which could potentially increase the demand for AET as compared to the preceding two decades.

10.3.1 The Coordination Side of ALS: Vocationalisation and Homogenisation

With its inclusion in the EU, Poland's AET policy became increasingly Europeanized. One of the outcomes of this process was the adoption of a new AET strategy in 2013—*The Lifelong Learning Perspective* and *The Human Capital Development Strategy*. These two policy documents defined the key framework for AET and utilised the same terminology as the EU. Additionally, the objectives of the Polish strategy aligned with the EU's objectives, with a primary focus on AET as a tool for improving employability and enhancing economic competitiveness (Holford, 2023; Hoford & Milana, 2023).

The MNAE remained the primary entity responsible for AET during this formation period. The former Department of Vocational and Continuing Education was transformed into the Department of Strategy, Qualifications, and Vocational Education, which was newly responsible for the AET agenda. This unit not only dealt with the strategic planning of AET but also with the development of the Integrated Qualification Standards (IQS) system and the quality assurance of educational institutions. The IQS played an important role in the state agenda, as it aimed to standardise and homogenise the supply of AET. In this regard, all state-related or co-financed providers were expected to offer educational courses according to the IQS.

One of the policy outcomes of a substantial increase in the number of higher education graduates in the previous decade (OECD, 2013) was the development of a new framework for upskilling individuals with higher education. In this area, the government enacted a new Act on School Education in 2016 that introduced provisions for non-degree postgraduate programs as part of the third role of universities, awarded partial qualifications at levels 6–8 of the ISCED, and complemented IQS (Eurydice PL, 2022).

In addition to the MNAE, the MLSA still had a vital position in coordinating AET. Organised learning was part of the Labour Market Department's agenda, which cooperated with MNAE to ensure a skill match between basic and formal education outputs and labour market requirements. To support proactive reskilling among employers and employees, the ministry established the National Training Fund in 2014.

10.3.2 The Supply Side of ALS: Persistent Pattern

Although Li and Wei (2019) reported an increase in the number of training institutions and offered courses in Poland since 2010, the provision of AET remained predominantly focused on FAE. Consequently, the diversity of AET remained low (AET PL, 2020).

The most common public institutions for AET remained Continuing Education Centres and Vocational Education Centres, with their numbers increasing to 3200 and 600 respectively, according to Eurydice report (Eurydice PL, 2022). The majority of these centres were publicly funded and co-financed by local governments. The provision of public NFE for the unemployed and job seekers stayed similar to the previous decade. Due to the declining unemployment rate, which reached 5% in the late 2010s, the MLSA was not under any pressure to increase the number and diversity of training provision.

The primary change in the supply side of ALS during this period was the entrance of universities into NFE provision. Based on the new Act on School Education from 2016, universities began offering non-degree postgraduate programs. These programs were open to applicants with at least an ISCED 6 level of education and were required to last at least 2 years. This model of organised learning slowly gained popularity, with both public and private universities enrolling 152,000 students by 2019 (Eurydice PL, 2022).

10.3.3 The Demand Side of ALS: Slow Rise in Demand

According to Večerník (2022), there has been a steady transformation in the occupational structure of Polish society during the previous two decades, resulting in a significant increase in both high-skilled workers and the proportion of adults with a tertiary level of education in the labour force. The percentage of high-skill workers in services rose from 22% in the early 1990s to 35% in 2018, the levels comparable to other CE countries. Similarly, the percentage of employed persons with tertiary education increased from 19% in 2004 to 36% in 2014, which was a much higher proportion compared to the rest of the post-socialist block (CEDEFOP, 2022). Theoretically, this trend should increase the demand for AET across Poland; however, the job requirement for skilled adults remained low, leading to more cases of overqualification than underqualification and the need for upskilling (CEDEFOP, 2015). Furthermore, the low level of unemployment throughout most of the decade reduced the demand for reskilling. Despite this trend, the proportion of manual workers in the labour force declined only marginally, representing 30% of the labour force at the end of the 2010s, more than double the levels of Western European and Scandinavian countries. Additionally, employers did not encourage large-scale AET of their employees and tended to focus only on selected higher-educated and qualified workers (Eurydice PL, 2022), leading to the limited overall demand for AET.

***

The formation of ALS in Poland has exhibited significant differences compared to the other countries in CE. Poland faced not only a higher accumulation of structural constraints hindering the demand for organised adult learning but also adopted a distinct approach to AET provision since the 1990s, specific path dependency, which has been reinforced over time. Instead of relying on a more deregulated market for AET, Poland established an extensive network of formal educational institutions during the 1990s, and this network continued to expand during the 2000s. While other CE countries increasingly pushed toward job-related NFE, Poland maintained its orientation towards formal education and expanded access to higher (formal) education. However, this type of provision was accompanied by significant tuition fees for non-traditional learners, exacerbating educational inequalities rather than alleviating them. These shifts have positioned Poland as the most formal education-oriented ALS in the CE region. Due to the persistence of strong structural constraints in the country, Poland's overall participation rates in AET (see Part V) and related inequality (see Part VI) lag behind those of the other countries analysed.

Part V
CE ALSs in Global Adult Learning Space

This chapter turns attention toward analyses of the position of CE ALSs in GALS. This position is identified with the help of key available quantitative characteristics of AET in investigated countries, which were proposed earlier. Beyond the overall volume of participation, a vertical axis of GALS, my analysis explores the following five dimensions that constitute horizontal axes of the model (for details see Part III):

1. *The extensification of ALS* (extensive/intensive ALSs): identifying variation among ALSs based on the number of training hours per participant. This dimension enables me to understand whether CE countries belong to extensive or intensive ALSs.
2. *The role of FAE* (ALS with low/high FAE orientation): determining the position of the FAE system within the country. Understanding this position serves me to show how profound its role is in offer of organised learning opportunities.
3. *Employers' support of NFE* (ALSs with low/high employers' financial support): by measuring the proportion of NFE participation financially supported by employers, the research is able to show how much is the involvement of adults in NFE driven by employers' contribution and intentions.
4. *The supply of public NFE* (ALSs with low/high public provision of NFE): identifying a proportion of NFE provided by the state. By incorporating this axis, the analysis shows whether the presence of public institutions in NFE is profound in CE countries or not.
5. *The demand side of AET* (ALSs with high/low demand for AET): measuring a perceived demand for AET or its absence among adults. Revealing findings regarding this dimension clarify whether ALSs in CE have demand for organised learning among their population.

Following these dimensions, my research not only investigates the characteristics of CE ALSs but also their relation to other selected European ALSs. By examining their relative distance or proximity in GALS, it is possible to determine how unique or similar CE ALSs are compared to others ALSs—whether they belong to some specific set of countries or constitute a unique group. Furthermore, my analysis not only offers a snapshot of these systems, but also capturse the evolution of GALS over time, which reveals key formation pathways of CE countries between 1989 and 2019, which are crucial preconditions for understanding of their institutional formation after the fall of communism.

Chapter 11
Vertical Axis: Volume of Participation

As one of the primary internal characteristics of ALSs, the global volume of AET participation is examined in this chapter. For this purpose, the chapter uses three different measures of the vertical position of ALS—participation in AET. The first is based on a 12-month referential period utilised in large-scale international surveys like AES, IALS and PIAAC, which is also the most commonly used measurement of participation in international comparative research. The second employed data from the EU's LFS, which measures participation with a 4-week referential period. The last is focused on time spent by adults who participated in AET in the year prior to the survey—'time' counting instead of 'head' counting.

11.1 Participation in AET with a 12-Month Referential Period

Over the past two decades, there has been *significant growth in participation in organised learning among CE ALSs*, resulting in increased upward mobility in GALS. Table 11.1 presents data indicating significant increases in participation levels, from around *one-quarter* of the adult population to *nearly half of the population* by the mid-2010s. From the historical perspective, participation levels in CE countries were much lower than those in Nordic and Western European countries in the 1990s. However, by the 2010s, most CE countries had *almost caught up* with them, with the exception of Poland, where adult involvement in organised learning remained relatively low. In the case of the Czech Republic, Slovakia, and Hungary, participation levels were only slightly lower in 2016 compared to representatives of the western and northern parts of Europe. However, they were higher than in the Mediterranean, Eastern European and Balkan countries.

Table 11.1 Participation levels in AET in 12 months before the survey: 1997–2016

	1997[a]	2007	2011	2012	2016	IALS and PIAAC Change (1997–2012)	Annual growth (1997–2012)	Relat. growth (%)	AES Change (2007–2016)	Annual growth (2007–2016)	Relat. growth (%)
EU	N.A	35	40	51	45	N.A.	N.A.	N.A.	+10	1	29%
Central European countries											
CZ	26	38	37	49	46	+23	1.2	88%	+8	0.8	21%
HU	20	9[b]	41	N.A	55	N.A.	N.A.	N.A.	+46	4.6	511%
PO	15	22	24	32	26	+17	0.9	113%	+4	0.4	18%
SK	N.A	44	42	33	46	N.A.	N.A.	N.A.	+2	0.2	5%
Scandinavian countries											
FIN	59	55	56	66	54	+7	0.4	12%	−1	−0.1	−2%
NOR	57	45	59	65	50	+8	0.4	14%	+5	0.5	11%
DEN	47	45	59	67	50	+20	1.1	43%	+5	0.5	11%
Southern European countries											
ITA	23	32	36	24	42	+1	0.1	4%	+10	1	91%
PRT	14	26	44	N.A.	46	N.A.	N.A.	N.A.	+20	2	77%
Western European countries											
UK	45	49	36	56	52	+11	0.6	24%	+3	0.3	6%
BEL	21	41	38	48	45	+27	1.4	129%	+4	0.4	10%
GER	N.A.	45	50	50	52	N.A.	N.A.	N.A.	+6	0.6	13%
NED	38	45	59	65	51	+27	1.4	71%	+6	0.6	13%

Source: IALS (1997), AES (2007, 2011, 2016), OECD (2000), and PIAAC (2012)

Note: Data in percent

[a]Data were collected in those countries in the period of 1994–1997. Participation was measured as the involvement of adults (25–64 years) in any AET in the 12 months prior to the survey, with the exception of IALS. This survey collected data from respondents aged 16–51 years, where adults aged 16–19 participating in full-time studies (4 or more days per week) toward ISCED 0-3, and who are not financially supported by an employer or union are excluded. Similarly, adults aged 16–24 in full-time studies (4 or more days per week) toward ISCED 4-7, and who are not financially supported by an employer or union are excluded

[b]Low reliability of data. Change is measured within the same type of survey (AES vs. IALS/PIAAC). Annual growth rates are calculated distinctly for the time frames spanning from 1997 to 2012 (IALS/PIAAC), or from 2007 to 2016 (AES). Relative growth is assessed as the relative percentage increment in participation

N.A. data not available

In a previous series of national case studies, it was demonstrated that the augmentation of adult engagement in organised learning within Hungary and Czechia stemmed primarily from the establishment of a free, semi-regulated market since the late 2000s. This growth was further propelled by a rising demand for job-related NFE (NFE-Voc), a trend that gained momentum after 2010. Conversely, despite a nearly twofold increase in participation, Poland's involvement in organised learning remained notably lower. This discrepancy can be attributed to a predominant emphasis on the front-end model of skill formation and the prevailing focus on FAE, as detailed in the corresponding chapter on Poland's ALS in Part IV. Notably, Slovakia stands as an exception, experiencing a mere two-percentage-point rise in participation between 2007 and 2016. This may be attributed to the lack of data from the 1990s and the fact that monitoring of development in Slovakia began only after 2007. On the other hand, an examination in the preceding section of this book (Chap. 9) revealed minimal dynamism within the ALS in Slovakia. This is evident in the realm of coordinating AET, establishing avenues for participation, and the limited demand for organised learning up until the 2010s. As a result, the ALS in Slovakia has demonstrated a deficiency in vertical dynamics within the GALS.

Furthermore, Table 11.1 also shows that the *growth rate in CE ALS has been comparable with* other selected countries. While most Nordic and Western European countries experienced annual growth of between 0.7% and 1.4%, CE ALSs have grown by 0.9% and 1.2% in the period from 1997 to 2012. Generally, their growth was much quicker in the 2000s than during the 2010s, when it slowed down to 0.2–0.8% annually. This finding should not be surprising, as initial measured levels of participation in the 1990s were very low, due to both low demand and supply of educational opportunities. The exception among them represented Hungary, which experienced a much higher turnover. However, its available participation data from AES 2007 has low reliability, which should be considered. Data limitations also further restrict the possibility of making certain types of comparisons, specifically because data from PIAAC 2012 is unavailable for Hungary. Consequently, a comparison between the participation rates in the 1990s (IALS) and the 2010s (PIAAC) cannot be conducted.

11.2 Participation in AET with a 4-Weeks Referential Period

Table 11.2 covers the development of participation in AET from a different angle, using a 4-week referential period. Its data reveals significant shifts in the involvement of adults in organised learning across CE ALSs for a little bit shorter period than the previous analysis (2002 and 2019) but with a much higher (annual) density of data. Concerning this indicator, the participation growth rate varied profoundly between countries. While Hungary and the Czech Republic saw 100% and 45% increases in their participation levels, Poland experienced only a 14% rise. Slovakia, on the other hand, had a minor decline in comparison (−2.7%). Overall, this trend confirms previous findings in Table 11.1, with (1) a very high increase in

Table 11.2 Participation levels in AET in CE countries 4 weeks before the survey: 2002–2019

	2002	2003	2004	2005	2006	2007	2008	2009	2010	2011	2012	2013	2014	2015	2016	2017	2018	2019	Change 2002–2019	Annual change	Relative change	Annual relative change
EU28	7.1	8.4	9.1	9.6	9.4	9.4	9.5	9.5	9.3	9.1	9.2	10.7	10.8	10.8	10.8	10.9	11.1	11.3	**+4.2**	**0.23**	59.2	3.3
CZ	5.6	5.1	5.8	5.6	5.8	6	8	7.1	7.8	11.6	11.1	10.8	9.6	8.5	8.8	9.8	8.5	8.1	**+2.5**	**0.14**	44.6	2.5
HU	2.9	4.5	4	3.9	4	3.9	3.4	3	3	3	2.9	3.2	3.3	7.1	6.3	6.2	6	5.8	**+2.9**	**0.16**	100.0	5.6
POL	4.2	4.4	5	4.9	4.7	5.1	4.7	4.7	5.2	4.4	4.5	4.3	4	3.5	3.5	4	5.7	4.8	**+0.6**	**0.03**	14.3	0.8
SK	3.7	3.7	4.3	4.6	4.3	4.1	3.6	3.1	3.1	4.1	3.2	3.1	3.1	3.1	2.9	3.4	4	3.6	**–0.1**	**–0.01**	–2.7	–0.2

Source: LFS (2022)

Note: Data in percent. Participation was measured as involvement of adults (25–64 years) in any AET in 4 weeks prior to survey. Relative change is measured as a relative percentage increase in participation between 2002 and 2019. Annual relative change is calculated as an annual percentual increase since 2002 participation level in Hungary, (2) a medium increase in the Czech Republic, and (3) a minor growth in the Polish system of organised learning, accompanied by (4) stagnation of adults' involvement in Slovakia. In summary, this means significantly different dynamics in their vertical position in GALS since the 2000s.

Furthermore, long-term LFS data allows me to reconstruct more *detailed trends* in AET participation. Several shifts should be highlighted in this regard. Until 2007, all countries experienced zero to mild annual growth. Only after 2007, the Czech Republic began to increase its participation significantly. However, its growth lasted only until 2011 before gradually declining to a level of participation in 2019 that was similar to that in 2007, prior to the period of growth. This trajectory mirrors the patterns observed within ALS in Czechia, as previously discussed. Specifically, it reflects the adoption of a robust supply-oriented policy, leading to an expansion in the availability of AET opportunities post-2007. This expansion was accompanied by the emergence of increased demand within regulated public professions for additional on-the-job training. The zenith of these dual processes occurred approximately in 2011 and 2012. Subsequently, the government diminished its support for the supply-side of AET provision. Concurrently, a substantial demand persisted for training in regulated public professions. Both these processes were probably behind the fall of participation rates in Czechia in the second half of the 2010s.

Hungary's participation rate rose significantly between 2014 and 2015. Despite a slight decrease in 2016, participation remains higher than it was in the 2000s. The abrupt surge in numbers can be attributed to the introduction of a systematic 'workfare policy' in Hungary during 2015. This policy was designed to address unemployment by mandating many unemployed individuals to enter unfamiliar job roles (Albert, 2019), thereby necessitating their acquisition of fundamental training (NFE-Voc) for these positions.

In addition, Poland recently increased its participation in the pre-COVID-19 period from 2018 to 2019. Nevertheless, the rate of Poland's expansion was not comparable to previous Czech or Hungarian growth of organised learning opportunities. Until these years, participation rates in Poland remained notably low, amounting to only one-third of the EU average when considering a 12-month time frame, which only supports a claim that ALS here belongs among low-participation regimes.

Only Slovakia demonstrates a stable pattern of participation with no significant deviation in the total volume. With the exception of 2016, the level of AET participation there has never continued to rise above 5% of the adult population or fallen below 3%. Rather than experiencing upward mobility, Slovakia's ALS witnessed the reproduction of its position inside GALS. This finding reinforces the argument presented in the preceding chapter regarding the interconnectedness between the relatively subdued dynamism within ALS and its inherent vertical stagnation.

In summary, it is important to note that all of these changes in participation levels do not represent long and steady growth trends. Instead, they *are sudden year-to-year changes that increase adult involvement by more than 50%*. Hence, the chapter posits that there exists a strong likelihood that these developments were responsive to alterations in policies within ALS or the societal challenges encountered by these systems. It is intriguing to note that the timing and magnitude of these processes vary significantly across CE ALSs, implying that they are not indicative of a single process or challenge, but rather, they appear to be connected to diverse processes.

11.3 Getting Closer to the EU?

LFS data are also useful in assessing whether CE countries are truly *catching up* to Western and Nordic countries in terms of participant numbers—whether they *experienced convergence* in participation levels or not. This question is answered in Fig. 11.1, which captures the long-term change of participation in CE countries as a percentage of the average participation in the EU 28. The figure shows that CE ALSs began between 40% and 78% of the EU 28 average in 2002, with the Czech Republic having the best starting position and Hungary having the worst. Nevertheless, all of them *finished in a worse situation in 2019*, when Poland, Czechia, and Slovakia all dropped to lower levels. For example, the participation levels of Slovakia and Hungary were only 32% and 51% of the EU average in 2019. Therefore, the data from LFS indicate that rather than a convergence process, CE ALSs *experienced divergence* from EU levels.

In relation to average EU participation (see also Fig. 11.1), we can observe the same historical pattern that mirrors participation levels in AET measured by a 4-week referential period. First, an increase in convergence of the Czech Republic in 2011, when even overgrowth in the EU 28 average levels occurred for a brief period of time (2011–2013). Sharp growth in Hungary from 30% to 65% of the EU average in 2015, and late growth in Poland from 37% to 51% of EU levels in 2018.

Identification of divergence in participation levels holds particular significance for two primary reasons. Firstly, the EU has employed participation in AET over a 4-week reference period as a pivotal benchmark for assessing the effective advancement of ALS within a country (EC, 2009). Despite the Visegrad countries' endeavour to attain the ambitious objectives of 12.5% participation by 2010 and 15% by 2020, as stipulated within the 4-week reference framework, they not only fell short of achieving these targets but also demonstrated comparatively inferior performance when compared to nearly two decades prior. Consequently, their AET policies fail to garner success from both the EU's perspective and in a broader comparative context.

Secondly, a notable empirical incongruity emerges between the participation rates based on the 12-month and 4-week reference periods, necessitating resolution. While the extended timeframe implies a trend towards convergence, the shorter span suggests the presence of a contrary trend. In the forthcoming chapter, which delves into the extensification of AET in CE countries, one of the potential explanations for this enigmatic finding will be posited. The central premise of this argument revolves around the substantial reduction in training duration per learner across CE over the past three decades, leading to an escalation in participation rates within the

11.3 Getting Closer to the EU?

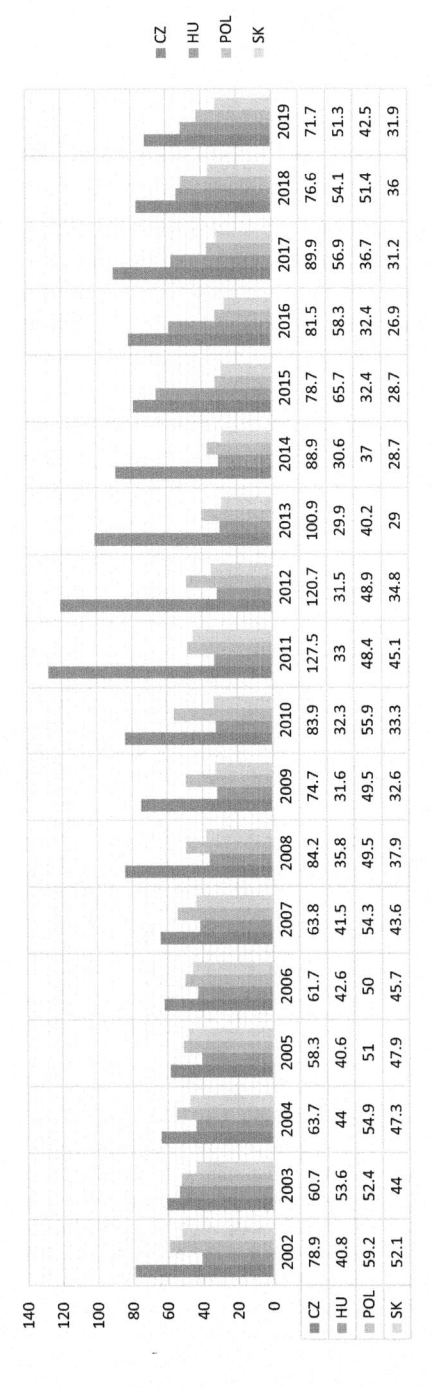

Fig. 11.1 Participation levels in AET in CE countries as a percentage of EU28 average: 2002–2019. (*Source:* LFS (2022)).
Note: Data in percent. Participation was measured as involvement of adults (25–64 years) in any AET in 4 weeks prior to survey

	2002	2003	2004	2005	2006	2007	2008	2009	2010	2011	2012	2013	2014	2015	2016	2017	2018	2019
CZ	78.9	60.7	63.7	58.3	61.7	63.8	84.2	74.7	83.9	127.5	120.7	100.9	88.9	78.7	81.5	89.9	76.6	71.7
HU	40.8	53.6	44	40.6	42.6	41.5	35.8	31.6	32.3	33	31.5	29.9	30.6	65.7	58.3	56.9	54.1	51.3
POL	59.2	52.4	54.9	51	50	54.3	49.5	49.5	55.9	48.4	48.9	40.2	37	32.4	32.4	36.7	51.4	42.5
SK	52.1	44	47.3	47.9	45.7	43.6	37.9	32.6	33.3	45.1	34.8	29	28.7	28.7	26.9	31.2	36	31.9

12-month horizon (higher occurrence of short-duration training among the population) but stagnation within the 4-week horizon (less training that would last 1 month or more).

11.4 Participation in AET Based on Training Hours

Not only participation levels based on the 4-week referential period and data regarding convergence to the EU, but also the volume of training reveals a less flattering aspect of the "growth story" of CE countries. With the exception of Hungary, all countries ended up in a worse position in the late 2010s than they had in the early 2000s (see Table 11.3). In contrast to both previous measures of participation,

Table 11.3 The average number of hours spent by participants in AET: 1997–2016

	1997[a]	2007	2011	2016	Change	Relative change in %
EU28	N. A.	124	131	119	**−5**	−4%
Central European countries						
CZ	123	91	86	51	**−72**	−59%
HU	177	220[b]	76	89	**−88**	−50%
PO	151	171	154	145	**−6**	−4%
SK	N.A.	95	83	49	**−46**	−48%
Scandinavian countries						
FIN	208	156	139	156	**−52**	−25%
NOR	219	198	171	167	**−52**	−24%
DEN	190	137	81	82	**−108**	−79%
Southern European countries						
ITA	193	113	92	115	**−78**	−40%
POR	N.A.	209	181	133	**−76**	−36%
Western European countries						
UK	157	72	167	121	**−36**	−23%
BEL	125	156	104	112	**−13**	−10%
GER	N.A.	147	141	124	**−23**	−16%
NED	240	59	127	89	**−151**	−63%

Source: IALS (1997), AES (2007, 2011, 2016), OECD (2000)
Note: Data in hours
[a]Data were collected in those countries in the period of 1994–1997. Participation is measured as the average number of hours spent by participants (25–64 years) in any AET in the 12 months prior to the survey with the exception of IALS. This survey collected data from respondents aged 16–51 years, where adults aged 16–19 participating in full-time studies (4 or more days per week) toward ISCED 0-3, and who are not financially supported by an employer or union are excluded. Similarly, adults aged 16–24 in full-time studies (4 or more days per week) toward ISCED 4-7, and who are not financially supported by an employer or union are excluded
[b]Low reliability of data. The calculation of change is conducted for the timeframe spanning from 1997 to 2016, whenever data is accessible. In instances where such data is not available, the calculation encompasses the period from 2007 to 2016. The determination of relative change is executed by expressing the percentage shift between the years 1997 and 2016, as well as between 2007 and 2016
N.A. data not available

11.4 Participation in AET Based on Training Hours

training hours have been steadily declining since the 1990s. During the monitoring period, the Czech Republic, Slovakia, and Hungary lost 48–59% of their hour training volume per participant. This is a significant change, especially when compared to other EU countries. Although this decline has been a common trend in Europe since the 2000, CE countries experienced one of the most profound changes in this direction. The only exception was Poland, which underwent only a slight decrease in training volume (−4%).

The modest alteration within this aspect of Poland's ALS is likely attributed to the enduring emphasis on FAE that has persisted since the 2000s. Broadly speaking, FAE involves the implementation of more comprehensive and extended courses compared to NFE training programs. This particular approach has aided Poland in maintaining its training volume per participant. Conversely, other CE countries, while transitioning toward a greater focus on workplace and employer-organised NFE and training (for more details see the upcoming chapter about employers' supported NFE), have observed a reduction in training volume. This can be attributed to the fact that company-based training (NFE-Voc) tends to be less formalised and of shorter duration (Brunello et al., 2007; CEDEFOP, 2022).

Beyond that, Table 11.3 also shows that, excluding Poland, CE countries had the lowest level of training hours spent by adults who were involved in organised learning. Their volume was usually less than half that of Western or Nordic countries. Such a finding supports my contention regarding the "extensification" of CE ALSs, a concept that is comprehensively expounded upon in the subsequent chapter focused on the first horizontal axis of GALS.

Chapter 12
First Horizontal Axis: The Extensification of AET

According to Desjardins (2011; see also Desjardins et al., 2006), combining the participation of persons and training hours provides a much *more nuanced picture* of the global development of the volume side of ALSs. The following section represents insight into this issue as it includes a series of analyses focusing on the interaction of AET participation and training volume. The first of them (Fig. 12.1) reveals that CE countries began their development as ALSs with low-level participation and a medium number of training hours in the 1990s, especially if we compare them with Nordic countries and the UK in the same period. Unlike to CE ALSs, they had significantly higher levels of participation and training hours per participant in organised learning.

Over time, CE countries have transformed into *highly extensive ALSs* with almost as high participation in AET (vertical dimension of participation) but a very low volume of training hours (horizontal dimensions of participation). As Fig. 12.2 shows, most of their growth between the 1990s and the 2010s has been due to the shortening of the time dedicated to organised learning. The regression analysis in this figure also reveals a strong relationship between the percentage growth of participation and the decline in hours of participation for CE ALSs (see Fig. 12.2). This suggests that the increase in participation levels in the Visegrad region and the process of extensification of AET have been closely linked. The results of this analysis provide additional evidence for the argument that the *growth in participation in CE ALSs is associated with a decline in the volume of training hours*. This implies that the expansion of participation in AET in CE countries has been driven primarily by the *expansion* of *low-intensity, low-volume forms of learning*, rather than high-intensity, high-volume modalities of AET—like longer courses in the area of ABE, AGE and AHE.

Drawing on this insight, the comparatively low participation levels in LFS metrics for CE ALSs can be explained by the shorter (4-week) frame of participation measurement used in the LFS. This shorter time frame may not adequately capture

© The Author(s), under exclusive license to Springer Nature Switzerland AG 2024
J. Kalenda, *Formation of Adult Learning Systems in Central Europe*, Lifelong Learning Book Series 32, https://doi.org/10.1007/978-3-031-59827-2_12

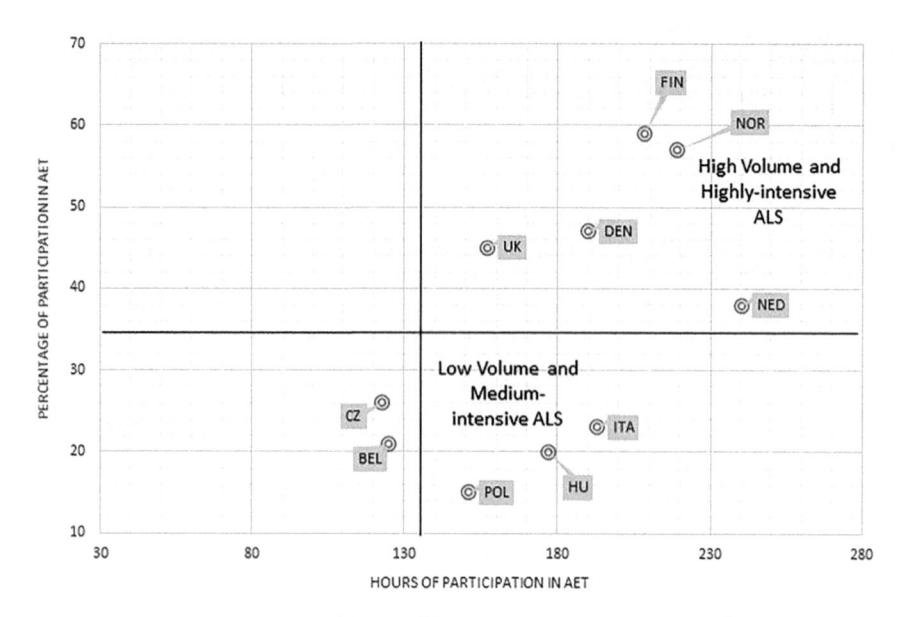

Fig. 12.1 Selected European ALSs in 1997: Percentage of participation in AET in CE ALSs and average number of hours spent by participants in AET. (*Source*: own calculation based on the data from IALS, 1997; OECD, 2003)

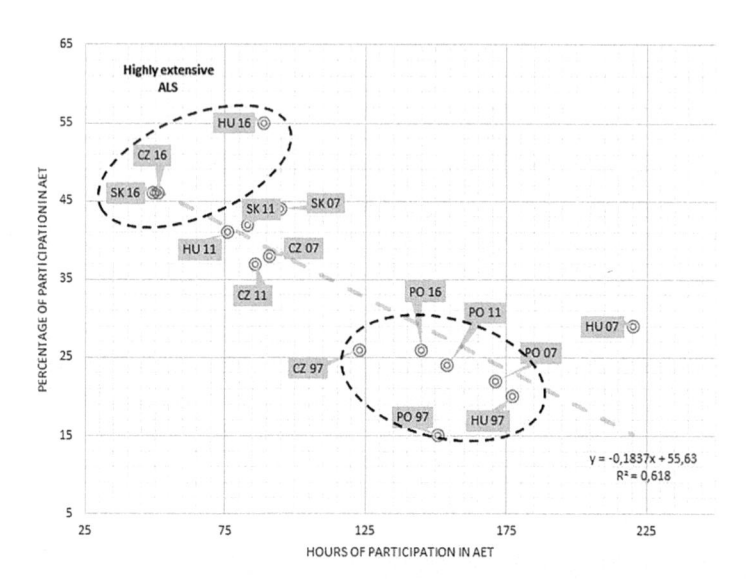

Fig. 12.2 Percentage of participation in AET in CE ALS and average number of hours spent by participants in AET: 1997 to 2016. (*Source*: own calculation based on the data from IALS, 1997; AES, 2007, 2011, 2016; OECD, 2003)

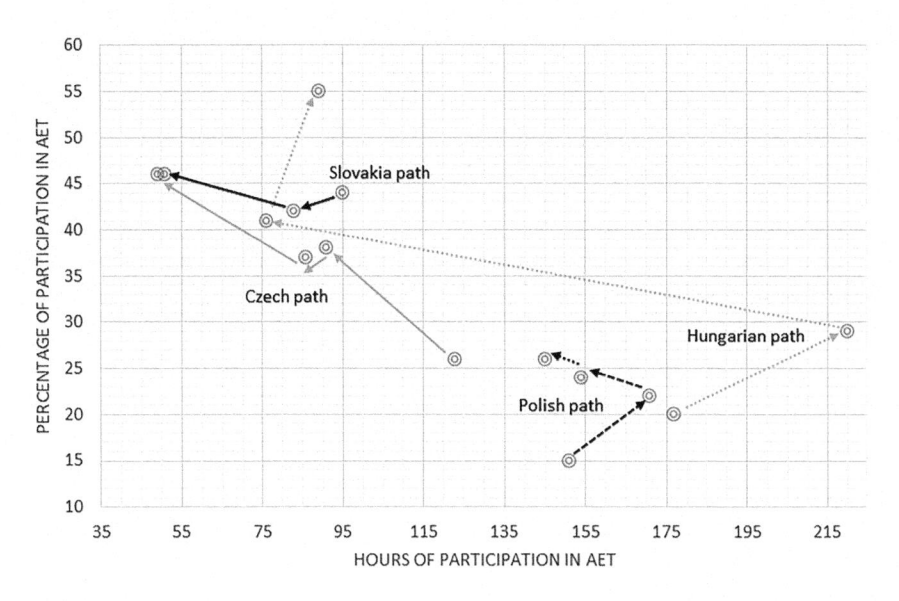

Fig. 12.3 Trajectories of CE ALSs between 1997 to 2016: From medium-intensive ALSs to highly extensive ALSs. (*Source*: own calculation based on the data from IALS, 1997; AES, 2007, 2011, 2016; OECD, 2003)

short-duration NFE training activities, which are more common for CE countries than for other European ALSs, leading to lower reported participation levels in the LFS data. Therefore, CE ALSs have exhibited closer vertical alignment with Western and Nordic countries in terms of absolute participation levels, measured by 12-month period; however, they have maintained a greater distance from these countries in relation to training volume. The origins of this discrepancy can be attributed to a confluence of parallel processes within CE countries: (1) there has been a notable surge in demand for training among individuals with lower skill levels and limited education post-2010 in the region. This training is typically less time-intensive compared to the training required for many highly skilled professionals (OECD, 2019a, b); (2) there has been a relative decline in participation in FAE, which generally encompasses longer-duration courses (for details see the upcoming chapter about orientation of ALSs toward FAE); (3) The CE population contains a significant proportion of adults possessing at least a secondary education (ISCED 3) when compared to other nations (WB, 2023). Consequently, this demographic typically requires less supplementary AGE, which is again time-consuming.

As shown in Fig. 12.3, specific formation trajectories of CE ALSs are depicted. The various lines in the figure display the paths that national lifelong learning systems have followed since 1997 within GALS. The process of extensification has not been straightforward, as Poland and Hungary initially moved towards more intensive ALS during the late 1990s and early 2000s. This initial direction can probably be associated with their early focus on FAE (Poland) and support of long-duration NFE courses (Hungary) during that time. Only after 2011 did they begin to pursue a path towards higher extensification. Especially, Hungary bet on short-duration NFE-Voc, while the introduction of this type of organised training in Poland has been much more limited. Additionally, there are small differences between Czechia and Slovakia. Czechia underwent extensification of AET with significant growth, whereas this process in Slovakia was not accompanied by a notable increase in participation rates, only by a horizontal move toward higher extensification. However, ultimately, all of these trajectories *led to the evolution into some of the most extensive ALSs among advanced industrial countries.*

Chapter 13
Second Horizontal Axis: Orientation Toward FAE

13.1 Long-Term Trends in FAE

The FAE represents a smaller but important part of AET. Usually, it indicates the extent to which a state is involved in the provision of certified adult education opportunities and the scope to which opportunities are made available for non-traditional learners (Table 13.1 shows data on participation rates in FAE in selected European countries between 2007 and 2016. The table differentiates between participation in FAE with educational outcomes of ISCED 3–4 level, typical AGE (left part of the table), and AHE of ISCED 5–8 levels (right part of the table). We can see that with the exception of Hungary, the general *trend across CE ALSs has been decreasing since 2007*, indicating that FAE has been in decline in this region. In the case of Hungary, we must take in mind the low reliability of their national data for 2007. If we use more reliable data, for a shorter period (2011–2016), we can also identify decline (for category ISCED 3–4) and stagnation (for category ISCED 5–8). Last but not least, the overall decline in the Visegrad region was even more profound in AGE than in AHE.

Also, data from LFS (Table 13.2) reveal the same pattern for CE countries in approximately the same time period (2004–2019), an overall loss of 15–58% of participation volume in FAE in the age category of 25–64 years. Only a minor exception here is represented by Czechia, which experienced stagnation. In comparison, most of the other European countries not only already had much higher participation rates in FAE in the early 2000s, but they even expanded it over time—like France, Austria, Ireland and many Nordic nations. For comparison, participation in this form of organised learning in Nordic countries was six to seven times higher in 2019 than in CE.

In regard to this finding, it is worth noting that Poland, despite emphasising FAE since the 1990s, observed a reduction in participation within this organised adult learning category. This outcome can likely be attributed to a significant portion of

Table 13.1 Participation levels in formal adult education in 12 months before the survey: 1997–2016

	ISCED 3–4 AGE					ISCED 5–8 AHE				
	2007	2011	2016	Growth	Relative change (%)	2007	2011	2016	Growth	Relative change (%)
Central European countries										
CZ	3	3	1	−2	**−62**	10	10	8	−2	**−22**
POL	3	3	2	−1	**−28**	16	14	10	−7	**−41**
HU	2[a]	9	6	3	**+142**[a]	6	11	12	7	**124**
SK	5	4	N.A.	−1	**−16**	11	14	3	−8	**−70**
Nordic countries										
SWE	7	10	9	2	**+33**	25	21	21	−3	**−14**
FIN	12	13	15	4	**+33**	13	14	14	1	**8**
NOR	7	N.A.	8	1	**+12**	17	10	17	0	**0**
DEN	10	11	11	1	**+15**	13	18	18	5	**35**
Southern European countries										
ITA	6	4	4	−2	**−28**	14	7	6	−8	**−56**
POR	14	15	5	−9	**−62**	15	13	8	−7	**−45**
FRA	5	3	3	−2	**−40**	9	7	6	−3	**33**
Western European countries										
BEL	11	7	7	−4	**−40**	19	11	9	−10	**−53**
NED	6	13	8	2	**+36**	11	17	11	−1	**−4**
GER	4	3	3	−1	**−26**	7	5	5	−2	**−28**
AUT	3	5	4	1	**+33**	8	13	13	5	**66**
Anglo-Saxon countries										
UK	17	15	12	−6	**−33**	21	19	16	−5	**−25**
IRL	N.A.	6	6	0	**0**[b]	N.A.	10	13	3	**30**[b]

Note: Participation levels in percent. N.A. data not available. The calculation of growth is conducted for the timeframe spanning from 2007 to 2016, whenever data is accessible. In instances where such data is not available, the calculation encompasses the period from 2007 to 2011 or 2011 to 2016. The determination of relative change is executed by expressing the percentage shift in the category of growth
Source: AES (2007, 2011, 2016)
[a]Low reliability of data for Hungary in 2007
[b]Calculated as change between 2011 and 2016 for Ireland. ISCED 3–4 = participants of AET aged 25–64 years with upper secondary and post-secondary non-tertiary education. ISCED 5–8 participants of AET aged 25–64 years with tertiary education

Poland's AET provision being directed towards younger adults (aged 16–24) in AGE, a realm not encompassed within the scope of data employed for assessing this aspect of the ALS and targeted adults aged 25–64 years.

For the remaining CE countries, this trend can be linked to their predominant focus on job-related NFE, which is predominantly facilitated by employers and private organisations. Moreover, the HE expansion that these countries experienced during the 2000s was also mainly focused on young adults in the initial phase of

13.1 Long-Term Trends in FAE

Table 13.2 Development of participation levels in formal adult education: 2004–2019 (4-week referential period)

	2004	2005	2006	2007	2008	2009	2010	2011	2012	2013	2014	2015	2016	2017	2018	2019	Change	Rel. change (%)
CZ	1.6	1.9	1.8	1.9	2.3	2.4	2.5	2.5	2.6	2.3	2.3	2	2	2	1.9	1.7	+0.1	6
HU	2.8	2.5	2.7	2.6	2.3	2.2	1.9	2	1.7	1.5	1.2	1.2	1.2	1.3	1.4	1.4	−1.4	−50
POL	3.1	3.2	2.9	3.1	2.9	3	3.1	2.8	2.7	2.6	2	1.7	1.6	1.5	1.5	1.3	−1.8	−58
SK	1.3	1.5	1.6	1.9	2	1.9	2	2	1.5	1.4	1.4	1.2	1.2	1.1	1.1	1.1	−0.2	−15
Average	2.2	2.3	2.3	2.4	2.4	2.4	2.4	2.3	2.1	2.0	1.7	1.5	1.5	1.5	1.5	1.4	−0.8	−38
SWE	7.8	6.2	6.1	6.3	6.2	6.4	6.9	6.9	7.2	7.5	7.7	7.6	8	8.2	8.7	9.6	+1.8	23
FIN	7.6	7.6	7.9	8.2	8.2	8	8.3	8.6	8.7	8.9	8.8	9.1	9.4	9.5	9.7	9.9	+2.3	30
NOR	7.6	7.6	7.9	8.2	8.2	8	8.3	8.6	8.7	8.9	8.8	9.1	9.4	9.5	9.7	9.9	+2.3	30
DEN	7.3	6.8	6.2	5.8	5.4	5.3	5.6	6	5.8	6.5	6.8	6.9	7.8	6.9	6.5	6.5	−0.8	−11
Average	7.6	7.1	7.0	7.1	7.0	6.9	7.3	7.5	7.6	8.0	8.0	8.2	8.7	8.5	8.7	9.0	+1.4	18
ITA	3	3	3.1	3.1	3	2.9	2.7	2.6	2.7	2.5	2.6	2.6	2.5	2.5	2.5	2.5	−0.5	−17
POR	2.9	2.9	3	3.2	3.9	4.8	4.1	6.3	4.8	3.3	3.1	3.2	2.9	3	3	2.9	+0.0	0
FRA	0.7	0.7	0.7	0.7	0.7	0.6	0.6	0.7	0.7	1.6	1.8	1.8	1.8	1.8	1.8	1.9	+1.2	171
Average	2.2	2.2	2.3	2.3	2.5	2.8	2.5	3.2	2.7	2.5	2.5	2.5	2.4	2.4	2.4	2.4	+0.2	11
GER	2.8	3.1	2.9	2.9	3.1	3.1	3.1	3	3.1	3.3	3.5	3.6	3.6	3.7	3.6	3.5	+0.7	25
AUT	2.9	3	3.1	3.2	3.4	3.9	4.1	4	4.1	4.2	4.3	4.5	4.4	4.7	4.4	4.3	+1.4	48
BEL	1.9	2.2	2.2	2.1	2.3	2.4	2.5	2.8	2.7	2.4	2.5	2.6	2.5	2.5	2.6	2.4	+0.5	26
NED	7.1	6.6	7	7.3	7.4	7.5	7.5	7.5	7.5	7.1	6.8	6.8	6.7	6.9	7.3	7.6	+0.5	7
Average	3.7	3.7	3.8	3.9	4.1	4.2	4.3	4.3	4.4	4.3	4.3	4.4	4.3	4.5	4.5	4.5	+0.8	21
UK	7.5	6.6	6.7	6.4	6.5	6.7	6.7	6.1	5.8	5.8	5.7	5.3	4.1	4	4	3.9	−3.6	−48
IRL	3.4	3.2	3.3	3.8	3.8	4	4.2	4.3	4.5	5	4.7	4.3	4.2	4.3	4.5	4.5	+1.1	32
Average	5.5	4.9	5	5.1	5.2	5.4	5.5	5.2	5.2	5.4	5.2	4.8	4.2	4.2	4.3	4.2	−1.3	−23

Note: Participation measured by 4-week referential period. Adults aged 25–64 years. Data in per percent
Source: LFS (2022)

their professional preparation rather than being an integral component of broader upskilling and reskilling pathways across a life course. The amalgamation of these processes further exacerbated the already weakened state of FAE during the 1990s, a fragility that persisted and even intensified throughout the last decade.

13.2 Changes in the Role of FAE

Figure 13.1 offers insight into differences between recent ALSs based on their orientation towards FAE, which is measured by the share of FAE on the total volume of participation in AET (in percent). This indicator enables us to capture the relative size of the FAE in various ALSs. According to this criterion, we can locate ALSs that have a comparatively high focus on FAE and those where this focus is minor. Following this logic, we can see that *recent CE countries fall surprisingly into both categories.* On the one hand, the Czech Republic, Slovakia, and Hungary represent typical ALSs with *weak FAE orientation* and medium to high overall participation. On the other hand, Poland is a country characterised by a *strong orientation towards FAE.* Participation in this type of AET included almost 12% of all provided AET in 2016. However, unlike other ALSs oriented towards FAE (e.g., Finland or Denmark), it had much lower overall levels of adult involvement in AET.

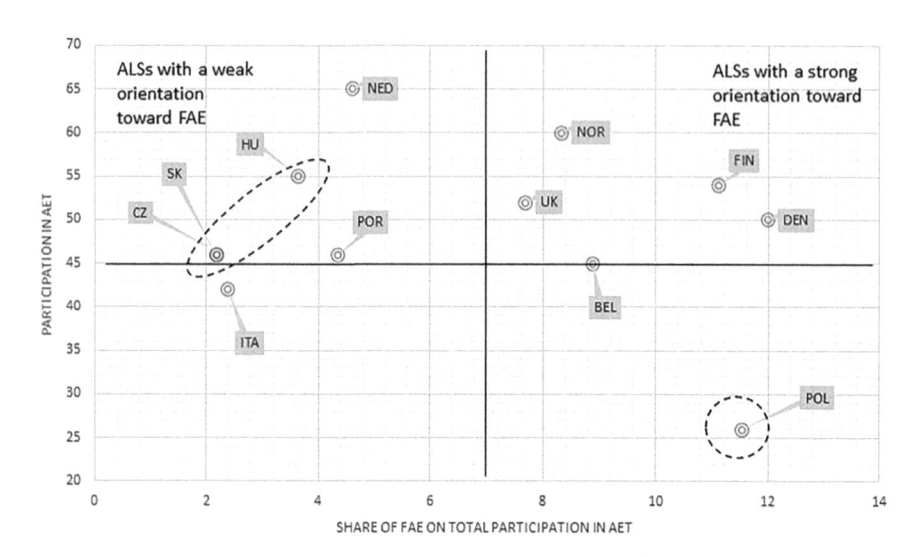

Fig. 13.1 Selected European ALSs in **2016**: Percentage of participation in AET and the share of FAE on the total participation in AET. (*Source*: own calculation based on the data from AES, 2016) *Note*: The data presented in this figure are reported in percentages. Participation is measured as the involvement of adults aged 25–64 years in AET within the 12 months preceding the survey. Share of DAE measure as a share of participation in FAE on the total participation in AET

13.2 Changes in the Role of FAE

The next figure (Fig. 13.2) maps the formation trajectories of selected European countries in GALS in relation to the change in the share of FAE on the total volume of AET participation. It clearly demonstrates that the importance of FAE for the overall level of participation has slowly disappeared across analysed ALSs, with the exception of Nordic countries. Contrary to other regions, development in Northern Europe has led to a relative increase in FAE participation. Furthermore, we can track down two regular formation pathways towards ALS with low FAE orientation. First, it is growth trajectories with a decreasing proportion of FAE, which is typical not only for Southern European countries but also for the Netherlands. The second pathway is a trajectory without significant overall growth in participation, which is common, for example, in Belgium or the UK. This pathway, rather than representing a change due to an increase in participation (outcome of quantitative change within ALS), indicates a change in the internal ratio of various forms of organised learning and thus a reorientation of the country's system.

The last figure (Fig. 13.3) provides insight into the formation trajectories of CE countries. As is common among many countries that have started building their ALSs late, countries across CE have typically been characterised by a growth trajectory accompanied by a decline in FAE participation. The results of the regression analysis presented in the figure indicate that these two processes have been strongly interrelated among CE ALSs. The growth went hand in hand with the decline of FAE proportion on a total of participation. The most dynamic change occurred in

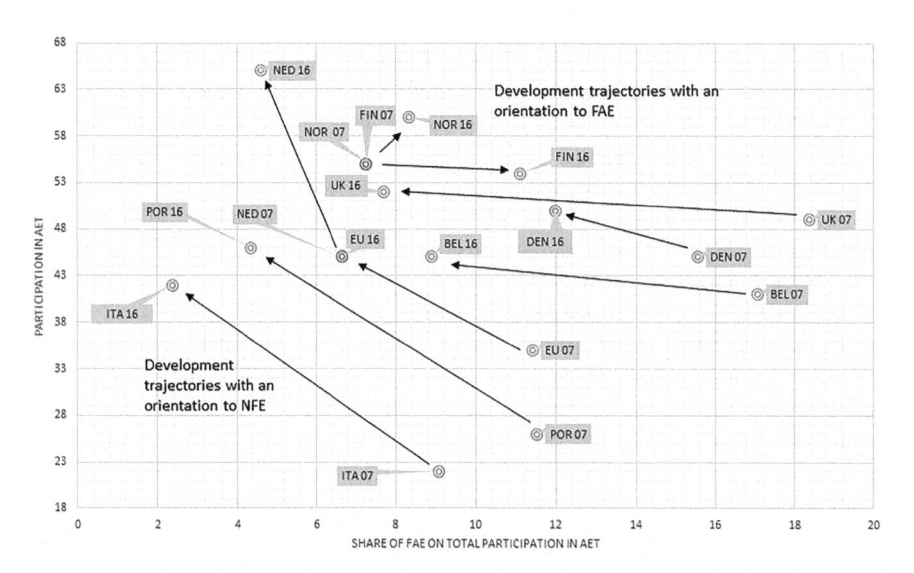

Fig. 13.2 Trends in share of FAE among selected European ALSs: 2007–2016. Percentage of participation in AET and the share of FAE on the total participation in AET. (*Source*: own calculation based on the data from AES, 2007, 2016)
Note: The data presented in this figure are reported in percentages. Participation is measured as the involvement of adults aged 25–64 years in AET within the 12 months preceding the survey. Share of FAE measure as share of participation in FAE on the on total participation in AET

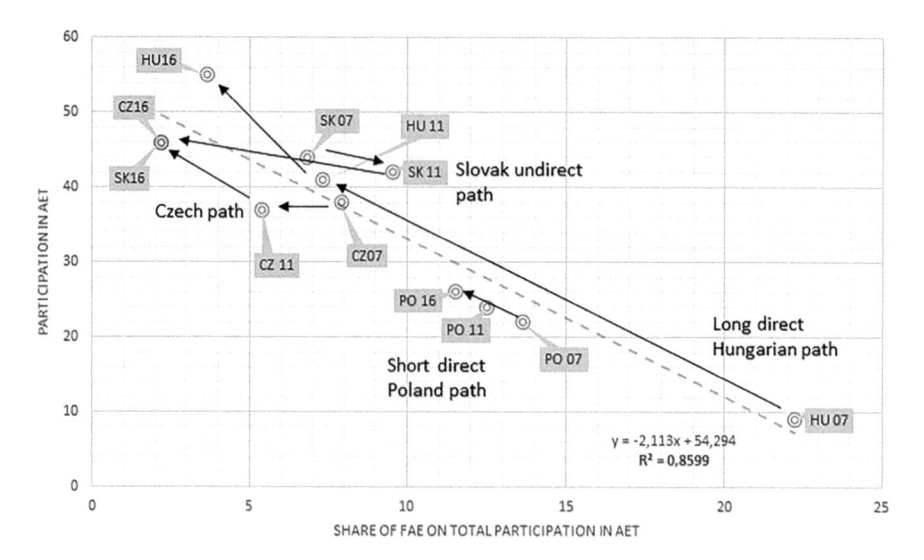

Fig. 13.3 Trajectories of CE ALSs between 2007 and 2016. (*Source*: own calculation based on the data from AES, 2007, 2016)

Note: The data presented in this figure are reported in percentages. Participation is measured as the involvement of adults aged 25–64 years in AET within the 12 months preceding the survey. Share of DAE measure as share of participation in FAE on the on total participation in AET

Hungary and the Czech Republic, while in Poland, it was only minor. As a result, the Polish lifelong learning system *has remained strongly oriented to FAE*.

In a series of case studies (see Part IV), I explained that the majority of CE ALSs have encountered challenges in establishing a robust framework for FAE intended for adults. On the one hand, the attainment rate for secondary education (ISCED3) among adults aged 18 has reached around 90% of the population, with the sole exception of Slovakia, which exhibited a slightly lower score (WB, 2023). Consequently, the social demand for 'second chance education', specifically AGE, has historically remained restricted within the region.

On the other hand, investment in formal education has primarily focused on the expansion of tertiary education systems for the youth, with comparatively less emphasis on older adults. As these two dynamics intersected with the limited fiscal resources available to the state, particularly exacerbated during the period of austerity following economic crises, the CE countries encountered both motivational and financial constraints that hindered the expansion of their FAE provision.

Chapter 14
Third Horizontal Axis: Employers' Support of NFE

14.1 Long-Term Trends in Job-Related NFE

The following chapter addresses the extent to which ALSs in CE countries are embedded in the economic market, specifically, how focused they are on *job-related NFE* that is primarily delivered in work-related settings (OECD, 2019b), and relies on employers' support. Investigating these aspects helps me understand the level of companies' involvement in current AET and the changes that have occurred since the 1990s. To what extent has AET across CE shifted towards meeting the needs and requirements of employers and their financial involvement in training their employees? This is important because job-related NFE currently constitutes the majority of participation rates in AET (Desjardins, 2017, 2020; Kureková et al., 2023; Rubenson, 2018; Wotschack, 2020).

The first presented table (Table 14.1) covers long-term development trends in participation in job-related NFE between 1997 and 2016, while the second (Table 14.2) shows changes only in employer-sponsored job-related NFE. In this regard, the first offers a good picture of the global orientation of ALSs to the formation of job-related skills, i.e., the level of 'vocationalisation' of lifelong learning (Boeren & Holford, 2016), while the second provides data regarding the level of AET directly supported by employers.

Both forms of AET grew significantly in the CE region, as Poland, Czechia and Hungary *doubled their participation rates in both subtypes of NFE*. The only exception was Slovakia, which experienced only modest growth in both job-related and employer-financed job-related NFE after 2007. However, its level was even higher than in Hungary and the Czech Republic, which means Slovakia had the highest orientation towards the job-related training of all CE lifelong regimes. On the other end of the spectrum, Poland historically had the lowest level of participation in this type of NFE, which remained half the size of other CE countries despite an increase in participation levels.

Table 14.1 Participation levels in job-related NFE in 12 months before survey: 1997–2016

	1997	2007	2011	2012	2016	IALS/PIAAC Change (1997–2012)	IALS/PIAAC Annual growth (1997–2012)	IALS/PIAAC Relat. Growth (%)	AES Change (2007–2016)	AES Annual growth (2007–2016)	AES Relat. Growth (%)
EU	N.A.	26	30	N.A.	35	N.A.	N.A.	N.A.	+9	0.9	35
Central European countries											
CZ	20	33	29	38	39	+19	1.0	95%	+6	0.6	18
HU	13	6*	34	N.A.	39	N.A.	N.A.	N.A.	+33*	3.3	550*
PO	10	16	18	26	20	+16	0.8	160%	+4	0.4	25
SK	N.A.	38	35	26	42	N.A.	N.A.	N.A.	+4	0.4	11
Scandinavian countries											
FIN	49	44	44	45	42	−4	−0.2	−8%	−2	−0.2	−5
NOR	40	47	52	35	52	+5	0.3	13%	+5	0.5	11
DEN	43	35	46	47	38	+4	0.2	9%	+3	0.3	9
Southern European countries											
ITA	16	14	25	18	33	+2	0.1	13%	+19	1.9	136
POR	N.A.	19	33	N.A.	40	N.A.	N.A.	N.A.	+21	2.1	111
Western European countries											
UK	40	31	22	38	41	−2	0.1	−5%	+10	1	32
BEL	12	29	30	35	35	+23	1.2	192%	+6	0.6	21
GER	N.A.	38	42	40	43	N.A.	N.A.	N.A.	+5	0.5	13
NED	25	36	49	44	54	+19	1.0	76%	+18	1.8	50

Note: Data in percent. *N.A.* data not available. *Low reliability of data. Change is measured within the same type of survey (AES vs. IALS/PIAAC). Annual growth rates are calculated distinctly for the time frames spanning from 1997 to 2012 (IALS/PIAAC), or from 2007 to 2016 (AES). Relative growth is assessed as the relative percentage increment in participation

Source: IALS (1997), AES (2007, 2011, 2016), OECD (2003), PIAAC (2012)

14.1 Long-Term Trends in Job-Related NFE

Table 14.2 Participation levels in employer-sponsored job-related NFE in 12 months before survey: 1997–2016

	1997	2007	2011	2012	2016	IALS/PIAAC Change (1997–2012)	IALS/PIAAC Annual growth (1997–2012)	IALS/PIAAC Relat. growth (%)	AES Change (2007–2016)	AES Annual growth (2007–2016)	AES Relat. growth (%)
	N.A.	22	30	N.A.	30	N.A.	N.A.	N.A.	+4	0.4	15
Central European countries
CZ	20	32	27	35	37	+15	0.8	75%	+6	0.6	16
HU	13	6*	29	N.A.	35	N.A.	N.A.	N.A.	+33*	3.3	483*
PO	18	16	16	21	17	+13	0.7	163%	+4	0.4	6
SK	N.A.	37	33	21	39	N.A.	N.A.	N.A.	+4	0.4	5
Scandinavian countries
FIN	38	39	41	41	39	+3	0.2	8%	−2	−0.2	−5
NOR	38	45	51	42	47	+4	0.2	11%	+5	0.5	4
DEN	35	34	43	43	35	+8	0.4	23%	+3	0.3	3
Southern European countries
ITA	8	10	21	15	27	+7	0.4	88%	+19	1.9	170
POR	N.A.	18	29	N.A.	36	N.A.	N.A.	N.A.	+21	2.1	100
Western European countries
UK	33	27	19	35	40	+2	0.1	6%	+10	1	48
BEL	11	26	27	31	36	+20	1.1	182%	+6	0.6	23
GER	N.A.	32	38	35	38	N.A.	N.A.	N.A.	+5	0.5	19
NED	19	33	46	40	48	+21	1.1	111%	+18	1.8	45

Note: Data in percent. *N.A.* data not available. *Low reliability of data. Change is measured within the same type of survey (AES vs. IALS/PIAAC). Annual growth rates are calculated distinctly for the time frames spanning from 1997 to 2012 (IALS/PIAAC), or from 2007 to 2016 (AES). Relative growth is assessed as the relative percentage increment in participation

Source: IALS (1997), AES (2007, 2011, 2016), OECD (2003), PIAAC (2012)

As I have shown in national case studies, the crucial traction of this horizontal move inside GALS has been both diffusion of modern workplace training from Western countries during the 2000s and the building of systematic HRD practice in medium and large enterprises. This trend has even strengthened during the 2010s when many firms (and in the case of Hungary also the government) in the region changed their approach toward workplace NFE for lower-skill occupations.

Figure 14.1 presents a comparison of CE ALSs with other European countries based on differences in the relationship between absolute participation in AET and the percentage of job-related NFE financially supported by employers in 2016. Results indicate not only big differences between all analysed ALSs, but also significant variation among CE countries. Poland and Hungary had low levels of employer financial support for NFE, while the Czech Republic and Slovakia had high rates. This suggests that the *degree of direct employers' involvement in AET among CE ALSs varies greatly*. In Slovakia and Czechia, 80–85% of NFE participants were financially supported by employers, while in Poland and Hungary, it was 65% or less.

In line with the current literature (Holford & Mohorčič Špolar, 2012, 2014; Thelen, 2014), one of the main global trends in lifelong learning and VET is *liberalisation*, which is characterised, among other things, by the role of employers in providing AET and the growing number of adults participating in

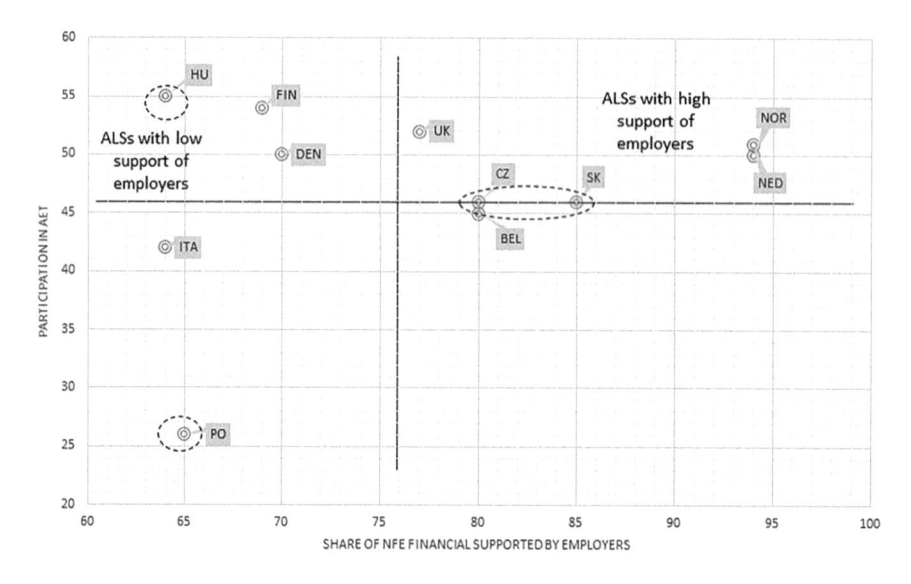

Fig. 14.1 Selected European ALSs in 2016: percentage of participation in AET and share of NFE financially supported by employers. (*Source*: own calculation based on the data from AES, 2016). *Note*: The data presented in this figure are reported in percentages. Participation is measured as the involvement of adults aged 25–64 years in AET within the 12 months preceding the survey. Share of employers' financial support of NFE measure as a share of participation in job-related NFE supported by employers on total participation in NFE

14.2 Uneven Paths of CE ALSs

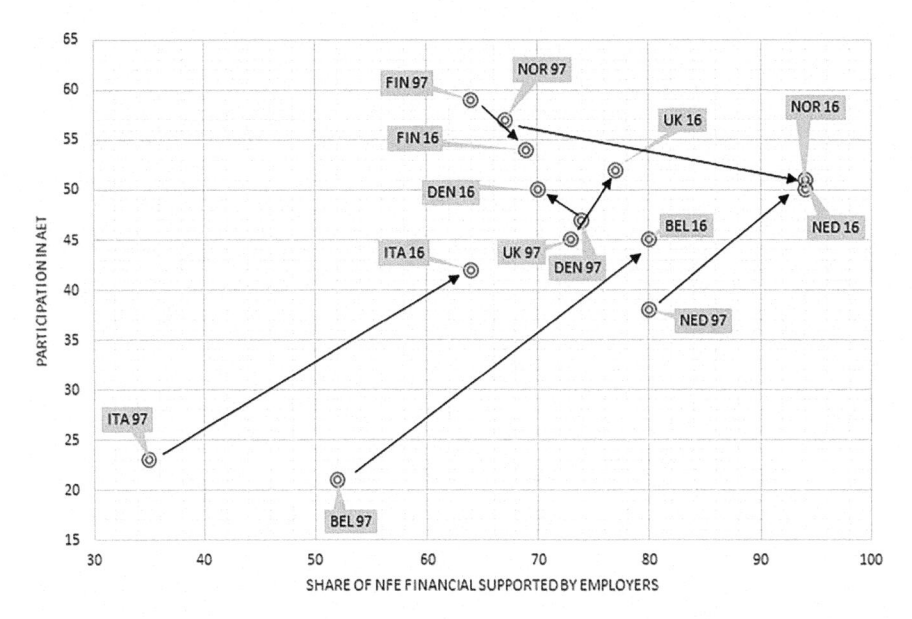

Fig. 14.2 Formation paths of selected European ALSs based on employers' financial support: 1997 to 2016. (*Source*: own calculation based on the data from IALS, 1997; AES, 2016; OECD, 2003).
Note: The data presented in this figure are reported in percentages. Participation is measured as the involvement of adults aged 25–64 years in AET within the 12 months preceding the survey. Share of employers' financial support of NFE measure as a share of participation in job-related NFE supported by employers on total participation in NFE

employer-supported forms of organised learning. Figures 14.2 and 14.3 present data on the historical pathways of selected European countries and specific formation trajectories of CE ALSs in relation to this process. First (Fig. 14.2), the data show that Western European and Nordic countries have experienced significant growth in the share of employer-supported NFE with a focus on job-related skills since the 1990s, with the exception of Denmark. However, this transformation was not necessarily accompanied by a corresponding increase in total participation in AET, as seen in the case of some Nordic countries (Norway and Finland) where higher financial support from employers in NFE did not lead to an increase in adult involvement in AET.

14.2 Uneven Paths of CE ALSs

Figure 14.3 illustrates that the *formation trajectories of CE countries differ from the rest of European ALSs*. While Hungary and the Czech Republic saw significant increases in overall participation, there was little change in their share of employer-supported job-related NFE. Both countries experienced *growth without significant*

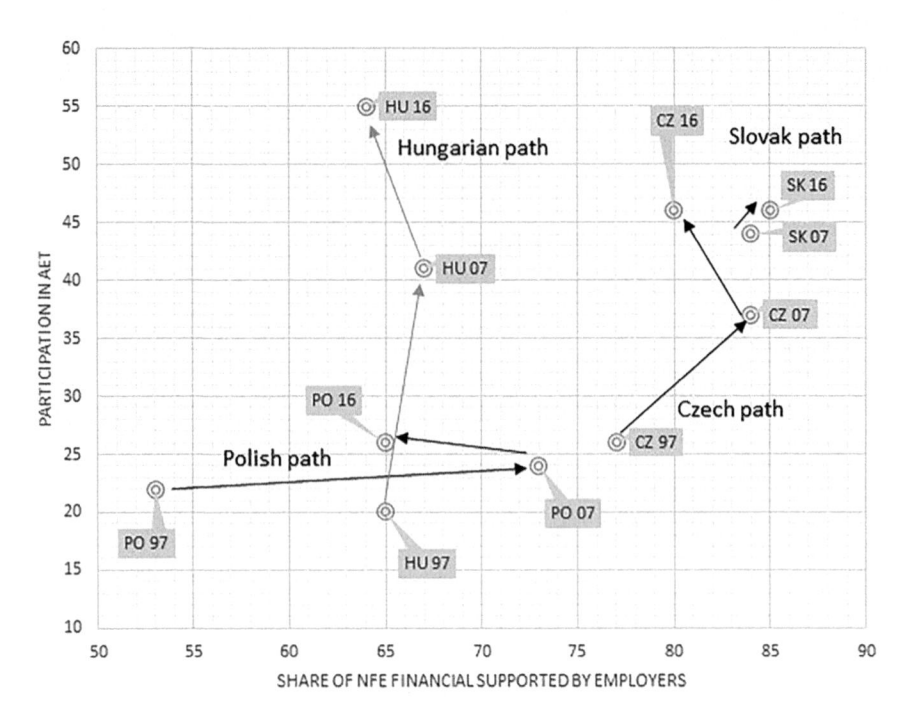

Fig. 14.3 Formation paths of CE ALSs based on employers' financial support (1997–2016). (*Source*: own calculation based on the data from IALS, 1997; AES, 2007, 2016; OECD, 2003). *Note*: The data presented in this figure are reported in percentages. Participation is measured as the involvement of adults aged 25–64 years in AET within the 12 months preceding the survey. Share of employers' financial support of NFE measure as a share of participation in job-related NFE supported by employers on total participation in NFE.

change in employers' sponsorship of NFE (vertical trajectory without horizontal change), although they differ from each other in internal characteristics (i.e., Hungary had a much lower share of employers' support). On the contrary, the proportion of adults participating in employer-sponsored NFE in Poland expanded between 1997 and 2007 but then decreased and was accompanied by very modest growth. Therefore, we can describe the Polish path as *partial liberalisation of NFE without growth*. The substantial horizontal movement has not been accompanied by similar vertical dynamics. However, it should be added that Poland only moved from a position of very low employer support, where only approximately half of the employers were responsible for financial support of job-related NFE, to a situation where two-thirds of them financially supported this type of organised learning. In Slovakia, we observed only a negligible shift, indicating a lack of development in this aspect of ALS. The position of employers has remained stable over the last two decades.

14.2 Uneven Paths of CE ALSs

A fundamental structural distinction between Czechia and Slovakia on one end, and Poland and Hungary on the other, can be attributed to the early emphasis on workplace learning in the former countries (Koubek & Brewster, 1995). This orientation was closely intertwined with a higher concentration of medium and large enterprises within those nations (Berend, 2009), which typically possess greater financial capabilities for employee training (Bassanini et al., 2005; Brunello et al., 2007). While Poland did observe an expansion in this sector during the 2000s, potentially influenced by a substantial influx of FDI into the country, it never attained the same level as that of Slovakia and Czechia, and then even decreased during the 2010s.

Chapter 15
Fourth Horizontal Axis: Public Provision of NFE

15.1 Public Provision of NFE

The supply side of AET describes the general structure of providers in a specific country. According to many previous theoretical insights (Busemeyer & Trampusch, 2012; Desjardins, 2017; Verdier, 2017, 2018), this network is critical because it is responsible for the content of the delivered training. Results of AES 2007 to 2016 allow us to not only distinguish between various types of NFE providers, but also to construct an empirical model of ALSs based on the key characteristics of NFE provision. Following Desjardins (2017), we recognise two main forms of NFE provision—*private* and *public*.

In this regard, the analysis primarily quantifies the proportion of NFE provided by public institutions, which allows me to account for the state's involvement in NFE activities. For instance, training and retraining programmes in the sphere of ALMP are typical representatives of this type of public provision. Based on this framework, it is possible to distinguish between ALSs with low and high NFE public provisions.

Figure 15.1 demonstrates distinctions between selected European countries according to the previously mentioned criteria in 2016. In this case, we can observe a substantial variation between ALSs. Although many countries have almost identical levels of participation, usually between 45% and 55%, they differ greatly in the public provision of NFE. For instance, while Germany or Nederlands had almost minimal involvement of public institutions in organising NFE activities, the volume of this type of public training in Finland and Denmark was three times higher.

From my analytical standpoint, it is interesting that *for CE countries is common overall medium to low involvement of the public sphere in NFE provision*. In all four representatives of CE, it never reached more than 10% of the total NFE provision. Therefore, these countries are textbook *examples of ALSs with low public NFE provisions*.

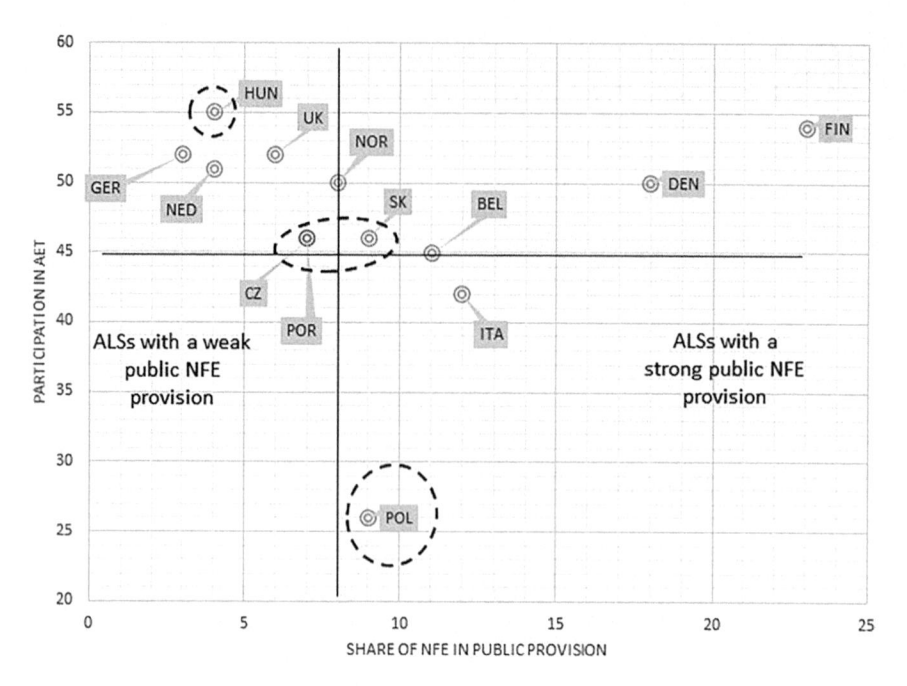

Fig. 15.1 Selected European countries in 2016: Share of NFE provided by public and private educational institutions. (*Source*: own calculation based on the data from AES, 2007, 2011, 2016) *Note*: The data presented in this figure are reported in percentages. Participation is measured as the involvement of adults aged 25–64 years in AET within the 12 months preceding the survey. NFE public provision is measured as a percentage of all NFE provided by public institutions

This outcome is a result of the delayed implementation and development of social investment policies within the Visegrad region, encompassing NFE programs directly administered by the state. Notably, while the Nordic countries adopted social investment policies as early as the 1970s, their implementation in other regions occurred much later (Bonoli, 2007; Hemerijck, 2017). Specifically, in the context of the CE countries, initial albeit limited endeavours in this direction were undertaken only during the 1990s.

As it is described in prior case studies, CE countries have predominantly relied on passive welfare policies along with a decommodifying of initial education and healthcare systems, supplemented by an extensive pension system. This emphasis has inhibited the substantial expansion of this category of welfare policy in these countries.

15.2 Pathways of CE ALSs

Figure 15.2 provides an overview of the development of CE ALSs over time. Initially, these systems had a higher level of involvement of public institutions in providing NFE. However, between 2007 and 2016, there was a significant decrease in public provision across all selected countries. Slovakia and the Czech Republic experienced the largest decrease, while Hungary had the lowest decline due to its already low percentage of public provision in NFE in 2007. Although the impact on the horizontal position of CE ALSs in GALS was not as profound as in the cases of extensification and employers' financial support, it is clear that the state's role in NFE has diminished since the 2000s. As discussed in the previous chapter, the liberalisation of CE ALSs coincided with an increase in job-oriented and employer-sponsored NFE, accompanied by a decrease in state involvement in NFE provision. In most cases, the states in CE reduced their NFE provision by half during the late

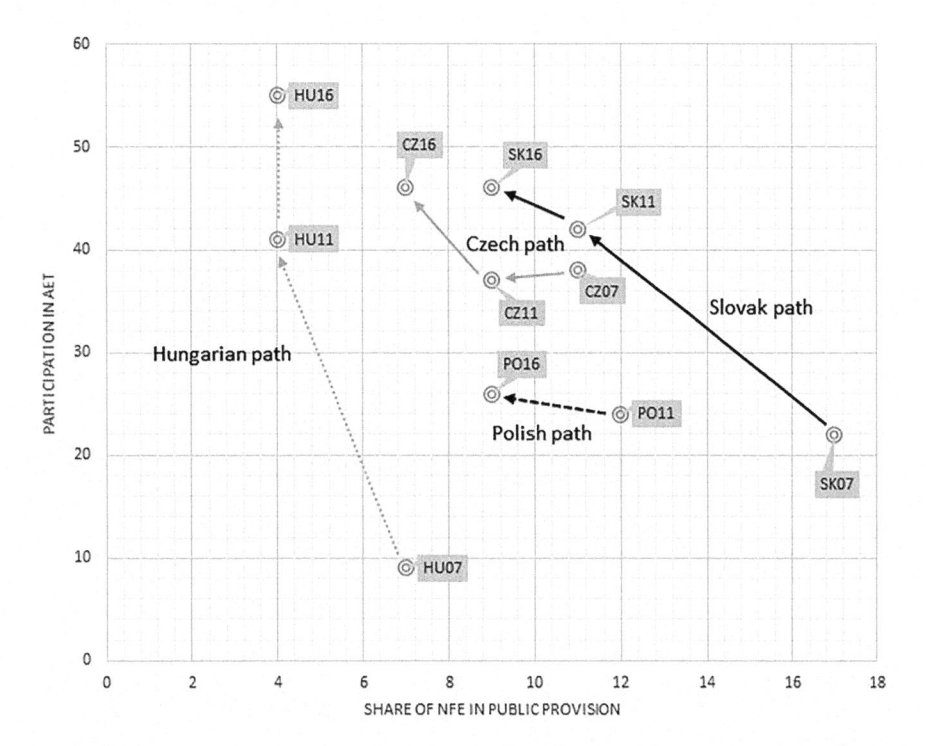

Fig. 15.2 Trajectories of CE ALSs between 2007 to 2016: Paths toward ALSs with medium to weak public NFE provision. (*Source*: own calculation based on the data from AES, 2007, 2011, 2016)

Note: The data presented in this figure are reported in percentages. Participation is measured as the involvement of adults aged 25–64 years in AET within the 12 months preceding the survey. NFE public provision is measured as a percentage of all NFE provided by public institutions

2000s and early 2010s. This transition aligned with their "austerity approach" amid an economic crisis, which, on one hand, was coupled with a low-policy priority attributed to social investment policies. This lower emphasis was not only an outcome of a different welfare philosophy since the 1990s but also a consequence of the rapid economic recovery post-crisis, along with the remarkably high demand for labour during the 2010s.

Chapter 16
Fifth Horizontal Axis: Demand for AET

Although ALSs have similar participation levels, they vary significantly in their demand for AET, which refers to how much the population perceives a need for further education and training. To distinguish between ALSs with low and high demand for AET, the chapter first looks at the role of perceived demand for organised learning, which also forms a fifth horizontal axis of GALS.

16.1 Perceived Demand for AET

Figure 16.1 illustrates the differences among European ALSs in 2016 based on the percentage of adults who declared demand for participation. The figure shows a wide variation. On one side, there are countries with high demand for AET such as Belgium, Denmark, and the United Kingdom, where 35% to 45% of the adult population expressed a desire to participate in AET. On the other side, there are ALSs with very low demand for AET such as Hungary, the Czech Republic, and Germany, where less than 15% of adults declared their intention to participate in the future. Regarding CE countries, we can observe that while *Hungary, Czechia, and Slovakia belonged to ALSs with low demand, Poland* is an example of a country *with a high proportion of adults who want to participate*. It is worth noting that ALSs in CE are located at the extreme ends of this spectrum.

Historical paths of CE countries to this pattern are shown in Fig. 16.2. From the figure is obvious variability in formation paths regarding the declared demand of adults for organised learning. While for Slovakia and the Czech Republic was typical a mild growth of participation in AET accompanied by a significant decrease in the share of those who want to enter AET activities, in the case of Poland, the percentage of adults who wanted to participate rise from less 20% to almost 40% over two decades. Finally, Hungary followed a growth trajectory without a profound change in the number of adults with demand for AET.

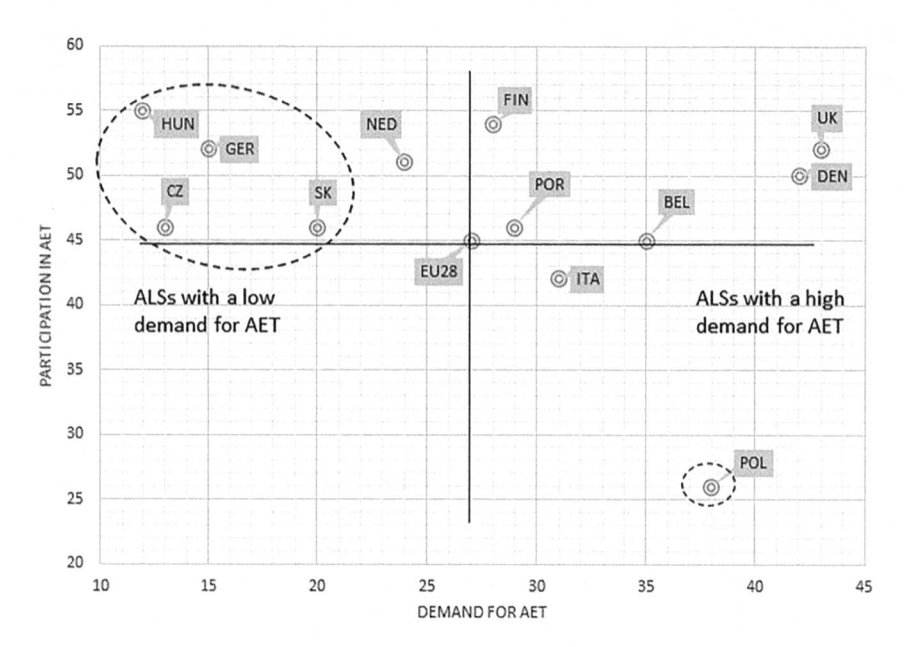

Fig. 16.1 Selected European countries in 2016 based on the variations in demand for AET. (*Source*: own calculation based on the data from AES (2016))
Note: The data presented in this figure are reported in percentages. Participation is measured as the involvement of adults aged 25 to 64 years in AET within the 12 months preceding the survey. Demand for AET is measured as percentage of adults who participated in AET and *want to participate* more and those who did not participated and *want to participate*

This analysis holds particular interest as it uncovers a noteworthy trend in Poland, where the number of adults expressing a desire to participate in adult education has grown. The current ALS has ineffectively met this escalating demand since the 2000s. The continuous trajectory of this growth can likely be attributed to the increasing number of individuals with higher levels of education. Poland, as the sole representative from the Visegrad region, has continued its expansion of higher education throughout the 2010s (for details see Chap. 10). As we know, these adults are usually those who have high motivation to participate in AET (Boeren et al., 2012a, b). Therefore, this educational expansion, coupled with limited educational opportunities, has given rise to a significant cohort of adults seeking AET.

Conversely, the decline in the proportion of adults with demand for AET in Czechia and Slovakia can be attributed to relatively advanced general skill levels within their populations, and overachieving skill requirements of the labour market, which has been pointed out by several studies (CEDEFOP, 2022; Koucký et al., 2014; NTF, 2017; OECD, 2022).

16.2 Adults with No Demand for AET 163

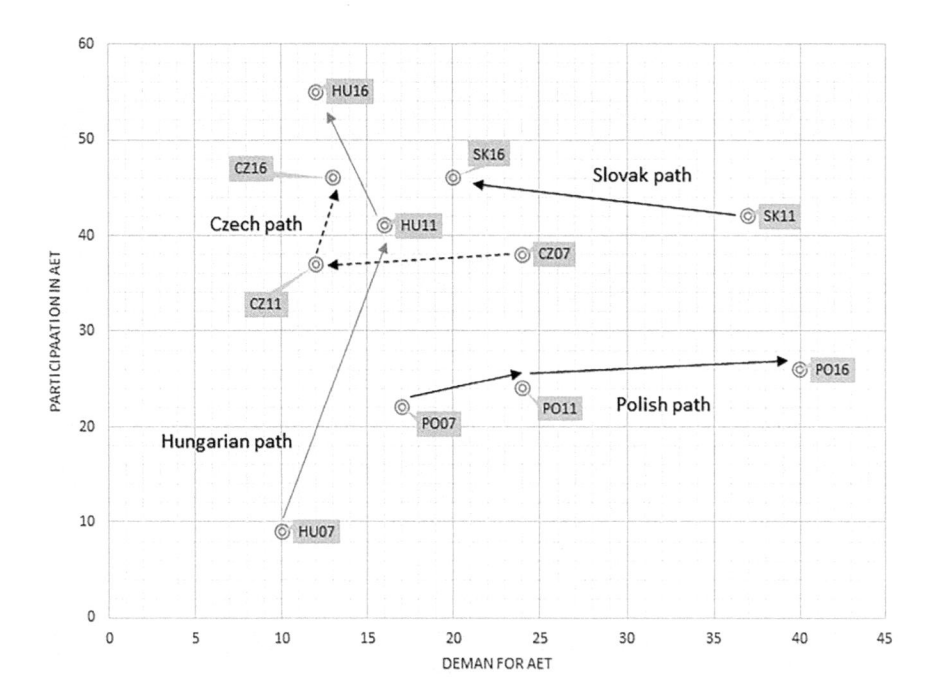

Fig. 16.2 Formation paths of CE ALSs based on demand for AET: 2007 to 2016. (*Source*: own calculation based on the data from AES (2016))
Note: The data presented in this figure are reported in percentages. Participation is measured as the involvement of adults aged 25 to 64 years in AET within the 12 months preceding the survey. Demand for AET measured as percentage of adults who participated in AET and *want to participate* more and those who did not participated and *want to participate*

16.2 Adults with No Demand for AET

As an addition to the previous analysis, this chapter also includes the opposite side of demand for organised learning—those who declared no demand for AET. Figure 16.3 shows data for this additional dimension. Although the differences among selected ALSs are smaller in this feature than in the previous analysis, they reveal an interesting pattern that is not identical to the previous one. Most countries have between 35% to 45% of the adult population who do not want to be involved in AET—i.e., typical non-participants. The Netherlands has the lowest proportion among the analysed ALSs (28%), while in Poland, it was a staggering 62%. As a result, Poland has an extremely polarised model of demand for AET, where a high portion of adults want to participate, but an even higher share of the population completely refused to be involved in organised learning (see Fig. 16.3). Other CE ALS belong to countries with a slightly above-average proportion of adults with no demand for AET (Slovakia and Czechia) or slightly below average (Hungary).

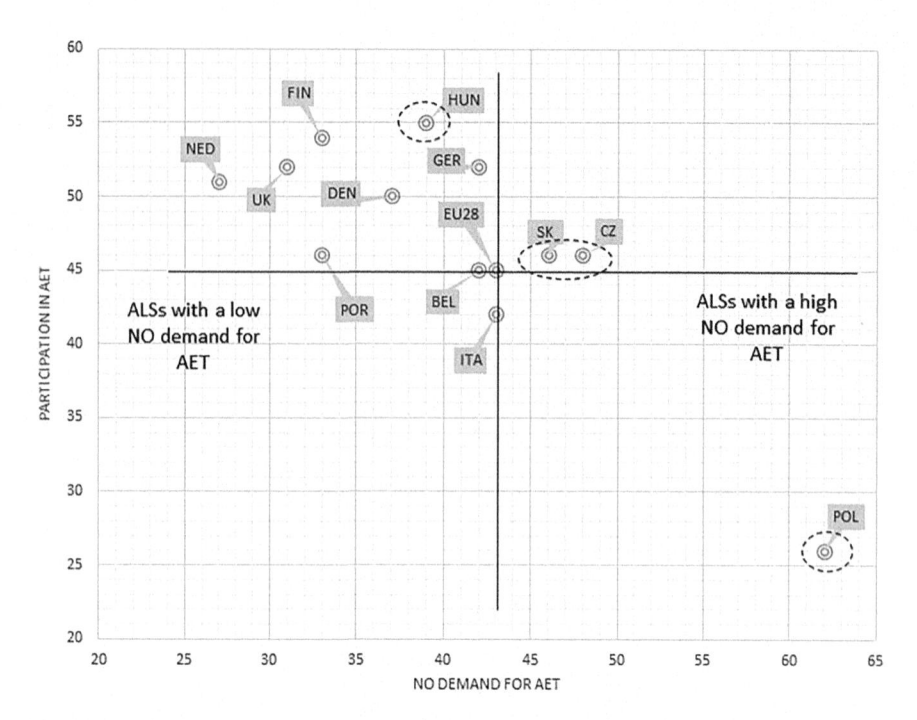

Fig. 16.3 Selected European countries in 2016 based on the variations in demand for AET. (*Source*: own calculation based on the data from AES (2016))
Note: The data presented in this figure are reported in percentages. Participation is measured as the involvement of adults aged 25 to 64 years in AET within the 12 months preceding the survey. The absence of demand for AET is measured as the percentage of adults who did not want to participate in AET

16.3 A Decline in No Demand for AET in CE ALS

The final figure (Fig. 16.4) illustrates the formation trajectories of CE ALSs. In this context, I identified the most straightforward formation path between 2007 and 2016. For all four countries, it is typical to have a simultaneous increase in participation levels with a decline in the number of adults who have no demand for AET. *The higher the overall participation, the lower the proportion of adults without the intention to enter organised learning.* This relationship has almost a perfect linear dependence in the analysed data, as shown in the result of the regression analysis. Such a finding strongly corroborates findings (Boeren, 2016, 2023; Kalenda et al., 2020; van Nieuwenhove & De Wever, 2021) that one of the crucial preconditions for participation in AET is previous participation in organised learning for adults.

16.3 A Decline in No Demand for AET in CE ALS

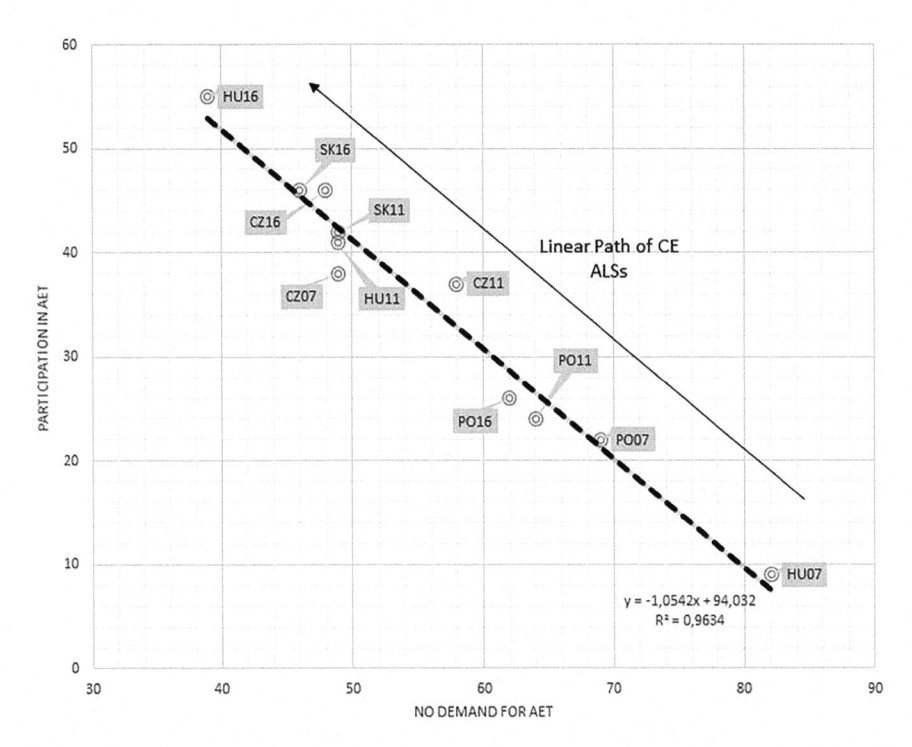

Fig. 16.4 Trajectories of CE ALSs between 2007 and 2016 based on the number of adults with no demand for AET. (*Source*: own calculation based on the data from AES (2007, 2011, 2016))
Note: The data presented in this figure are reported in percentages. Participation is measured as the involvement of adults aged 25 to 64 years in AET within the 12 months preceding the survey. The absence of demand for AET is measured as the percentage of adults who did not want to participate in AET

Summary of Part V

Based on the previous analysis, it can be concluded that the quantitative characteristics of CE ALSs differ significantly from those of other European ALSs. This indicates that CE ALSs *operate under a distinct model of AET coordination and provision, which is different from WSR and VoC models of ALSs proposed* (see Part III for details). When examining ALSs features in more detail, I observed further uniqueness and variability, both in comparison to Western European countries and among the CE countries themselves.

These *differences are not solely attributed to the structural characteristics of CE ALSs but also to the specific pathways of their formation* that I tried to explain in relation to their previously described institutional histories. In addition to the overall growth of these systems reflected in upward vertical movement in GALS, based on the 12-month participation framework, the analysis has identified the five following distinct horizontal trajectories of CE ALS inside GALS:

1. a process of extensification of their participation;
2. a shift towards job-related and employers' supported NFE;
3. and reduced state provision of FAE;
4. decline in public NFE provision;
5. decline in demand for AET.

Especially, extreme extensification, the low perceived demand for AET and medium to strong orientation towards the private provision of job-related and employers' supported NFE are key factors that make CE ALSs distinct in the current GALS, using the latest data from the 1990s to 2010s.

However, even though they share some of these structural characteristics, ALSs in *CE differ not only from other European ALSs but also among themselves.* For a summary of these differences, see Table 1. Looking at their position in GALS, it is difficult to classify CE ALSs as having a shared type or pattern (Green, 2006, 2011; Saar et al., 2013a, 2023). For instance, Hungary experienced the most significant growth dynamic with increased private provision of NFE, but at the same time, had

Table 1 Empirical features of CE ALSs in the late 2010s

Features	Hungary	Czech Republic	Slovakia	Poland
The overall participation	High	Medium	Medium	Low
1. Extensification	Highly extensive ALS	Highly extensive ALS	Highly extensive ALS	Intensive ALS
2. The role of FAE	NFE-oriented ALS	NFE oriented ALS	NFE oriented ALS	FAE-oriented ALS
3. Employers' financial support	ALS with low employers' financial support	ALS with high employers' financial support	ALS with high employers' financial support	ALS with low employers' financial support
4. Supply of public NFE	ALS with low public NFE provision	ALS with medium public NFE provision	ALS with medium public NFE provision	ALS with medium public NFE provision
5. Demand for AET	Low-demand ALS	Low-demand ALS	Low-demand ALS	A mix of high demand and no demand for AET

low financial support from employers and a significant role of the state in providing FAE. Poland saw modest growth with very polarised demand for AET and has been significantly different in its very strong direction toward FAE. Compared to the other three CE countries, the level of extensification and liberalisation of AET has been very low in Poland, as overall participation. The Czech Republic and Slovakia share many common features, such as a high level of extensification of AET and job-related NFE, as well as employers' financial support of NFE. However, Slovakia underwent less transformation in its ALS development, with the lowest dynamic observed among the countries. In summary, if we place all these organised learning systems on an imaginary continuum, Hungary has reached the highest level of liberalisation of AET, while Poland has the lowest. Generally, the ALS in Poland is the most distinctive from the rest of CE ALSs.

Drawing upon these data and employing the principle of constructing typologies from below (see Part II), my research contends that among the examined countries, only Hungary, Czechia, and Slovakia *can be classified as closely aligned with a single empirical type of ALS*. These countries demonstrate a convergence across diverse dimensions within GALS and collectively embody the CE model of ALS. In contrast, Poland's trajectory appears to indicate a distinct future orientation, potentially aligning it more closely with Baltic countries as suggested by Saar et al. (2023). However, it is important to note that this classification should not be regarded as a definitive conclusion, given that the evolution of ALSs is an ongoing process influenced by shifting institutional configurations and emerging challenges (see Part III). Only forthcoming data can unveil whether Hungary's early divergence, particularly the path it embarked upon after 2010, will lead to further differentiation, distancing it from the characteristics shared by Slovakia and Czechia. In such an instance, and acknowledging the speculative nature of this assertion, the viability of categorising it as the CE type or model of ALS may become a subject of contemplation.

Part VI
Patterns of Participation and Barriers in CE ALSs

Chapter 17
Participation Patterns in AET

The impact of ALSs extends beyond the level of participation in AET (their vertical dimension in GALS) and encompasses the involvement of diverse social groups in organised learning. These two phenomena, ALSs and social group involvement in AET, are profoundly interconnected and contribute to participation inequality (Boeren, 2023; Boyadjieva & Ilieva-Trichkova, 2021; Lee, 2017, 2018; Lee & Desjardins, 2019). This chapter argues that specific institutional complementarities exist at the empirical level between characteristics of CE countries, their institutional clusters, which were delineated in Parts IV and V, and the level of participation inequality in AET, which are unpacked further in this section. Generally, they are:

1. The connection between the welfare system and involvement in AET based on age—i.e., *age-related inequality*. Especially retirement/pension scheme plays an important role here.
2. The interrelationship between women's workforce participation, their employment rate, and women's active participation in AET—i.e., *gender-based inequality*.
3. The alignment between the initial formal education system, the match/mismatch of skills within the labour market, and the involvement of higher-educated and low-educated adults in AET—i.e. *education-based inequality*.
4. The concurrence between a pronounced demand for lower-skilled employment and the participation of adults with lower educational attainment, along with those in low-skill occupations, in AET—i.e., *occupation-related inequality*.

My analysis shows that these inequalities grow up from specific characteristics of national institutional clusters, and their strength is interlinked with the ability or inability of ALSs to mitigate them. In this regard, this chapter examines the long-term changes in participation patterns both among and within CE countries. To achieve this aim, a combination of data from the AES covering the years 2007 to 2016 is utilised to identify participation patterns based on the key sociodemographic factors (see Part III). Specifically, the following analysis uncovers participation patterns related to (1) age, (2) gender, (3) economic status, (4) highest attained education, and (5) occupation status. Simultaneously, the research draws their link to particular social mechanisms that produce the inequality and the role of ALSs in them.

17.1 Participation Based on Age

Current literature (Desjardins, 2019; Kalenda & Kočvarová, 2022b; Schuller, 2019; Schuller & Watson, 2009) generally agrees that participation declines with age. However, this drop comes especially after the age of 55 and generally interferes with the retirement age in a particular country. Thus, it is dependent on general welfare policy, mainly the pension system, and the inclusion of older persons in the labour market. CE ALSs are not an exception as they have shown *significant age-related inequality*.

Table 17.1 presents the participation levels in AET for two age cohorts of older learners: individuals aged 45–54 and those between 55 and 64 years. The data reveals significant variations among older learners. While the younger age group (45–54 years) exhibited slightly above-average participation in AET, adults over 55 years old displayed considerably lower engagement in organised learning. The participation index in the last column of the table indicates that the oldest age cohort's participation levels ranged from 54% to 63% of those 10 years younger. These differences in CE ALSs mirror the overall participation pattern, which is accompanied by growth of volume in AET across all CE countries after 2007, with Hungary exhibiting the highest dynamics and Slovakia the lowest.

Table 17.2 provides insights into the dynamic nature of age-related inequality in participation rates. The table presents the participation levels of two age groups as a percentage of the average participation in the country during a specific year. Notably, Czechia and Slovakia did not witness any significant changes in participation levels for the age group between 45 and 54 over the analysed period. However, Poland and

Table 17.1 Participation in AET among age cohorts over 45 years: 2007–2016

	Aged 45–54				Aged 55–64				
	2007	2011	2016	dif.	2007	2011	2016	dif.	Index
CZ	41	40	49	+8	22	20	29	+7	59
POL	16	20	24	+8	7	10	13	+6	54
HU	8	43	60	+17*	3	22	38	+16*	63
SK	46	44	48	+2	24	22	30	+6	63

Source: AES (2007, 2011, 2016)
Note: Participation levels in percent. dif. = difference between 2007 and 2016. *Low reliability of data for Hungary in 2007; the difference for Hungary computed only for a period of 2011–2016. Index = Index of participation, i.e., participation of adults aged 55 to 64 years as a percentage of participation levels of the adults aged 45 to 54 years in 2016

17.2 Participation Based on Gender

Table 17.2 Relative levels of participation in AET among age cohorts over 45 years: 2007–2016

	Aged 45–54				Aged 55–64			
	2007	2011	2016	**dif.**	2007	2011	2016	**dif.**
CZ	108	108	107	**−1**	58	54	63	**+5**
POL	73	83	92	**+20**	32	42	50	**+18**
HU	89	105	109	**+20**	33	54	69	**+36**
SK	105	105	104	**+0**	55	52	65	**+11**

Source: own calculation
Note: Participation levels in the percentage of average adult participation (25 to 64 years) in the country in a particular year. dif. = difference between 2007 and 2016

Hungary experienced a substantial increase in participation for this age group, with a notable twenty percentage point change between 2007 and 2016. Consequently, age-related inequality for adults aged 45 to 54 significantly decreased in these countries.

Furthermore, across all CE ALSs, there was a *positive trend in participation inequality for the age group over 55*. In 2007, typically only one out of three or two older adults were engaged in organised learning, whereas 10 years later, it increased to two out of three individuals in most countries. In summary, although CE ALSs still show a high age-related inequality, it has declined since the 2000s.

However, this trend has not been the fruit of the implementation of specific age-sensitive social investment policies in the region—i.e., a provision of better target training for this age group. It was a result of higher utilisation of labour power in the age category 55 to 64 during the 2010s and a simultaneous extension of retirement age from early 60 s to more mid-60 s for men, and from late 50s to early 60s for women (Hwang & Roehm, 2022). Due to that, the proportion of older adults in retirement in the oldest cohort declined, and their chances to receive on-the-job training increased. Also, the high demand for labour power during the 2010s made employers invest more frequently in the skills of their older workers that would not normally support them (for a detailed discussion see Part IV).

In summary, ALSs within the CE context exhibit limited success in addressing the pronounced inequality in participation linked to age, notably prevalent among individuals aged 55 and above. Given the demographic aging within these countries, fostering the involvement of older adults in AET emerges as a prominent challenge to contend with (EC, 2019).

17.2 Participation Based on Gender

Across all CE ALS, *men tend to participate more frequently than women*. These differences are mainly caused by a lower employment rate of women, as being employed is a crucial precondition to having access to organised learning opportunities in CE (Dämmrich et al., 2014, 2015; Vaculíková et al., 2021). In general, women's participation levels in 2016 were approximately 85% of men's levels (see

Table 17.3 Participation in AET among Men and Women: 2007–2016

	Men 2007	2011	2016	dif.	Women 2007	2011	2016	dif.	Index
CZ	45	43	51	+6	34	37	43	+9	84
POL	26	29	30	+4	22	25	26	+4	87
HU	11	47	61	+14*	10	39	53	+14*	87
SK	51	48	51	0	43	42	45	+2	88

Source: AES (2007, 2011, 2016)
Note: Participation levels in percent. dif. = difference between 2007 and 2016. *Low reliability of data for Hungary in 2007; the difference for Hungary computed only for a period of 2011–2016. Index = Index of participation, i.e., participation of women as a percentage of participation levels of men in 2016

the index in Table 17.3). However, there were variations among countries regarding the dynamics of women's participation. Hungary and the Czech Republic experienced more significant growth in women's involvement over the past 20 years compared to Poland and particularly Slovakia, where the gender pattern of participation underwent only minimal changes.

This result is logical as both Poland and Slovakia have had much lower involvement of women in the labour market, where people have the highest chance to receive training as I showed in the previous part of the book (see Chap. 14). Further, both countries introduced conservative family-oriented policies during the 2010s that rather than stimulate the involvement of women in the job market, they constrained it (Szelewa & Polakowski, 2020, 2022).

Table 17.4 presents the developmental trends in gender-related inequality with regard to involvement in AET. The table demonstrates a decline in the advantage of men over women in AET participation. Men's gender has become less substantial for involvement in organised learning over time. However, it is essential to underscore that the relative involvement of women has demonstrated limited progress since the 2000s in both Slovakia and Poland. This lack of advancement can likely be attributed to a less proactive social policy. Similarly, while there has been a modest improvement in this aspect within Czechia and Hungary, the progress remains incremental. As a result, addressing this form of inequality within CE ALSs will require a considerable amount of time, given the persistently lower representation of women in the labour market, which consequently constrains their opportunities for participation. Moreover, Vaculiková et al. (2021) discerned that gender-related disparities in access to participation are even more deeply entrenched and less overt when it comes to employer support, a realm in which investment in women is historically less substantial—a phenomenon that extends beyond mere employment rates.

17.3 Participation Based on the Highest Attained Education 177

Table 17.4 Relative levels of participation in AET based on gender: 2007–2016

	Men				Women			
	2007	2011	2016	**dif.**	2007	2011	2016	**dif.**
CZ	118	116	111	**−8**	89	100	93	**+4**
POL	120	121	115	**−4**	100	104	100	**0**
HU	122	115	111	**−11**	91	95	96	**+4**
SK	116	114	111	**−5**	98	10	98	**0**

Source: own calculation
Note: Participation levels in the percentage of average adult participation (25 to 64 years) in the country in a particular year. dif. = difference between 2007 and 2016

17.3 Participation Based on the Highest Attained Education

The level of highest attained education plays a pivotal role in shaping participation in AET within the CE context. *"Matthew's principle"* holds true, wherein individuals with higher educational attainment exhibit greater involvement in organised adult learning. Nevertheless, trends observed in CE countries also reveal the emergence of a distinct process of *partial equalisation* among those possessing the lowest educational qualifications. Both these are linked to the formation of ALSs and specific processes—(1) raising the number of persons with tertiary education diplomas (education expansion) and (2) governments' and firms' approaches toward training low-educated workers.

Table 17.5 shows a main pattern. Generally, we can see that adults with tertiary education (ISCED 5–8) have much higher participation rates in both AET and NFE than adults with only primary or secondary education without the state exam (ISCED 0–2). In all CE ALSs, half to two-thirds of university graduates were involved in AET in 2016, while participation of low-educated adults was dramatically lower. Sometimes reaching only one-tenth of the higher educated levels.

The difference between high and low-educated adults depicts the *index of participation* (see the last column of Table 17.5), which shows the levels of participation of low-educated adults as a percentage of participation levels of adults with tertiary education. In this regard, we can see that Hungary had the smallest difference between these two educational groups, as it reached 62% of university graduates, while other countries had much more profound differences (between 10 to 36%). This finding also holds when we look at NFE specifically (see Table 17.5 for details).

As a result, all four countries have substantial inequality in participation in AET based on attained education. This finding supports the existence and persistence of "Mathew's principle" (Blossfeld et al., 2020; Boeren, 2009) and the effect of the

Table 17.5 Participation in AET and NFE based on the highest attained education: 2007–2016

	Adults with ISCED 5–8				Adults with ISCED 0–2				Index
	2007	2011	2016	**dif.**	2007	2011	2016	**dif.**	
Adult education and training									
CZ	62	64	67	**+4**	15	13	16	**+1**	24%
POL	54	52	48	**−6**	5	6	5	**+1**	11%
HU	19	58	67	**+9***	3*	32	42	**+10***	62%
SK	62	64	62	**0**	14	21	22	**+8**	36%
Non-formal education and training									
CZ	57	59	62	**+5**	15	13	16	**+2**	26%
POL	46	44	43	**−3**	4	5	4	**0**	10%
HU	15	53	62	**+9***	2*	30	40	**+10***	64%
SK	57	56	60	**+3**	14	21	22	**+8**	37%

Source: AES (2007, 2011, 2016)
Note: Participation levels in percent. dif. = difference between 2007 and 2016. *Low reliability of data for Hungary in 2007; the difference for Hungary computed only for a period of 2011–2016. Index = Index of participation, i.e., participation of adults with ISCED 0–2 as a percentage of participation levels of adults with ISCED 6–8 in 2016

"prolonged arm of education" (Rubenson, 2018) on participation patterns in AET in CE ALSs. More educated adults have a much higher chance of entering organised learning. This phenomenon is probably even exacerbated in the Visegrad region due to a very high graduation rate for secondary level of education, which has been around 90% in Czechia, Hungary and Poland, and around 80% in Slovakia (WB, 2023). Due to that, those without at least secondary education (ISCED 3) face profound educational inequality later in their life.

While low-educated adults in Poland faced the highest inequality, low-educated persons in Hungary had the highest probability of participating among CE countries. On the one hand, ALS in Poland is typical by the absence of training for low-educated adults over age 24, due to its overall focus on the 'front-end' modelof education. On the other hand, Hungarian reforms after 2010 specifically targeted this population to mobilise it as a cheap labour power for key segments of the national economy (for details see Chap. 7).

Table 17.6 sheds light on the evolution of education-related inequality since 2007. The table reveals divergent trends between high-educated and low-educated adults. Over time, the relative advantage enjoyed by tertiary-educated individuals has decreased, particularly in Hungary and Poland. On the other hand, the situation for adults with an ISCED 0–2 level of education has remained relatively stable in Poland and Czechia. However, there has been a significant improvement in Hungary and Slovakia, as these countries have experienced a decline in education-related inequality over the years.

If we look at trends over time, except for Poland, all countries experienced minor growth in the number of adults who entered into AET based on the highest attained education. In the case of the Czech Republic, the number of tertiary graduates involved in both AET and NFE was already high in the mid − 2000s, which was also

17.4 Participation Based on Economic Status

Table 17.6 Relative levels of participation in AET based on highest attained education: 2007–2016

	Adults with ISCED 6–8				Adults with ISCED 0–2			
	2007	2011	2016	**dif.**	2007	2011	2016	**dif.**
CZ	164	174	145	**−20**	39	35	35	−4
POL	247	215	185	**−62**	21	24	21	−1
HU	216	142	122	**−93**	29	78	76	+47
SK	140	151	134	**−6**	32	51	48	+16

Source: own calculation
Note: Participation levels in the percentage of average adult participation (25 to 64 years) in the country in a particular year. dif. = difference between 2007 and 2016

the case in Slovakia. Slovak's ALS differ only in the more rapid growth of adults with ISCED 0–2 between 2007 and 2011. However, after this rise, the levels flattened out, probably as a result of the limited absorption capacity of large industrial companies that demanded labour power in the western part of Slovakia (OECD, 2022).

In comparison to the rest of CE ALS, Poland is an interesting case, as the number of adults with tertiary education who participated in AET and NFE decreased. This trend seems to be continuous since 2007. This should indicate that Mathew's principle does not work here perfectly. Although adults with tertiary diplomas still have an advantage over other educational groups, they are involved less frequently in organised learning over time. This process went hand in hand with HE expansion in Poland, when the number of adults with higher education significantly rose during the 2000s and 2010s. Probably, because the occupational structure did not match the increasing skill supply in the 2010s, we can observe not only less participation and relative advantage over other social groups in those with the highest attained education, but also a much higher share of adults who declare no demand for AET (see Chap. 16).

In contrast, Hungary shows the greatest dynamics, especially in relation to the participation of low-educated adults after 2011, which numbers are exceptional, as the percentage of low-educated adults in Hungary almost matched the proportion of high-educated adults involved in NFE in Poland. Also, in this case, national policy played its role. Not by generating inclusive training schema for all adults over the country to enhance their long-term chances of improving their overall capability through AGE, but rather by introducing a semi-obligatory system of low-skilled jobs for the unemployed, including workplace NFE.

17.4 Participation Based on Economic Status

Inequality based on economic status is profound across CE. Table 17.7 depicts the participation pattern based on economic activity, and compares the participation of the employed and the unemployed adults in NFE. This type of organised learning

Table 17.7 Participation in NFE among the employed and unemployed: 2007–2016

	Employed				Unemployed				
	2007	2011	2016	**dif.**	2007	2011	2016	**dif.**	Index
CZ	46	43	53	+7	12	23	19	+7	36%
POL	26	29	31	+5	9	10	7	−2	22%
HU	10	53	66	+13*	5	17	24	+7*	36%
SK	52	47	57	+5	12	14	14	+2	24%

Source: AES (2007, 2011, 2016)

Note: Participation levels in percent. dif. = difference between 2007 and 2016. *Low reliability of data for Hungary in 2007; the difference for Hungary computed only for a period of 2011–2016. Index = Index of participation, i.e., participation of the unemployed adults as a percentage of participation levels of the employed adults

was used for the analysis of these two socioeconomic groups rather than participation rates in AET (combining FAE and NFE) because the unemployed rarely participate in FAE.

The table shows that the participation of employed adults in NFE is three to four times higher than the unemployed across all CE countries, and this pattern has been persistent since 2007. More than half of the employed adults participated in NFE in 2016, except in Poland, which had lower levels, around one-third of the employed. In summary, these participation levels are significantly higher than is average participation in NFE in a particular country, which confirms that the "long arm of the labour market" (Rubenson, 2018) profoundly impacts the chance of adults being part of lifelong learning by making it more easily accessible for those who have a job. In all CE ALSs, participation of the unemployed was between 22 to 36% of the participation levels of the employed adults (see Table 17.7 for details).

However, the involvement of both social groups in organised learning has improved over time, as their participation increased between 2007 and 2016. That was again, with the exception of Poland, which experienced a decline in participation in NFE among the unemployed in the same period. A higher increase in participation among the unemployed scored Hungary, and the Czech Republic, while the situation of this group in Slovakia only slightly improved.

Table 17.8 provides an overview of the trends in the relative participation of employed and unemployed individuals in AET over time. The four countries examined in the table exhibit substantial variations in these trends. The Czech Republic and Poland demonstrate a slight decline in the advantage of employed individuals. Conversely, Hungary and Slovakia experience the opposite trend, where the advantage of the employed in AET participation has increased over time. Moreover, significant differences are observed among unemployed individuals. Hungary and Czechia have witnessed an improvement in the relative participation levels of the unemployed since 2007, whereas Poland and Slovakia have not shown the same progress. In fact, in Poland and Slovakia, the relative participation level of adults without a job has either remained the same or even worsened compared to the 2000s.

Table 17.8 Relative levels of participation in AET based on economic status: 2007–2016

	Employed				Unemployed			
	2007	2011	2016	dif.	2007	2011	2016	dif.
CZ	121	116	115	−6	31	62	41	+10
POL	120	121	118	−2	40	40	27	−13
HU	107	130	120	+13	5	41	43	+38
SK	117	113	123	+6	28	33	30	+2

Source: own calculation
Note: Participation levels in the percentage of average adult participation (25–64 years) in the country in a particular year. dif. = difference between 2007 and 2016

The extent of participation by the unemployed in NFE and its temporal patterns are closely intertwined with the provision of public NFE in the form of ALMPs in CE ALSs, encompassing training and retraining endeavours tailored for this group. Countries that establish robust systems for retraining unemployed individuals and invest in this facet of welfare policy tend to experience reduced levels of associated inequality (Desjardins, 2017). However, within the CE ALSs, the development of this particular domain of AET has not been as extensive as in Western and Nordic countries (see Chap. 15; see also Cook & Inglot, 2022; Hemerijck & Ronchi, 2022; Szelewa & Polakowski, 2022). Support for this form of organised learning has been constrained, with a pronounced emphasis on passive labour market policies and broader welfare initiatives (Szelenyi & Wilk, 2010). Consequently, the progress made in boosting participation levels among the unemployed from 2007 to 2016 has been comparatively modest. Notably, Slovakia, in particular, introduced effective measures in this realm only after 2015 (see Chap. 9).

The oversight of this issue can also be attributed to the fact that these countries had some of the lowest unemployment rates in Europe, hovering around 3–5% by approximately 2016. These figures further diminished the prioritisation of social investment policy objectives.

17.5 Participation Based on Occupation Status

In the context of CE ALSs, a *reduction in inequality related to occupational status has transpired over the past decade*, notably evident among manual workers, particularly those classified under the ISCO 08 and 09 categories (skilled manual workers and elementary occupations). Of greater significance is the distinct characteristic of CE ALSs marked by *minimal inequality among skilled manual workers*. This section contends and expands upon this argument subsequently (see Part VII), that this attribute is intricately connected to a new approach adopted by firms in DMC toward skill development post-2010, along with specific lifelong learning policies within certain countries, such as Hungary.

Table 17.9 Participation in AET among the high-skilled and medium-skilled service workers: 2007–2016

	Managers, professionals (ISCO 01)				Clerical support workers (ISCO 02)				Index
	2007	2011	2016	**dif.**	2007	2011	2016	**dif.**	
CZ	63	63	69	**+6**	42	42	49	**+7**	70%
POL	52	55	53	**+1**	26	26	30	**+5**	56%
HU	20	64	73	**+9***	10	54	64	**+10***	88%
SK	64	62	69	**+5**	45	44	50	**+5**	72%

Source: AES (2007, 2011, 2016)
Note: Participation levels in percent. dif. = difference between 2007 and 2016. *Low reliability of data for Hungary in 2007; the difference for Hungary computed only for a period of 2011–2016. Index = Index of participation, i.e., participation of adults in clerical support occupations as a percentage of participation levels of managers/professionals in 2016

Table 17.10 Participation in AET among qualified and unqualified manual workers: 2007–2016

	Skilled manual workers (ISCO 08)				Elementary occupations (ISCO 09)				Index
	2007	2011	2016	**dif.**	2007	2011	2016	**dif.**	
CZ	42	33	45	**+4**	22	15	24	**+2**	34%
POL	15	18	18	**+3**	11	14	13	**+2**	24%
HU	7	54	64	**+10***	6	47	71	**+24***	97%
SK	48	40	55	**+7**	30	26	41	**+11**	59%

Source: AES (2007, 2011, 2016)
Note: Participation levels in percent. dif. = difference between 2007 and 2016. *Low reliability of data for Hungary in 2007; the difference for Hungary computed only for a period of 2011–2016. Index = Index of participation, i.e., participation of adults in elementary occupation as a percentage of participation levels of managers/professionals in 2016

Table 17.9 covers the pattern of participation in AET among high-skilled (managers and professionals, ISCO 01) and medium-skilled workers (clerical support workers, ISCO 02). Data shows that high-skilled service workers experience the highest participation level of all analysed sociodemographic categories in this chapter. Usually, more than three-quarters of them regularly participate in any type of AET during the previous 12 months. As in other sociodemographic factors, Czechia, Hungary and Slovakia show a much higher involvement of higher skills occupations in organised learning than Poland. The occurrence of AET among semi-skilled service workers is significantly lower. However, it is still higher than the average level of participation recorded in those countries. It is between 70 to 88% of the participation levels of the managers and professionals. Both categories experienced growth in participation over the previous two decades, especially in Czechia and Hungary, while their growth in Slovakia and Poland was less extensive. It is highly probable that this trend is an outcome of the massive proliferation of job-related NFE, including NFE financially supported by employers that I described in Part V (Chap. 14).

Table 17.10 reveals the participation levels among skilled and unskilled manual workers, two occupations that typically rarely participate in organised learning for adults. However, data shows very interesting participation patterns as well as surprisingly high differences among CE ALSs—the biggest variations among studied countries. First, the participation of 'blue-collar' workers is not as low as we may expect. *The involvement of skilled manual workers in AET is around the average participation level in the Czech Republic and even higher than average levels in Slovakia and Hungary.* In those two countries, the participation of skilled manual workers matched the participation of semi-skilled service workers in 2016. Only Poland had a comparatively lower involvement of adults in manual occupations, deeply under the average country participation level. Second, the differences among CE countries are even higher in the case of elementary occupations. While low-skilled manual workers in Hungary participated with almost the same frequency as high-skilled workers in 2016 (see previous Table 17.9), Czechia and Poland had a significantly lower occurrence of further education and training in this group of adults. This fact is effectively depicted in the last column of Table 17.10, which shows the participation of adults in elementary occupations as a percentage of managers'/professionals' participation.

Although firms in DMC should not intensively train their workers, especially those in low-skill occupations (see Part II., see also Magnin & Nenovsky, 2022; Nölke & Vligenthart, 2009), a practice of firm training for manual workers has changed since the early 2010s. My research posits that this shift can be attributed to a distinctive convergence of factors, including the prevailing economic conditions, heightened demand for labour, the evolution of corporate readiness to provide on-the-job training, the availability of financial resources, and intensified competition for key workers. This confluence of circumstances has directed firms' training strategies toward an increased emphasis on workplace-based NFE for manual workers (see Part IV for a discussion of these trends inside CE countries).

Moreover, countries also varied in their trends over time. While Hungary has seen a profound increase in participation of skilled manual workers already in 2011 and then, an extreme jump in the involvement of unskilled workers in AET from 2011 to 2016, Poland, and the Czech Republic had only a slight increase in participation of 'blue-collar' workers during the 2000s and 2010s. Slovakia's trend reminds much more of the Hungarian's trajectory but with less staggering improvement in the early 2010s.

The interpretation of these observed trends necessitates consideration of distinct processes occurring within CE countries. To begin with, Hungary underwent a significant shift post-2010, directing its focus predominantly toward job-related NFE tailored for skilled manual workers. This shift was facilitated by comprehensive governmental reforms encompassing legislative adjustments and partial financial support. Consequently, this shift elucidates the notably elevated levels of participation among manual workers in AET within Hungary.

In a parallel vein, Slovakia's industrial sector, grappling with pronounced labour demand throughout the 2010s, expanded opportunities for workplace learning among manual workers. However, this expansion occurred independently of state support, resulting in a level of growth that did not match the magnitude observed in Hungary.

Conversely, Czechia had a relatively established system of frequent training for manual workers as early as 2007, a system that did not experience subsequent expansion as the proportion of manual workers within the labour market gradually diminished.

Lastly, in the context of Poland, enterprises did not implement extensive workplace learning initiatives for manual workers, thus contributing to persistently low participation levels with minimal improvements. The circumstances in Poland reflect a combination of distinct factors, including a higher concentration of agricultural workers, lower levels of innovation within companies, smaller FDI, and a larger representation of small enterprises in comparison to other CE countries.

The data presented in Tables 17.11 and 17.12 offer valuable insights into the trends in occupational inequality within CE countries. Notably, there are substantial differences among them. Firstly, with the exception of Slovakia, all ALSs experienced a decline in the relative advantage of managers and professionals over time. The most significant decline occurred in Hungary, where high-skilled workers participated at only 133% of the country's average rate in 2016 (see Table 17.11). In contrast, the participation pattern of semi-skilled service workers in AET remained relatively stable, with a slight decline in advantage observed in Poland and Czechia, while Hungary and Slovakia displayed an opposite trend. Moreover, the relative advantage of skilled manual workers in Czechia declined between 2007 and 2016. In 2007, this occupational category exhibited above-average participation in organised learning but subsequently experienced an 11 percentage point decrease.

On the other hand, the relative participation of skilled 'blue-collar' workers significantly improved in Hungary and Slovakia, reaching 117% and 120% of the average country participation levels, respectively. This trend was also observed among unskilled manual workers in Hungarian and Slovakian ALS (see Table 17.12). In contrast, Poland did not witness any significant change in the relative involvement of elementary occupations, while Czechia experienced a slight decline.

These findings illuminate both the diverse temporal trajectories of occupational inequality in participation within AET across CE countries, as well as the contrasting outcomes in occupation-related participation inequalities despite similar economic models (DMC). My findings contend that the considerable reduction in occupational inequality stems from intentional government policies in Hungary

Table 17.11 Relative levels of participation in AET among the high-skilled and medium-skilled service workers: 2007–2016

| | Managers, professionals (ISCO 01) |||| Clerical support workers (ISCO 02) ||||
	2007	2011	2016	**dif.**	2007	2011	2016	**dif.**
CZ	166	171	150	**−16**	111	114	106	**−5**
POL	237	228	205	**−32**	116	109	116	**−1**
HU	220	156	133	**−87**	111	131	117	**+6**
SK	146	149	150	**+4**	103	104	108	**+5**

Source: own calculation

Note: Participation levels in the percentage of average adult participation (25 to 64 years) in the country in a particular year. dif. = difference between 2007 and 2016

17.5 Participation Based on Occupation Status

Table 17.12 Relative levels of participation in AET among qualified and unqualified manual workers: 2007–2016

	Skilled manual workers (ISCO 08)				Elementary occupations (ISCO 09)			
	2007	2011	2016	**dif.**	2007	2011	2016	**dif.**
CZ	109	88	98	**−11**	57	39	51	**−6**
POL	68	73	68	**0**	50	57	50	**0**
HU	78	132	117	**+39**	69	115	129	**+60**
SK	110	95	120	**+10**	68	62	89	**+21**

Source: own calculation
Note: Participation levels in the percentage of average adult participation (25 to 64 years) in the country in a particular year. dif. = difference between 2007 and 2016

following 2010, on the one hand, and from Poland's comparatively less pronounced transition to frequent training for manual workers. This variance can be attributed, in part, to the less advanced development of a workplace NFE culture in Poland.

Chapter 18
Barriers to Participation in AET

The upcoming chapter explores perceived barriers to participation, as overcoming them represents one of the crucial constraints that effective and impactful ALSs must overcome. Their analysis clarifies key perceived barriers that adults face and whether CE ALSs have a shared pattern of barriers or not. Specifically, my analysis focuses on what have been key barriers to participation in AET for adults from CE who did not participate in organised learning, according to data from AES 2007 to 2016.

Table 18.1 presents a condensed answer to this question as it shows perceived barriers to participation in organised learning reported by adults who wanted to participate but did not. Consistent with Cross's (1981, see also Chap. 4 for details) conceptualisation of barriers, the items representing different constraints are arranged in order, ranging from (1) *situational barriers* (e.g., family reasons, health issues, and AET costs) to *institutional barriers* (e.g., training schedule and suitability of educational offerings) and *dispositional barriers* (personal reasons). Regrettably, data on barriers for Slovakia are unavailable for both the AES 2007 and 2001 surveys. Therefore, it cannot be included in trend analysis.

18.1 Commonalities in Barriers

Analysing the table (Table 18.1), it becomes evident that the CE countries share certain common patterns of barriers. All of them have profound constraints regarding (1) *family-related reasons* and (2) *health/age-related reasons*. Approximately one-quarter to one-third of non-participants perceived family-related reasons as a barrier, while every tenth non-participant mentioned health/age as an obstacle. Not surprisingly, these two types of barriers have been shown in other studies (Roosma & Saar, 2017) as the most characteristic of CE countries. Moreover, as I have shown in the previous chapter, all CE ALSs scored a high participation inequality in both

Table 18.1 Perceived barriers to participation in AET among those who wanted to participate: 2007–2016

	2007	2011	2016	dif.	Rel. dif.
Family reason					
CZ	36	28	33	−3	**−8**
POL	29	33	34	+5	**+17**
HUN	37	23	26	−11	**−30**
SK	N.A.	N.A.	36	N.A.	**N.A.**
Health/age					
CZ	8	6	8	0	**0**
POL	6	5	7	+1	**+17**
HUN	13	11	11	−2	**−15**
SK	N.A.	N.A.	13	N.A.	**N.A.**
Distance					
CZ	15	11	12	−3	**−20**
POL	29	8	4	−25	**−86**
HUN	32	24	30	−2	**−6**
SK	N.A.	N.A.	14	N.A.	**N.A.**
Cost of AET					
CZ	18	25	22	+4	**22**
POL	52	38	21	−31	**−60**
HUN	41	55	42	+1	**2**
SK	N.A.	N.A.	33	N.A.	**N.A.**
Lack of support from employers or public services					
CZ	19	15	10	−9	**−47**
POL	21	10	11	−10	**−48**
HUN	39	20	20	−19	**−49**
SK	N.A.	N.A.	12	N.A.	**N.A.**
Schedule of AET					
CZ	41	26	21	−20	**−49**
POL	39	28	28	−11	**−28**
HUN	51	32	49	−2	**−4**
SK	N.A.	N.A.	49	N.A.	**N.A.**
No suitable offer					
CZ	N.A.	11	10	−1	**−9**
POL	N.A.	13	8	−5	**−38**
HUN	N.A.	10	24	+14	**+140**
SK	N.A.	N.A.	12	N.A.	**N.A.**
Personal reason					
CZ	8	13	48	+40	**+500**
POL	13	15	13	0	**0**
HUN	15	5	5	−10	**−67**
SK	N.A.	N.A.	20	N.A.	**N.A.**

Note: Perception of barriers in percent. Dif. = difference in percentage points between 2007 and 2016, or 2011 to 2016, if data for 2007 are not available. Rel. dif. = Relative difference in percent
Source: AES (2007, 2011, 2016)

areas, as age and family constraints are strongly interconnected with gender-based inequality (Boeren, 2011; Vaculíková et al., 2021) and age-related inequality (Kalenda & Kočvarová, 2022b; Schuller, 2019).

18.2 Differences in Barriers

However, significant differences also exist among them in various aspects of barriers. On the other hand, the most significant differences can be observed in terms of the *cost of AET*. For Hungarian adults who expressed that they wanted to participate, the cost of AET was perceived as a barrier by 40–55% of respondents. In contrast, for Czech adults, this barrier was reported by only 18–25% of individuals. Notably, in Poland, over half of the respondents mentioned the cost of training as a limitation to their participation in 2007, but this percentage decreased to 21% in 2016.

The differences between the Czech Republic and Hungary can be attributed to specific factors. In the case of Hungary, the comparatively (1) high cost of FAE (Hordósy & Szanyi-F., 2021; see also Chap. 7), (2) lower-extend of employers' support for NFE (see Chap. 14) and (3) very stratified and restricted model of state support for NFE-Voc (see again Chap. 7). Conversely, in Czechia, the prevalence of financial support from employers for AET plays a significant role in understanding the observed variations (see Chap. 14). As for Poland, the decline in the proportion of the population perceiving cost as a constraint to involvement in AET may be a result of two reinforcing mechanisms: (1) the decline in the cost of FAE for adults since the 2000s and (2) the improvement in living conditions in Poland, with average wages approaching the EU average during the 2010s (see Chap. 10).

A second significant difference worth noting is the perception of *distance* as a barrier (i.e., distance from site of education provision is too long). In Hungary, this barrier is strongly perceived, with 30% of respondents considering it an obstacle to participation. Surprisingly, in Poland, the largest country in the region, with the uttermost regional differences, only 4% of respondents view distance as a barrier. Slovakia and Czechia have much lower occurrences of this barrier.

In the case of Hungary, we should consider the geographical differences in educational opportunities between the East and West regions of the country, as they can pose strong constraints on participation. In contrast, the wide and dense network of formal educational institutions across Poland (see Chap. 10) may contribute to a weak perception of this barrier, despite the existence of significant participation inequality between adults residing in urban and rural areas.

Another notable difference is found in the case of *personal reasons* in the Czech Republic, this barrier has notably expanded, with nearly half of the respondents mentioning it in 2016. In contrast, in Poland, only 13% of respondents reported personal reasons as a barrier, and in Hungary, the percentage was even lower at 5%. This finding can be attributed to the very low demand for further education in

Czechia (see Chap. 16) as well as the weak perceived utility of organised learning among its population (Karger et al., 2022).

In addition to these barriers, there are also differences in the *perception of the schedule* of AET and the *suitability of the offered education and training*. Although the number of adults who perceive the schedule of AET as an obstacle has declined since 2007, it remains one of the most significant barriers in Hungary and Slovakia, with almost half of the adults considering it a key barrier. In contrast, in Poland and the Czech Republic, the schedule of AET is viewed as an issue by 21–28% of non-participants. It is worth mentioning that this item has witnessed a decline over time, particularly in Czechia, where it has been reduced by half. These findings are particularly significant when considering the supply-side perspective. They indicate that in the Czech Republic and Poland, there is an appropriate scheduling of AET provision, which aligns with the expectations of adults. However, in Hungary and Slovakia, the offer of educational opportunities does not meet the expectations of half of the potential learners.

Finally, *the lack of support from employers or public services* is noteworthy for two reasons. First, Hungary stands out with almost double the number of adults perceiving this factor as a barrier to their participation compared to other CE countries. Second, there is a common trend of declining perception of the "lack of support" across CE. Since 2007, the CE ALSs observed a significant decrease of approximately 50% in the number of non-participants stating "lack of support" as a constraint to their involvement in organised learning. Furthermore, when considering health/age-related barriers and the availability of a suitable provision, the lack of support emerged as the least perceived obstacle. This result and the overall trend can be attributed to the very high involvement of employers in the provision of NFE, which contains 65–85% of all organised training in the region (see Chap. 14).

18.3 Barriers Among Those Who Did Not Want to Participate

Table 18.2 covers the most typical barriers to AET among adults who did not want to participate in AET—*no need for AET*. In the case of need, a typical dispositional barrier, we can see that all CE ALSs in 2016 showed a *very high occurrence of this obstacle*, as more than 77% of adults stated this reason for non-participation. Differences among countries were rather small. It is worth mentioning that perception of this barrier grew between 2011 and 2016, especially in the Czech Republic and Poland. In comparison, it was comparatively high in Hungary already at the beginning of the 2010s.

In this context, it is pertinent to observe that this outcome is potentially associated with the perceived need for AET within the Visegrad countries. Czechia, Hungary, and Slovakia displayed some of the lowest levels of demand for AET among European nations in 2016 (see Chap. 16). The pronounced prevalence of the

18.3 Barriers Among Those Who Did Not Want to Participate

Table 18.2 Perceived barriers to participation in AET among those who did not want to participate: 2011–2016

	2007	2011	2016	dif.	rel.dif
No need					
CZ	47	42	77	+30	+60%
POL	69	60	77	+8	+12%
HUN	82	87	85	+3	+4%
SK	62	N.A.	80	+18.	+29%

Note: Perception of barriers in percent. Dif. = difference in percent points between 2007 and 2016, or 2011 to 2016, if data for 2007 are not available. Rel. dif. = Relative difference in percent
Source: AES (2007, 2011, 2016)

reason "no need for organised learning" within their non-participants contributes to an understanding of this diminished perceived demand. This phenomenon can be attributed to the commendable level of general skills present in these countries, which is a result of their notably elevated secondary education attainment (as introduced in the opening of Part IV), along with the frequent participation of individuals in low-skilled occupations.

Summary of the Part VI

This part of the book revealed an important insight: *ALSs in CE countries exhibit significant variations in their participation patterns and barriers*—who actually participate in them, and which barriers are perceived the most? From this point of view, they *cannot be considered members of one group of countries with similar levels of inequality in access to organised learning opportunities for adults* (Green, 2006, 2011; Saar et al., 2013a, b, 2023).

Once, we delve into differences in the involvement of their key sociodemographic groups in AET, we easily identify not only variation among who participates and how much but also contradictory trends in them. While some groups of adults have experienced an improvement in their access to AET, others have seen rising inequality.

To summarise my argument here. While certain CE countries, such as Hungary, Slovakia, and Czechia, may have similar levels of participation in AET, the involvement of different sociodemographic groups varies among them. Hence, their *ALSs have a different impact on the inequality inside them*.

These differences arise as an outcome of some key characteristics of these systems, their horizontal dimension. Notably, the effect of the position of FAE within a country´s approach toward skill formation, public NFE provision, the role of employers in support of AET and demand for job-related NFE. However, they also go beyond these ALSs characteristics, as they are rooted in institutional clusters that shape ALSs in a particular country and in their transformation processes: expansion of HE system in them, shift toward post-industrial occupational structure, general approach to economy (DMC), and welfare policy.

This finding is inherently rational, given that ALSs are intricately intertwined with a network of economic, political, educational, and cultural establishments. These encompass the labour market, the welfare state system, the formal education system, and industrial relations (Desjardins, 2023a, b; Kureková et al., 2023; Saar et al., 2023). Consequently, it is imperative to conceive of these systems as interconnected yet loosely structured, with overlaps existing among them. This intricate network (or ecology) addresses diverse forms of AET, which are continuously evolving and being employed for distinct purposes.

Table 1 Patterns in participation inequality based on key sociodemographic factors: 2007–2016

Differences in participation based on	Hungary	Czech Republic	Slovakia	Poland
Age	High	High	High	High
Gender	Low	Low	Low	Low
Attained Education	Medium	Medium-high	Medium-high	Very high
Labour market participation	Medium-high	Medium-high	Very high	Very high
Occupational status	Low	Medium	Medium	High

The next part of the text (see Part VII) comes back to these interconnections between ALSs and other institutional clusters in CE. Before that, this chapter generalises key patterns regarding observed participation inequality and perceived barriers. Table 1 serves as a comprehensive summary of the key findings from the preceding chapters.

Patterns of Inequality

Overall, the four countries display varying levels of participation inequality across different sociodemographic factors. Hungary exhibits the lowest level of inequality, while the Czech Republic and Slovakia show a slightly more unequal pattern. Poland, on the other hand, has high to very high levels of inequality across multiple factors, indicating significant disparities in participation rates. This finding aligns with Saar et al.'s (2023) recent analysis, which also revealed significant disparities in participation rates among CE countries based on occupational category and level of education attained. Their findings suggest that the four CE countries under consideration can be classified into three distinct empirical groups; the same can also be concluded based on our analysis.

As per Saar et al. (2023), the distribution of occupations is likely to have a significant impact on the inequality in AET participation in post-socialist countries, compared to their educational qualifications. However, my research shows that inequality is more pronounced based on the highest level of education attained, as opposed to occupational status. Individuals with the lowest education levels (ISCED 0–2) participated in organised learning at rates ranging from 21% to 76% of the country's average participation rates. Whereas individuals from the lowest occupational group (ISCO 8–9, skilled manual workers and elementary occupations) attended organised learning at rates ranging from 68% to 120% of the country average, which is approximately 50–129% of the average. Based on that, we can see that *educational structure has a much more profound effect on the level of inequality in the involvement in AET*.

The rationale behind this intriguing discrepancy can be attributed to the influence of two self-reinforcing factors. Firstly, individuals with lower levels of education (ISCED 0–2) within the Visegrad region experience heightened inequality due to the prevailing norm of attaining at least a secondary education (ISCED 3) in these countries. This norm is reflected in the education attainment rate among 18-year-olds, exceeding 80% in Slovakia and surpassing 90% in the remaining CE countries (WB, 2023). Consequently, adults with such educational backgrounds often find themselves ensnared in the "grey economy," precarious employment, or unemployment. These circumstances result in limited opportunities for work-related training (NFE-Voc). Furthermore, CE countries generally curtail their FAE programs, which encompass ABE and AGE for those older than 24, and the overall schema for public NFE training is relatively underdeveloped.

Secondly, when compared to CMEs or LMEs, DMEs from CE have displayed a greater inclination to provide training for low-skilled workers (ISCO 8-9) within crucial industries, particularly during the 2010s. Certain DMEs, such as Hungary, have even bolstered these efforts with specialised, even though contradictory, labour market policies aimed at supporting such initiatives.

Trends in Inequality

Trends in participation inequality vary across the four countries. Hungary and Slovakia have generally experienced decreasing participation inequality across multiple factors, while the Czech Republic has shown slight improvements in certain areas. On the other hand, Poland has observed only minor improvements in the overall high level of participation inequality. Therefore, I can conclude that Poland's ALS has been the least successful in mitigating educational inequality.

Table 2 provides a detailed overview of these trends. Starting with Hungary, its ALS underwent the most profound changes in patterns of participation since the 2000s. There has been a decreasing trend in participation inequality based on age, attained education and labour market participation, as well as occupational status. This suggests that the disparities in participation rates have been gradually reducing across these factors. The only one sociodemographic category that shows an increase in inequality over time is gender. The trend of unequal gender access to AET and lifelong learning opportunities in Hungary was driven by policies that favoured professions with a higher proportion of men and lower rates of women employment.

The Czech Republic has also experienced some positive developments. Participation inequality based on age, gender, and attained education has slightly decreased, indicating more balanced participation across these three factors.

Table 2 Trends in participation inequality based on key sociodemographic factors: 2007-2016

Differences in participation based on	Hungary	Czech Republic	Slovakia	Poland
Age	Decreasing	Slightly decreasing	Decreasing	Decreasing
Gender	Increasing	Slightly decreasing	Stable	Stable
Attained Education	Decreasing	Slightly increasing	Decreasing	Stable
Labour market participation	Decreasing	Decreasing	Stable	Stable
Occupational status	Decreasing	Slightly increasing	Decreasing	Stable

Similarly, it has experienced a substantial decrease in participation inequality related to the unemployed. However, participation inequality based on occupational status slightly increased after 2007. This trend could be an effect of the continuous shift toward a post-industrial occupational structure where more adults works in service sector.

In many respects, Slovakia has a pattern very similar to Czech ALS—an overall decreasing trend in participation inequality based on age and attained education, however, with much higher intensity than in Czechia. On the other hand, participation inequality based on gender and labour market involvement has remained stable over the examined period. As in the case of the overall level of participation and many axes of the GALS model, Slovakia shows only minor dynamics in its participation inequality.

Participation patterns in Poland have undergone the smallest change among CE ALS. It has seen only a consistent decrease in participation inequality based on age. However, this type of inequality has been still comparatively very high. Other types of inequality have remained stable, indicating no significant changes over time.

Patterns of Barriers

Regarding barriers to participation in AET, several significant differences have been observed among CE ALSs (see Table 3). Although they *share strong dispositional barriers* to AET, they *slightly differ in perception of other types of barriers* to organised learning.

The most common barriers reported by non-participants are "no need for AET," with all countries showing a high occurrence of the former, which corroborates the previous finding regarding a high occurrence of dispositional barriers in CE countries, although they have operationalised differently from Cross's (1981) original conception, as mainly health and age-related constraints (see Roosmaa & Saar, 2017, Saar et al., 2023).

Regarding differences, one notable is the perception of *distance* as a barrier, with Hungary having a strong perception of this obstacle compared to Poland, Slovakia, and Czechia. Geographical differences within Hungary pose constraints on participation, while Poland benefits from a wide and dense network of educational institutions. *Personal reasons* also vary, with the Czech Republic having the highest occurrence of this barrier, followed by Poland and Hungary. The schedule of AET is viewed as a significant obstacle in Hungary and Slovakia but less so in Poland and

Table 3 The pattern of barriers to participation in CE ALSs

Barriers to AET	Hungary	Czech Republic	Slovakia	Poland
Situational	Medium	Weak-Medium	Medium	Weak-Medium
Institutional	Medium-strong	Weak-Medium	Medium	Medium
Dispositional	Strong	Strong	Strong	Strong

Summary of the Part VI 197

the Czech Republic. Lack of support from employers or public services is another noteworthy barrier, with Hungary having the highest perception of this factor. However, there has been a declining trend in the perception of a "lack of support" across the Visegrad region.

Part VII
Discussion and Conclussion

This part of the book links findings from the previous three empirical parts. Both the history of institutions responsible for lifelong learning in CE countries and available empirical patterns regarding AET in them are putted together and discussed relation to two key topics related to ALSs formation. First, it is a periodisation of this process—i.e., how a sequence of formation processes has looked like and what has been the main drivers of this process (Chap. 19). Second, it is debateted how traditional forces, which are according to the literature responsible for institutional building and rebuilding in the sphere of AET, specifically influence the construction of national ALSs in the Visegrad region. In this regard, Europeanisation, national governmental policy, the evolution of social structure, DMC and Welfare policy are putted under the spotlight. By doing so, this chapter also highlights how ALSs are shaped by institutional clusters that are responsible for these processes (Chap. 20). In conclusion, the final part of the book brings synthesise of the principal findings, proposes major policy recommendations derived from these insights, and suggests potential avenues for future research (Chap. 21).

Chapter 19
Three Stages of ALSs Formation in CE

Based on the key configurations of institutional development, three phases of the formation of ALSs in CE between 1989 and 2019 could be distinguished. Each of them is characterised by a specific set of *societal challenges*, which have influenced the coordination, supply and demand side of ALSs. These challenges produced either *drivers* or *constraints* that worked for or against the overall accumulation of the "mass of organised learning opportunities available to adults" (Desjardins & Ioannidou, 2020, p. 145) and its even concertation across various social groups. My previous findings identified:

1. the *transition period* (1989–2003);
2. the *accession period* (2004–2012);
3. the *period of economic recovery* (2013–2019).

While each of these phases contained similar types of institutional pressures, it is important to note that their progress and impact on the structure of ALSs, i.e. vertical and horizontal movements of the country within the GALS, and related inequality in access to AET opportunities were not uniform. The internal characteristics of each ALS, the strength of these pressures as well as specific responses of stakeholders to them led to the differentiation in the construction and reconstruction of ALSs. Sometimes, it caused the establishment of new institutions and centralisation of coordination over the lifelong learning field, while sometimes it produced a disruption of institutions responsible for AET, i.e. change of their goals, function, funding scope or decentralisation of their management. In other words, while all these phases demonstrate similarities in the building of the institutional framework of organised adult learning across the investigated countries, outcomes of the formation process differ among the countries. These key variations are fully unpacked later.

19.1 Years of Transition (1989–2003)

The first phase, which commenced shortly after 1989, was typical of extensive decentralisation and the removal of ideological influences in AET. The socialist model of organised learning for adults was abolished, paving the way for widespread liberalisation in the field of AET. As a result, the level of state direct coordination for AET remained relatively low across most countries in CE until the early 2000s. This was not only a case of the state apparatus but also other prolific stakeholders, like the unions and other professional representative organisations, which were much weaker in CE countries than in Western Europe, because were understood as a relic of old times and constrain toward transformation into capitalist societies (Cook, 2007; Spieser, 2007; Vanhuysee, 2006).

The lack of state interventions in this domain can be attributed to multiple factors. Firstly, there was a negative ideological perception of AET, which hindered state action, as well as policy preference toward other areas that had a bigger relevance for transforming societies: e.g., privatisation of the public property, formation of a free market, and establishing new law and independent judicial system and institutions of democratic representation. Additionally, two other factors played a significant role in AET decentralisation: (1) *weak state capacity* and (2) the *transitional nature of the newly established state institutions*. Although all CE countries inherited comprehensive welfare state institutions from the socialist era encompassing free healthcare, initial formal education, and pension systems, the countries lacked the necessary resources to build institutions beyond these foundational pillars of the nascent and financially burdensome democratic welfare state (Cook, 2007; Cook & Inglot, 2022; Szelenyi & Wilk, 2010). Consequently, the allocation of funds towards state-building efforts aimed at AET or enhancing training in the labour market was severely limited from the outset. Moreover, there was a lack of state-legislated frameworks, methodologies, and general expertise ("know-how") in the field of AET, including both the establishment of effective ALMP through public NFE (Szelewa & Polakowski, 2022) and strategies for promoting workplace learning within a market economy that was still in its early stages of development during the 1990s (Łobos et al., 2020).

The second key institutional juncture in the development of ALSs in CE represented the emergence of an *unregulated market* for organised learning provision. During this process, the growth of new private providers played a pivotal role. However, the extension of AET provision was relatively slow, and the demand for learning opportunities remained generally low throughout most of this early period. Moreover, it is necessary to mention, that there were variations among CE countries in their approach to supporting FAE—both AGE and AHE. Some countries, like Poland, prioritised AGE as a key component of their AET provision, while others, such as Slovakia and Czechia, considered it a secondary priority and open space for private provision.

A notable lack of demand for AET also characterised the years following the fall of Communism. Several processes contributed to this situation. First, the transition from socialism to capitalism had its undisputable price. The economic performance of national economies experienced a temporary downturn, leading to limited financial capacity for both firms and households to invest in learning and development initiatives. Second, as the economies underwent reconstruction, newly established firms and individuals seeking new employment or starting their own businesses had different priorities that took precedence over investing in education and organised training. Third, all CE countries inherited occupational and educational structures with a significant proportion of adults employed in manufacturing industries and a relatively small share of tertiary education graduates. Although the severity of these structural conditions varied across the region (with Poland facing greater challenges than the rest of the Visegrad countries), the social structure consisting of a high proportion of adults with low training requirements in the workplace, combined with a low proportion of employees with high training needs, significantly constrained the demand for AET in the 1990s.

19.2 Years of Accession (2004–2012)

The second phase of ALSs formation introduced a new factor that drove the establishment of lifelong learning institutions—the construction of the 'European Education/Learning Space' (Lawn, 2006; Lawn & Grek, 2012) and consequently also 'European lifelong learning space' (Holford, 2023; Holford & Milana, 2023). The accession of CE countries to the EU greatly expedited the development of ALSs, particularly in terms of their coordination side and introduction of multilevel supranational government. The diffusion of the lifelong learning agenda from Brussels to the CE region resulted in the adoption of new vocabulary, understanding, objectives and indicators that later translated into national AET strategies and partially influenced legislative frameworks related to lifelong learning. Although all CE countries adopted this framework, there were variations in the timing and implementation of these initiatives as well as the depth and systematisation of this adoption. Nevertheless, it is worth noting that the implementation of these policy measures heavily relied on external resources, primarily the EU funds, as the institutional capacity of CE states in this area was still weak.

Despite the state institutions becoming less transitory and better equipped to implement various measures related to organised learning due to the "socialisation" of public servants through mechanisms of peer learning by the EC (Milana et al., 2020), the substantial expenses allocated to the core welfare triad in CE countries limited large-scale investments in the AET policy domain. This situation was further complicated by the fact that all CE countries simultaneously expanded their costly tertiary education systems during the same period (Garitzmann, 2016; Garritzmann et al., 2022; Jungblut et al., 2023), focusing on widening access to tertiary education, considering it more important for economic competitiveness than enhancing opportunities for AET. Therefore, research results highlight that despite AET being considered a secondary policy priority also in more economically advanced countries (Regmi, 2020), its starting position in the competition for public funding in CE was more unfavourable compared to countries that switch to a policy of so-called social investment already in the 1970s or even the 1980s (Bonoli, 2007; Hake, 2022).

In the years following the turn of the millennium, there was a significant expansion of AET offerings throughout various segments of the market for organised adult learning. In all CE countries, the number of providers increased until the economic crisis, which resulted in some providers experiencing bankruptcy. Concurrently, the growth in supply was accompanied by a diversification of provision. Not only did the number of private providers increase, but there was also an expansion of workplace training, particularly in large international companies that began to adopt HRM/HRD practices from Western countries. The public sector also made advancements, providing opportunities for non-traditional learners to participate in AHE, and delivering more training to employees in selected public sectors.

Most CE economies had already recovered from the economic transition of the 1990s and experienced a positive economic upturn until 2009 when the global economic crisis hit the region. However, the impact of the crisis on CE economies was lower than in other parts of Europe (Hall, 2018). Consequently, living standards improved during the 2000s, reducing financial constraints to AET participation that were prevalent in the previous decade. Additionally, all CE governments began exerting more pressure on upskilling public employees by introducing new qualifications and regular training requirements for workers in healthcare, the education system, social services, and other regulated professions.

Nevertheless, two robust mechanisms continued to hinder high social demand for AET across CE countries. Firstly, despite changes in the social structure, the occupational composition still included a significant proportion of low-skilled manual workers, and the social structure had a small number of adults with university degrees. Secondly, the dominance of DMC drove firms to invest less in training of their employees, focusing instead on low wages and minimal innovation enhancements. This strategy limited the demand for AET within the workforce.

19.3 Years of Economic Recovery (2013–2019)

Following the end of the economic crisis, CE countries experienced significant economic growth, deviating from the trajectory of many countries in Southern and Western Europe (Hall, 2018). This led to a substantial increase in the demand for labour, presenting a new societal challenge that governments and economies in the region had to confront.

As the EU framed lifelong learning primarily for enhancing employability and sustaining economic competitiveness and growth, which CE countries both experienced during the 2010s, the policy attractiveness of supporting AET diminished. While the EU discourse continued to be adopted at the national level, the implementation and funding of its key measures were deprioritised by governments or utilised for their own purposes. Consequently, the focus of the lifelong learning agenda in the CE shifted even more toward vocational orientation, while losing the political urgency it had in the previous decade. In many cases, it was possible to see various examples of *institutional conversion* in the area of lifelong learning policy due to this unexpected situation; for instance, states started to use measures originally intended to support the supply side of AET to co-financing their own apparatus.

The vast expansion of the AET market, which was characteristic of the 2000s, slowed down and, in some CE countries, even experienced a slight contraction in the early 2010s (due to the economic crisis). Rather than continue to grow and diversify, the trend shifted toward a narrower focus on private job-related learning, particularly provided by employers or specialised education providers for companies. Consequently, public provision of both FAE and NFE declined across the region, with the exception of Poland. Additionally, countries began to grapple with new phenomena such as skill mismatch among university graduates and shortages of labour in lower and middle-skilled occupations, especially in Hungary and Slovakia. This phenomenon heavily influenced inequality in access to AET, as they pushed employers to invest more in lower-educated and lower-skilled workers.

In comparison to the previous phase of their formation, CE ALSs experienced an increased demand for organised learning among adults. This trend can be attributed to the convergence of two socioeconomic processes that unfolded within CE countries after 2010. First, there was a culmination of a transformation in the educational and occupational structure, characterised by significant growth in the number of higher education graduates and expansion of the service sector. Secondly, the exceptionally high demand for labour power, surpassing that of other European nations during this decade, compelled firms to revise their strategies, previously typical for DMC. Instead of relying predominantly on cheap and easily available labour, companies recognised the need to train workers with lower levels of education for effective integration into their workforce, as well as to update the skills of low-skilled employees to retain them within the organisation for more complex tasks that were unable to fill from external candidates.

19.4 Multidimensionality and Multipath of Institutional Change

Table 19.1 presents a summary of the three stages of ALSs formation in CE countries. As we can see, the formation did not have a main societal driver during the 1990s and did happen mainly as a deconstruction of the institutional apparatus of organised learning from a previous era and the emergence of a free market with AET. During the second period, the leading driver of the institutional building was the adoption of the policy framework from the EU and state activity in the field, while in the last period, it was overall demand for training at the workplace. The labour market replaced the state as a main traction of ALSs transformation.

Table 19.1 General periodisation of ALSs formation in CE: 1989–2019

	Coordination of AET	Supply of AET	Structural demand for AET
Transition period (1989–2003)	Low	Low-medium	Low
Accession period (2004–2012)	High	Medium-high	Low-medium
Period of economic recovery (2013–2019)	Medium-low	Medium-low	High

From a historical institutionalism point of view (Mahoney & Thelen, 2015), we can see that time-oriented/processual analysis reveals some of the crucial elements of the institutional development of ALSs in the Visegrad countries—their multicausality as well as variation in the timing of the effect of institutional pressures on these systems, their tipping points. In this context, it is important to note that not all societal challenges have an equal impact on the formation of ALSs, particularly in terms of immediate outcomes for both state-building activities in the field of AET and the changes in strategies of firms and individuals with regard to upskilling and reskilling. They represent distinctive dimensions not only theoretically but also empirically. For example, while the integration of CE countries into the European lifelong learning arena had a significant influence on all countries immediately during the 2000s, its effects on both vertical and horizontal changes in ALSs within GALS were less profound a decade later. A different story is a case of deindustrialisation and opening access to higher education in the CE region. Although these processes started as early as the late 1990s, their impact on mechanisms related to participation in AET and related inequality came only later, after 2010.

Chapter 20
Key Drivers of ALSs Formation in CE

In the following chapter, my focus turns to the various facets of ALSs development that set CE countries apart from each other. Primarily, it proposes summarisation of the critical drivers behind the formation of ALSs in the countries under study. Specifically, a discussion here explores how major societal challenges influenced the creation and evolution of institution responsible for coordinating adult education, the extent of organised learning provided, and the associated inequalities.

20.1 Europeanisation of ALSs Matters, but...

The creation of the European learning arena and the development of lifelong learning policies by the EU since the 1990s have had a big impact on the formation of ALSs in CE, especially between 2004 and 2012. The EU has introduced key elements of lifelong learning policies across the region, including terminology, concepts, manifest functions, and a predominant focus on vocational goals such as upskilling and reskilling of the workforce. However, this is not very surprising, as some scholars (Scharpf, 2008; Streeck, 2013) have considered the EU as a vehicle of liberalisation. Additionally, the EU has provided essential policy tools like a shared qualification framework and a system for recognising prior learning. However, this process has involved *two distinct levels*—(1) the discursive level, which primarily includes policy documents and reports with background philosophy, strategies, goals and a repertoire of the proposed policy tools; (2) the *implementation level,* which covers actual measures put into practice.

On the one hand, the dissemination of key concepts and policy objectives has been *highly successful at a discursive level*. On the other hand, the implementation of these policy objectives across countries, and even within their regions, *has been less effective in terms of the implementation of direct policy measures* and *achieving policy aims*. None of the CE countries has achieved the targets set by the Lisbon

Strategy for 2000–2010 or its "double", the "Europe 2020" strategy for lifelong learning, despite incorporating their objectives into national agendas. We can only concur with Olsen's (2002) assertion, made over 20 years ago that "The actual ability of the European level to penetrate domestic institutions is not perfect, universal or constant" (Olsen, 2002, p. 936). Brussels's agenda of lifelong learning has penetrated mostly discursive level of ALSs coordination and then has been adapted toward an existing environment of national ALS rather than vice-versa.

In addition to the diffusion of lifelong learning discourses and their associated policy aims and indicators, the actual implementation of measures to promote participation in AET and reduce related inequalities *varied significantly among CE ALSs*. This variation can be attributed primarily to the (1) diverse approaches taken by national governments in utilising AET to address specific national socioeconomic challenges or their lack of, as well as that (2) implementation was done without a deeper understanding of the complementarity of lifelong learning to other institutional packages. Also, (3) political preferences of the ruling governments regarding European integration or nationalist orientation played their role in specific periods.

For example, *Hungary* emerged as an "early adopter" of the EU's lifelong learning strategy among the Visegrad countries, formulating its initial strategy in 2005. Furthermore, Hungary implemented extensive legislation aimed at enhancing the provision of certified job-related courses to low-skilled and semi-skilled adults, based on this strategy. Subsequently, after 2010, Hungary further intensified this approach by focusing on the training of low-skilled workers in specific industries with high labour demands, utilising shorter training programs outside the formal education system. However, during this period, the nationalist government also restricted support for other forms of AET, including non-job-related organised learning and specific groups of potential learners such as women, older adults, and minority groups.

The *Czech policy* approach to the adoption of the EU's lifelong learning agenda was slightly slower compared to Hungary, as it formulated its first dedicated strategy in 2007. However, the Czech government demonstrated more initiative in utilising the EU structural funds to support the provision of organised learning in both the public and private sectors. Nevertheless, the systematic enhancement of this area has decreased over time as the resources from the EU funds have diminished, the national economy has improved, and the demand for urgent retraining has waned during the 2010s. Consequently, the Czech Republic has formally embraced the EU's lifelong learning agenda, but with minimal government initiative in this domain.

In contrast to Czechia and Hungary, *Slovakia* exhibited a more reluctant approach to adopting the EU policy framework, primarily due to the nationalist tendencies, which opposed Slovakia's full integration into the EU and slowed down the accession process. Consequently, despite publishing its first lifelong learning strategy in the same year as the Czech Republic, Slovakia only introduced AET-related legislation 2 years later. Additionally, resources for directly enhancing organised learning became available only during the mid-2010s, and the country was unable to establish its own national system of recognition of prior learning during the analysed period. AET policy in Slovakia remained primarily at the discursive level, with advancements in support of ALMP occurring mainly in the latter half of the 2010s.

Finally, *Poland* formulated its lifelong learning strategy in 2005, aligning with European guidelines. Although Poland's adoption of the strategy was quicker compared to Czechia and Slovakia, the national discourse on lifelong learning in Poland diverged significantly from the terminology used in Brussels. Moreover, the focus remained heavily on formal education for both youth and adults—the so-called 'front-end model' of learning (Desjardins, 2017). As a result, little attention was given to training outside the formal education system until the second half of the 2010s. The lack of innovation in this area was exacerbated by the high instability of the Polish educational system following its accession to the EU. If resources from EU funds were utilised to support AET, they were primarily directed towards the existing network of formal educational institutions and their programs, or the implementation and standardisation tools of national policies such as the NQF. Essentially, these resources were used for co-financing already existing activities of the state apparatus, which could serve as an example of institutional conversion. This means that the government utilised resources intended to enhance access to participation and equality in AET to reduce the cost of its own activities and enhance their legitimacy by aligning them with a new policy goal.

Based on my findings we can conclude that while institutional isomorphism is noticeable in the implementation of the EU's lifelong learning policy discourse, the actual implementation of policy tools and measures to support the supply and demand for AET has been widely varied. This heterogeneity can be attributed to regional and national differences in the demand for skills, as well as the availability of governmental and firm solutions to address them, including financial resources and expertise. In this regard, Milana et al. (2020) are right when they argue that the Europeanisation of lifelong learning had a rather a *form of domestic adaptation than direct implementation*. Beyond supranational policymaking, national and subnational policymaking still matters in the field of AET.

20.2 National Policy Matters, but…

Although the national policies adopted by CE ALSs have played a *significant role in shaping their unique characteristics*, it would be a mistake to reduce the formation process to governmental practice in the AET field. As Busemeyer and Trampusch (2012) rightly argued, "policy matters" for the evolution of skill-formation regimes, including, in this case, also their extension in the form of ALSs. Each country, albeit for a limited period, *implemented specific approaches towards AET that influenced the trajectory of ALS and temporarily impacted various aspects of the system*. These measures often resulted in increased participation rates among specific social groups, primarily determined by their educational and occupational status, and reshaped the pattern of participation-related inequalities. However, these policy interventions have not been the only drivers of the progressive development of ALSs in the Visegrad region. Many times, they worked against balancing fair access to organised learning opportunities across all adults or ended with united consequences for the effectiveness of AET coordination—e.g., leading to an oversupply of some particular type of AET or prioritising some groups of participants over others.

In the case of *Hungary*, the government led by Orbán made a radical move after 2010, introducing a new workfare policy for the unemployed, targeting low-skilled workers in selected sectors of the national economy while also making adjustments in tertiary education—deprioritising some segments of the HE system. This strategy, combined with improved conditions for workplace learning across some parts of the industrial sector, resulted in a significant surge in AET participation among low-skilled workers, surpassing the levels observed in many Western European countries. Concurrently, the inequality in participation in organised learning based on occupational status decreased in Hungary at a historically low level (Chap. 7). However, these reforms did not improve the living conditions of many of these adults, as they were forced to work in low-income professions. As an outcome, the reforms rather toughened up income and social inequality (Albert, 2019).

The *Czech government*, between 2004 and 2012, provided massive support to the supply side of AET in job-oriented NFE. This support was made possible through resources from the EU funds. While this strategy resulted in increased participation rates during that period (Chap. 8), it also had notable side effects. These included an oversupply of training programs, a decline in the quality and credibility of the training offered, and an inflation of the effects of certified NFE on employability. Because the focus of AET shifted from its intended purposes, and the state reduced its support for AET after this period.

In *Poland*, the emphasis was primarily placed on utilising the existing network of formal education institutions during the 1990s, and this reliance has persisted over time. As an outcome, Poland developed a distinctive *path dependency* within its ALS, which has been heavily oriented towards the public provision of FAE at the secondary level (ISCED 3-4). In comparison to other CE countries, Poland also directed more attention towards tertiary education for young adults (aged 18–24) after 2010, rather than promoting on-the-job training within companies across the country (Chap. 10). The overall approach toward the competitiveness of the national economy was driven by an emphasis on the initial level of schooling, including extending the number of young higher-educated graduates.

During the 1990s, *Slovakia* pursued highly neoliberal policies towards AET, particularly under the leadership of Mečiar's government in the 1990s. This approach minimised not only various types of ALMPs but also substantially restricted passive labour market policies, in contrast to other CE countries. Consequently, Slovakia experienced extreme inequality among the unemployed and low-skilled adults, which persisted into the 2000s (Chap. 9). However, the situation gradually improved during the 2010s, driven by increased employer investment in job-related training for low-skilled workers and the implementation of the first well design and targeted ALMP programs.

20.2.1 Institutional Instability and Secondary Priority of AET

In addition to the aforementioned characteristics, the national lifelong learning policy in CE countries exhibits several other significant features that have influenced the coordination aspect of ALSs. First, the policy has often been *short-lived*, rarely spanning the tenure of a single government, resulting in limited effectiveness and impact. The institutional instability of key ministries responsible for AET over the studied period exacerbated this situation. For instance, Poland witnessed nine different ministers of education during the 2000s, while Czechia had eight, and Slovakia and Hungary had six each; generally, one every 15 to 16 months.

Second, in comparison to other areas of education and general welfare policy, lifelong learning has received *secondary priority*. Visegrad countries inherited costly general welfare institutions that consisted the core of their welfare policies, rather than developed specialised and targeted tools of ALMPs and other specialise social investment policies (Cook & Inglot, 2022; Hemerijck, 2017, 2018; Hemerijck & Ronchi, 2022; Szelewa & Polakowski, 2022). This has created a specific path dependency within the CE region with dominant reliance on general welfare as a key domain of decommodification. Moreover, at a time when CE countries should have been expanding and developing their ALSs, they instead focused on another education priority—opening up higher education and expanding their formal education systems for the youth. As a result, resources allocated to formal education increased, further limiting the available resources for the development of AET, particularly within the labour market context.

To conclude, while national policies play a crucial role in the formation of ALSs, it is important to acknowledge that this process cannot be solely attributed to them. ALSs formation is often influenced by external organisations such as the EU (see discussion above) and is significantly constrained by the educational and occupational structure, logic of the national economy, and the overall integration within the national welfare framework. Especially, the last factor can represent the 'institutional lock' for governments from different ideological spectrums to change the direction of the current ALS. Therefore, ALSs formation is always a complex interplay of various factors, including national policies, external influences, social structures, economic considerations, and the preservation of existing institutional frameworks. ALSs in CE have not only been made up of formal rules that have been just implemented, but they have involved national-specific interpretation and adaptive implementation by both government, firms and social actors in response to emerging challenges of post-socialist societies.

20.3 Social Structure Matters, but…

The development of ALSs in CE has been tightly interlinked with the country's social structure, particularly the evolution of the *educational* and *occupational groups*. This subchapter argues that changes in both these social structures—expansion of the number of higher educated people and rise of the number of jobs in the knowledge-intensive services—matter for the overall level of participation in AET and related inequality, but the relationships between them, at least in CE countries, has not been straightforward. If the rise in high-skilled occupations does not coincide with a proportional decline in low-skilled occupations and the creation of structural opportunities for training (the creation of more jobs with new/ higher skills requirements), along with the potential utilisation of new skills for life-related goals, participation in AET does not increase in tandem with changes in social structure.

At the beginning of the analysed period, CE countries had lower levels of higher education attainment compared to Western European countries, with only about half or one-third of the rates observed in the West. Moreover, a substantial proportion of the workforce in CE countries was employed in 'blue-collar' occupations, exceeding 45% prior to the fall of the Berlin Wall. The transformation of this initial occupational structure was not uniform. While certain periods experienced rapid changes, such as the early 1990s, other periods saw limited progress and remained relatively stagnant for almost a decade. Despite this uneven development, all CE countries underwent a *transition from a predominantly industrial social structure*, characterised by a significant presence of skilled and unskilled labour workers, to an *occupational structure with a higher representation of service workers, including those with advanced skill sets*. However, by the end of the 2010s, the proportion of manual workers in CE countries still remained twice as large as in most Western European nations. The region's reliance on qualified manual labour acted as a hindrance to a more pronounced shift towards knowledge-based societies, impeding the march towards a more knowledge-intensive economy and 'growth regime' (Hall, 2022).

The impact of social structure on AET participation in CE countries has yielded unique outcomes and shed light on related inequalities. It explains the weak association between changes in occupational structure and overall AET participation in the region. Despite the growth of workers in service sectors, particularly in high-skilled professions, the persistent *presence of a large number of low-skilled workers has impacted limited linear growth in overall participation in AET*. This has resulted in two specific effects. Firstly, although facing participation inequality, adults from low-skilled occupations have exhibited relatively high participation rates, thereby improving the chances of involvement in AET based on occupational status. Secondly, training programs for low-skilled workers tend to be shorter and require less investment compared to those for high-skilled workers (Brunello et al., 2007). This could be one of the factors that can help us explain the presence of very high extensification of AET participation (low number of training hours per learner) observed in Hungary, Slovakia, and Czechia (Chap. 12).

The changes in the educational structure have also been noteworthy. As mentioned earlier, the investment in widening access to HE during the 2000s limited public resources available for the development of robust and large-scale AET initiatives targeting adults aged 25–64 years. Moreover, the rise in the number of higher education graduates has affected participation patterns. On the one hand, with the growing number of tertiary-educated adults the number of actors who participated in AET has risen. On the other hand, the relative advantage of higher-educated adults in comparison to lower-educated has declined over time (for details see discussion in Part VI). This effect began to be profound by the beginning of the 2010s, after a decade of HE expansions (Garritzmann et al., 2022). Consequently, after 10 years of significant production of new graduates, some countries (CZ, HUN, SK) experienced skill mismatches and overqualification issues concentrated within specific age cohorts and shifted their policy approach. They preferred to stop HE expansion, as it has moved faster than the countries' occupational structure. As an outcome, the change in educational structure flattens by the end of the 2010s.

Beyond that, a higher proportion of HE adults among participants of AET escalated the extensification of participation in AET. As more adults have been generally more educated and have more general skills, they needed less time to acquire new skills. Therefore, they have been rather a target of shorter duration upskilling rather than time-consuming reskilling or upskilling with advancement to new ISCED level. Skill mismatch between the occupational structure of CE countries, which did not offer enough high-skilled jobs for HE graduates after 2010, only strengthens this tendency as partial reskilling for lower-demand job positions requires less time.

Although this process has had profound effects on all CE representatives, countries have a little bit varied in their trajectories. Especially Poland has followed a slightly different path compared to the other three CE countries. It has had an occupation structure that has been less conducive to large-scale demand for lifelong learning, including a notably high number of adults employed in agriculture. Additionally, Poland continued to prioritise higher education expansion, even after 2010, emphasising a front model of skill formation.

20.3.1 Matthew Effect and Partial Democratisation

While the analysis has identified the presence of the *Matthew effect* in CE ALSs concerning education and occupation status (see Part VI for details), which are commonly associated with participation inequality in AET (Blossfeld et al., 2020; Boeren, 2016, 2023; Kosyakova & Bills, 2021), it is important to clarify this finding in two ways.

First, the *Matthew effect has weakened over time*. As an outcome, CE countries *have witnessed partial democratisation* in the access to organised learning for many social groups. The chances of participation for low-educated and low-skilled adults have improved compared to the situation 10 or 20 years ago. However, the position of other social groups and typical non-participants, like older adults (over 55 years), have improved only sporadically or not at all.

Second, this *partial democratisation has not been geographically even.* The situation for low-educated and low-skilled adults has exhibited considerable *divergence* across CE countries and not only in general trends but also in situations of particular social groups. Both firm strategies and national policies have contributed to this variation, with Hungary and Slovakia experiencing significant improvements since the 2000s, while Czechia and Poland have seen minor or no improvement, even in the case of profound change in their social structure.

20.4 Dependent Market Capitalism Matters, but…

Although DMC (Magnin & Nenovsky, 2022; Nölke & Vliegenthart, 2009) has hugely impacted the strategies of firms in CE, *its internal logic regarding employee training has changed during the 2010s*. Unique concurrence of economic conjuncture, extreme demand for labour power, maturation of company readiness to deliver on-the-job training, available financial resources, and increasing competition for talents turned firms' training strategy 180°. This shift has not only led to increasing the presence of job-related NFE within CE ALSs but also positively influenced inequality in participation in AET, as it improved the situation of low-educated and low-skilled workers.

Originally, the enterprises, which largely depended on FDI, focused primarily on low-wage labour costs and minimal investment in employees and their development. This approach was common mainly during the 1990s and early 2000s, especially among firms in the automotive and other related industrial sectors. However, the situation changed after 2010, as many CE companies have extended workplace training. This shift was perfectly timed as the majority of medium and large companies had established HRM/HRD departments capable of on-the-job training programs for their employees by that time. When the demand for company training arose, many firms were institutionally prepared. They were not only organisationally but also financially ready because economic conjuncture in CE countries equipped them with enough financial resources for training.

The main reason behind this new HR strategy was that local companies desperately needed to cope with quickly rising international demand for their production. As the level of both digitisation and automatisation of work was still low in CE (CEDEFOP, 2022; NTF, 2017), the only available option was increasing the number of workers (CEDEFOP, 2018; OECD, 2020, 2021, 2022). However, the availability of workers for key industrial sectors was strictly limited by already high utilisation of labour power and less dense age cohorts of young graduates. Firms, therefore, had to extend their hiring process to workers (1) without direct qualifications (lower educated ones), (2) from other sectors of the economy and (3) migrants. All these three categories needed more systematic job-related training, even though they worked in professions commonly referred to as low-skilled with minimal requirements for training.

Moreover, undersupplied qualified and semi-qualified workers led to problems in the hiring process in general and increased competition for talent across all economic sectors. In such conditions, the availability of workplace training has quickly emerged as one of the competitive advantages of firms in hiring new workers and one of the desired benefits among job candidates (Misiak-Kwit et al., 2023; Smerek et al., 2021; Stachová & Smerek, 2023).

When all of these factors came together, participation in AET in DMC economies was suddenly not restricted but even supported by the firms' strategy. As it was mentioned above, firms even lower inequality in participation based on occupational status by supporting job-related employer-sponsored (Slovakia, Czechia) and partially public-supported (Hungary) NFE. This was especially prominent in Hungary and Slovakia which had the most profound orientation of national economies towards sectors with a high FDI. The impact of changes varied mainly between Poland and Hungary. In this regard, Poland had more low-skilled workers in agriculture and small businesses without FDI resulting in less significant changes. Meanwhile, Hungary's ALS systems were reformed under Orbán to meet the needs of a to-date industrial complex and maximise workforce participation, leading to even more pronounced changes. As a consequence of this dynamic, CE ALSs experienced a transition towards a greater emphasis on job-related NFE provided by employers with their financial support. Empirically, this change represented a distinctive horizontal move in GALS for all Visegrad countries (see Part V for details), although it was more profound in Czechia and Hungary than in Poland.

On this place, from a greater distance, my reserch concludes that the global rationalisation process through integration in the world economy has influenced only some parts of ALSs (especially the supply and demand side of these systems through the development and institutionalisation of more frequent workplace learning), while the coordination part rather developed into different national models.

In addition, although DMC had shaped the formation process across the CE region, its effects have been neither temporal nor spatial constant. The local adoption of workplace strategies has been specific—based on the overall level of dependence on global capitalism, mainly overall country export and FDI on the one hand and the level of post-industrialisation expressed by a proliferation of service sectors and share of high-skilled jobs on the second hand. Moreover, their impact seems to be more recent compared to other processes involved in the alternation of ALSs. Hence it is an open question whether training reconfiguration after 2010 is more a temporary adaptive strategy for unique economic conditions or a more stable feature of DMC in CE.

20.5 Welfare State Policy Matters, but…

Even though participation in AET is deeply interconnected with the idea of a new welfare policy focused on ALMP tools—*social investment policy*, this approach has never been very strong across the CE region (Hemerijck, 2017, 2018; Hemerijck & Ronchi, 2022; Palier et al., 2022; Szelewa & Polakowski, 2022). The commodification of a robust welfare state inherited from socialism has been limited in most CE countries (Cook & Inglot, 2022). The only exception represented Slovakia, which experienced a higher level of decommodification during the 1990s. As an outcome, ALMP in general and training and re-training activities, in particular, have had a low policy priority (Szelewa & Polakowski, 2022). Therefore, CE countries have been considered as 'newcomers' of the social investment approach toward welfare (Hemerijck & Ronchi, 2022).

It does not mean that CE countries have not developed their own version of a 'hybrid welfare state' (Vanhuysee, 2006), but it is a different type of WSR where adult learning has not had an important place. Instead, the social policy of CE countries has targeted different domains of social security. It has preferred a mostly free public education system for the youth, including tertiary education, that was even enhanced during the period of increasing access to HE after 2000. Then, it has been mostly free public healthcare, focusing on direct health aid for all patients with minimal fees. Finally, the wide pension system for older adults, which especially in the 1990s, when the retirement age was in many professions set in the mid-fifties, enabled transit of a large proportion of workers, threatened by structural unemployment, out of the labour market.

If some social investment strategies have been applied, they *have usually been stratified* (Avlijaš, 2022; Cook & Inglot, 2022; Szelewa & Polakowski, 2022), supporting mainly those who have been the key electorate of the ruling party and bore the brunt of the negative effects of the transformation (Vanhuysee, 2006). Alternatively, these policy measures have promoted a conservative view of women in society, showing the "ugly face" (Szelewa & Polakowski, 2020) of social investment by supporting conservative family policies that encourage women to take primary responsibility for childcare, lower their participation in the labour market and conserve inequality between genders. Not surprisingly, gender inequality has been high in the Visegrad region.

Due to this unique setting of welfare policy, public resources for investment in ALMP have always been limited and had a secondary preference.

Drawing from an institutionalist perspective, I would like to conclude that there exists a specific institutional complementarity, referred to as an 'institutional lock' (Streeck, 1992, 1994a, b), between the general welfare approach characterised by redistributive systems in CE countries and the limited presence of intensive social investment policy, including robust public NFE programs. This situation has been further intensified by the extensive utilisation of the labour force in key economic sectors of CE economies, such as the automotive industry and electrical engineering, which typically encounter substantial pressures related to skill obsolescence and the necessity for reskilling (CEDEFOP, 2022; OECD, 2019a, b), but not in the case of Visegrad countries. As an outcome of this structural setting of CE countries since the 1990s, ALSs there have become more and more liberalised with the prevalent provision of private forms of AET. As Part V. demonstrates, this trend represents another key direction in the GALS that has been typical for CE countries over the last two decades. However, it remains uncertain whether CE countries can maintain their current "ex-post" oriented welfare system or whether they will shift towards a new one that focuses on preventing risks and building capabilities for the future—i.e. "ex-ante risk prevention" (Hemerijck, 2017).

Chapter 21
Conclusion

The final chapter of this book offers a comprehensive synthesis of the preceding analyses, focusing on the evolution of ALSs within CE during the period from 1989 to 2019. Emphasis is placed on exploring the intricate interplay between ALSs formation and the resulting differences in AET participation, as well as related inequality and the perceived barriers to organised learning. Drawing insights from this analysis, the discussion culminates in the formulation of essential policy recommendations aimed at enhancing the efficacy of CE ALSs. These recommendations are designed to foster greater adaptability and responsiveness in catering to the diverse needs of adults who stand to benefit from involvement in AET activities. Concluding this section, potential directions for future research are outlined, extending the inquiry into ALSs dynamics within the Visegrad region and its broader implications.

21.1 Summary

Systematic mapping of the development of ALSs in CE subsequent to the fall of the Berlin Wall has yielded significant insights. First, in treating ALSs within the CE context as a distinct "laboratory case," intended to test current theories of ALSs, my analysis has demonstrated that the trajectories of their formation cannot be easily inferred solely from the characteristics of the institutional clusters within which they have been embedded, as many earlier theories have posited. This holds particularly true when the empirical foundations of these theories are predominantly derived from data from the 1990s. While features of the formal education system, capitalism, and welfare frameworks do interplay with certain elements of ALSs, as they are intricately interwoven, it is imperative to recognise that ALSs cannot be reduced to mere dependent variables of these encompassing institutional configurations. On the contrary, this book proposes an alternative ontological conceptualisation of ALSs—*one that views them as relational, non-systematic, evolving and ecological systems*. These systems not only undergo influence from other societal institutions and processes ("are structured by them") but also exert influence upon them ("structured them").

Furthermore, it is evident that CE ALSs have undergone evolution to some extent independently of these broader institutional clusters (see Part IV for details). This is due to the emergence of national and supranational policy frameworks in the domain of AET, which have come to form semi-autonomous spheres capable of steering the course of how organised learning is coordinated and provided across CE countries. This realisation has prompted the adoption and refinement of a different perspective in the study of ALSs—an approach centred on the *construction of these systems from below* (see Part II for details).

Second, employing the heuristic principles of the new political economy of ALSs and historical institutionalism, a novel theoretical framework has been devised for the investigation of these systems—the *Global Adult Learning Space* (GALS). This conceptualisation overcomes the conventional two-dimensional understanding of ALSs, which often revolves around dichotomous distinctions of low/high participation rates and low/high inequality concerning adult access to learning opportunities. GALS, however, affords a more encompassing perspective, capable of capturing other critical quantitative characteristics inherent to ALSs. This expanded framework facilitates the formulation of a novel analysis rooted in the inherent ontological characteristics of these systems (see Part III for details).

Application of the GALS framework to both CE and Western European countries has demonstrated its potential efficacy in understanding both shared traits and distinctions across ALSs that extend beyond their broader institutional contexts (see Part V for details). My analysis focused on CE ALSs revealed that *CE ALSs not significantly differ from other ALSs but also among each other*. As an outcome, Poland has evolved into a vastly different type of ALS than the rest of CE ALSs (Czechia, Hungary, Slovakia), even though also Hungary and Czechia and Slovakia have begun to evolve in a slightly different direction since the 2010s. In conclusion, the GALS model, with its inherent flexibility, holds promise as an initial foundation for the construction of a new typology of ALSs, employing data from a new wave of PIAAC 2022 and AES 2022.

Third, the process of ALSs formation in CE unfolded through three distinct phases from 1989 to 2019:

1. The transition period (1989–2003),
2. The accession period (2004–2012),
3. The period of economic recovery (2013–2019).

Each phase exhibited unique dynamics within ALSs, with three fundamental dimensions—coordination, supply, and demand—manifesting divergent structural configurations in terms of intensity, timing, and processes that drive institutional building. Consequently, the development of ALSs in CE materialised as a multifaceted and multipath process. During the *transition period*, a decentralised approach to AET predominated, accompanied by modest demand for organised learning. This

21.1 Summary

phase witnessed the emergence of a free market for organised learning provision. Subsequently, the *accession period* saw the integration of the EU's lifelong learning policy, marking attempts at AET coordination and the transformation of the free market to a partially regulated market for AET provisioning. However, the path dependence originating from the initial orientation of ALSs towards (NFE-Voc) in Czechia, Hungary, and Slovakia, or (FAE) in Poland, persisted and became more pronounced. Finally, after a period of limited AET demand following the fall of communism, an expansion occurred shortly after 2010. This growth in demand was a consequence of the vigorous *economic recovery* experienced in the Visegrad region subsequent to the economic crisis. During this time, the coordination side of AET experienced a decline across the region, except for Hungary, where a targeted AET policy focused on low-skilled workers was introduced. The combination of these processes led to the formation of distinctive national models of ALSs in the region (see Part IV for details), although countries have shared a lot of structural characteristics.

Fourth, the application of the GALS framework to elucidate the formation trajectories of ALSs in CE shows notable insights into key processes intertwined with their institutional establishment (see Part V for details). Within this context, Hungary, Czechia, and Slovakia have undergone the following significant changes in GALS:

1. An *increase in participation rates* in AET over a 12-month period before the survey, leading to a narrowing of the gap between CE ALSs and Western and Nordic ALSs from the 1990s.
2. However growing numbers of adults who were involved in organised learning have been accompanied by *enormous extensification* of their participation—lowering the time spent by AET.
3. Concurrently, there has been an ongoing transition *towards job-related and employer-supported NFE*, which has emerged as the prevailing mode of AET.
4. These preceding trends have coincided with a diminishing provision of FAE and NFE by the state, further accentuating the *liberalisation of AET* within the purview of these ALSs.
5. As participation rates have risen appreciably, the proportion of individuals perceiving a *demand for AET has declined* in their population.

In contrast to these trends, Poland's trajectory of formation has exhibited distinct characteristics. The growth in participation has been relatively modest and has not been paralleled by a considerable degree of extensification. Furthermore, while the role of FAE has been prominent in Poland since the 1990s, albeit showing a slight decline over time, the prominence of job-related employer-supported NFE and public NFE has been less pronounced compared to others CE ALSs. Consequently, adults in Poland perceive a higher demand for AET. As a result, the structural features of *Poland's ALS have become significantly different from the rest of the Visegrad countries*. Although Poland is part of the same geographical region, its ALS has probably more shared characteristics with Eastern European countries.

Fifth, the investigation of patterns of participation has highlighted the intricate dynamics of inequality within CE ALSs. On the one hand, these countries have shared profound age-based and gender-related inequality. Conversely, distinctions arise in terms of inequalities rooted in the highest level of education attained, economic status, and occupational position. Particularly in Hungary, Slovakia, and Czechia, the level of inequality based on occupational status has recently diminished due to the specific nature of in-firm training. Generally, a distinctive pattern of inequality in participation within AET across the CE region has not been identified. Instead, the countries exhibit variations in the involvement of diverse societal segments, along with evolving trends over time—specifically, in the ability of ALSs to mitigate these different forms of inequalities. Notably, Poland's ALS is emblematic of the highest degree of inequality. Moreover, CE countries collectively exhibit a shared trend of perceived barriers to AET, with dispositional constraints assuming key importance.

21.2 Policy Recommendations

Based on the previous findings regarding the formation of ALSs in CE, patterns of participation in AET and related inequality and constraints to participation, it remains imperative for CE ALSs to enhance their effectiveness in supporting prospective learners. This entails both diminishing existing inequalities in access, especially for those who are most in need, and overcoming dominant barriers. Grounded in this rationale and building upon the insights gleaned from the preceding parts, this chapter formulates a series of policy recommendations aimed at enhancing these systems:

1. *Strengthen Implementation of Lifelong Learning Policies:* While the EU has introduced key elements of lifelong learning policies in CE countries, there is a need to enhance the implementation of these policies at the national and regional levels. Governments should focus on translating policy objectives into direct measures and strive to achieve the targets set, especially for social groups at risk, as especially older adults and women still face substantial inequality across the region. Instead of building large-scale policy measures, that many times have undergone an institutional conversion, *tailored training programs for selected groups facing the highest level of inequality should be a main policy priority in the area.* This may require aligning national agendas with investing in the provision of public (highly decommodified) certified job-related courses, as well as non-job-related organised learning for specific groups such as women, older adults, and minority groups, and interlinked them with other tools of social policy for those groups.
2. *Improve Coordination and Stability of Lifelong Learning Policies*: In CE countries, national lifelong learning policies have often been characterised by short durations and frequent changes due to shifts in government and key ministries

responsible for AET. To ensure the effectiveness and enduring impact of lifelong learning policies, it is essential to *establish coordination and stability in policy development and implementation through the adoption of long-term strategies that transcend different government tenures*. The lack of a central or national coordination body for AET across CE ALSs is a primary factor contributing to policy inconsistencies and coordination inefficiencies. Establishing such a body could enhance the effectiveness of policies, as the supply and demand for AET are influenced by various institutional clusters and relationships between the labour market, welfare system, and initial education system. This requires a comprehensive understanding that often extends beyond the purview of a single ministry and can easily lead to erroneous conclusions regarding the causes of skill mismatches (Brown et al., 2001). Adopting a long-term perspective and establishing a centralised coordination body for AET would promote stability, coherence, and improved outcomes in lifelong learning policies. Such measures would facilitate effective collaboration among relevant stakeholders, which is another crucial factor of successful AET coordination, and contribute to a more comprehensive and integrated approach to addressing skill gaps and enhancing workforce development.

3. *Enhance Resources for AET*: CE countries should prioritise allocating sufficient resources towards the development of robust and large-scale initiatives in AET. This requires a *shift away from ALS with weak public provision of NFE and limited focus on FAE*. While investments in initial education, such as higher education, are important, it is equally critical to allocate resources for expanding and enhancing AET programs, encompassing both FAE and NFE. By investing in AET, CE countries can effectively address skill mismatches, promote on-the-job training, and support the upskilling and reskilling of their workforce. However, implementing this policy strategy poses challenges within the CE context, as we have previously highlighted due to the specific welfare orientation of Visegrad countries and firms' strategies. These countries encounter limitations in prioritising general social welfare over supporting ALMPs or enhancing on-the-job training in companies. To overcome these challenges, *smaller yet targeted policy initiatives focusing on these areas can serve as an essential transition towards a new socio-economic policy model—the social investment model* (Hemerijck, 2017, 2018; Hemerijck & Ronchi, 2022). This model should leverage AET more extensively to achieve both social inclusion and economic performance enhancement. It is crucial to act promptly because CE countries will soon experience rapid demographic ageing in their labour force (EC, 2019). This demographic shift will strain not only their pension system but also their mostly free healthcare system. Moreover, it will lead to a further decline in the available workforce, which has been the highest among Europe countries over the past decade. As the workforce becomes less easily available, as observed in the latter half of the 2010s, firms will likely need to adjust their strategies accordingly.

4. *Address Social Inequalities and Skill Mismatches*: Given the influence of the social structure of CE societies on AET participation and inequalities, policies should aim to address these disparities. Governments *should prioritise the*

provision of AET opportunities specifically for low-educated workers and adults in low-skilled occupations. Despite the relatively higher participation rates of these social groups in AET compared to other ALSs, significant inequality persists, particularly in light of the ongoing deindustrialisation of these societies. Additionally, it is important to note that older adults (aged 55–64 years) also experience high levels of observed inequality. This is important for overall inequality in access to AET, as it is expected that the proportion of this age cohort within the total population will grow. Efforts must be made to ensure that training programs are easily accessible, targeted, and relevant to the specific needs of these social groups. These programs should also be integrated with other measures and tools of ALMPs. This comprehensive approach is crucial because governments often tend to provide support to adults who already have access to AET, as highlighted by Desjardins (2013), particularly members of the (upper) middle class (Bonoli et al., 2017; Szikra, 2014). However, when targeted properly, government support can effectively reach those adults who are most in need. This requires earmarking funds and complementing them with outreach activities, even though it may involve higher costs. Without such targeted efforts, support rarely reaches the adults who require it the most. Additionally, addressing skill mismatches and overqualification issues should be a priority, with a focus on aligning educational offerings with the evolving demands of the labour market.

5. *Promote Employer Engagement and Workplace Learning*: Collaboration between employers and training providers is crucial for the establishment of durable and responsive ALSs. Governments should actively encourage and *incentivise employers to invest in job-related training for their workforce, employing strategies such as tax and training credits or levy systems.* While some support policy tools have been introduced in CE countries to enhance NFE provision in the workplace, these incentives have often been burdened by excessive bureaucracy and have yielded mixed results in terms of effectiveness and impact. In light of the forthcoming termination of EU funds allocated for this purpose by 2030, the development and implementation of a new generation of targeted economic incentives for employers to support on-the-job training emerge as a critical future challenge for CE ALSs. This initiative can be achieved through the establishment of partnerships, the provision of financial support, and the creation of favourable policy environments that acknowledge the value of workplace learning. By fostering increased employer engagement, CE countries can enhance the relevance and effectiveness of AET provision, addressing the evolving needs of the workforce.

6. *Addressing Geographic Disparities*: Recognize the strong perception of distance as a barrier in Hungary and consider implementing measures to improve access to education in rural regions, especially in Poland. This could involve establishing satellite campuses, mobile learning centres, or online education platforms to bridge the gap between urban and rural areas.

7. *Targeting Dispositional Barriers to Participation in AET*: Given the high occurrence of dispositional barriers in CE ALSs, it is crucial to develop targeted

campaigns that emphasise the value and usefulness of organised learning for the population. Additionally, improving the system of consulting to assist potential learners in navigating and orienting themselves in AET provision should be a high priority. Although some initial efforts have been made in the late 2010s, their impact on AET has been relatively modest.
8. *Continuous Monitoring and Evaluation:* To ensure effective policies and interventions in AET, it is crucial to regularly monitor and evaluate participation patterns, trends, and barriers. This monitoring helps identify emerging issues and assess the effectiveness of existing measures. However, it is important to note that the current methods of measuring barriers to AET are often lagging behind and may not encompass all the relevant constraints faced by adults (Desjardins & Rubenson, 2013). Expanding the scope of monitoring and evaluation is also necessary. This can involve conducting regional-level assessments or focusing directly on specific target groups of adults. It is a misconception to assume that adults from the same sociodemographic group face identical constraints or hold similar attitudes towards AET (Kalenda et al., 2022, 2023). By systematically utilising more nuanced findings, policymakers can make evidence-based decisions and adapt strategies accordingly. In summary, consistent monitoring and evaluation of AET participation, trends, and barriers are essential. This should include addressing the limitations of current measurement methods and extending the analysis to regional and target group levels. By using comprehensive and nuanced data, policymakers can make informed decisions and adjust strategies to promote adult education and training effectively.

By implementing these policy recommendations, CE countries can work towards reducing participation inequalities and barriers to AET, as well as fostering a culture of lifelong learning that promotes personal and socio-economic development.

21.3 Future Directions

Although GALS and other conceptual tools provide a new understanding of CE ALSs and their development since 1989, it is essential to acknowledge that these maps are still crude. Predominantly reliant on internationally available data spanning from 1997 to 2016, these are characterised by several blind spots. Certain facets of ALSs are absent from the dataset or exhibit unreliability. Therefore, we should not consider my previous exploration as a perfect mirror of these ALSs but as their crude estimation—as a preliminary stride towards attaining more precise maps of ALSs formation in the CE area—rather than a final picture. Guided by this presumption, there is a need to extend this research. The next steps should follow these directions.

The first of them involves an extension of the temporal scope to encompass the period following the emergence of the COVID-19 pandemic. The upcoming data from international surveys AES 2022 and PIAAC 2022, both expected to be available in 2024, should enable prolonged time analysis and construct a longer timeline. This extended timeframe should serve as the foundation for evaluating the quantitative evolution of these systems subsequent to 2016. By doing so, it becomes possible to elucidate the current trajectories of CE ALSs—specifically, how they have responded to prevailing challenges such as pandemic recovery, energy crises, inflation surges, and persistent labour shortages.

Another direction for research involves broadening the geographical scope of analysis to encompass the remaining post-socialist countries. As elucidated by previous scholars (Avlijaš, 2022; Cook & Inglot, 2022; Szelewa & Polakowski, 2022), countries within CE, the Baltic region, the Balkans, and those formerly under the direct influence of the Soviet Union have followed distinct institutional trajectories leading to the emergence of ALSs models (Saar et al., 2023). A systematic exploration of this aspect has the potential to establish a new comprehensive typology of post-socialist ALSs, while also identifying pivotal trends within them. This entails investigating whether these ALSs have undergone an expansion of participation in AET, shifts towards increased financial support for NFE from employers, and a decline in the state's role in providing AET.

Different, but not less important point of view, is an extension of our understanding of who are participants of organised learning for adults. This book specifically concentrates on individuals aged 25–64 years. Nonetheless, it is imperative to recognise that both young adults (aged 16–24) and older adults (individuals over 65) should be understood as pivotal target groups within the framework of lifelong learning policy. On the one hand, the flexible and responsive frameworks of Adult AGE and NFE-Voc assume a critical role in facilitating transitions between initial formal education and entry into the labour market. On the other hand, given that all advanced societies will face rapid population ageing, projected to peak between 2050 and 2060, there is a pressing need to devise strategies for maintaining the labour force engagement of older adults. In this adaptive response, AET will assume a paramount role (EC, 2019).

Moreover, it is both feasible and advantageous to broaden the thematic breadth of the analysis by introducing a novel and more intricate horizontal dimension within the GALS framework, along with the incorporation of new variables that facilitate the understanding of variations among ALSs and their internal variations. To accomplish this objective, the creation of new instruments capable of more effectively capturing both the supply and demand aspects of ALSs will be imperative. It is my contention that a significant proportion of forthcoming insights pertaining to ALSs will emanate from this avenue of research.

An auspicious research direction, with the potential to bridge an existing gap in our analysis of ALSs, draws significant inspiration from the principles of historical institutionalism. In essence, this approach entails a methodical examination of individual country cases and their development across time, spotlighting the intricate interconnections among social institutions within the framework of national ALSs and the broader national policies on lifelong learning. This exploration also encompasses an analysis of the roles played by pivotal stakeholders within these systems and specific national institutional complementarities between AET and various

21.3 Future Directions

institutional clusters, like mode of capitalism, welfare state and formal educational system. Rather than rely on theories from other social science disciplines (comparative education, politics, economy and sociology), we should directly explore the current notion of relations between them and AET.

Finally, the role of supranational governance in AET, particularly the process of Europeanisation within the context of the EU, plays a crucial role. This influence extends to various dimensions of ALSs, encompassing dimensions such as coordination, as well as the supply and demand aspects of these systems. While the dimension of coordination and the tracking of policies have garnered increasing attention in the past decade, the impact of supranational governance on the provision and demand for organised learning opportunities within these systems remains a relatively unexplored area.

References

Abbott, A. (1997). Of time and space. *Social Forces, 75*(4), 1149–1182.
Abbott, A. (2016). *Processual sociology*. University of Chicago Press.
Act on Promotion, PL. (2004). *Act on promotion of employment and institutions of the labour market*. Republic of Poland.
AES. (2007). *Adult Education Survey 2007: Survey data*. Eurostat.
AES. (2011). *Adult Education Survey 2011: Survey data*. Eurostat.
AES. (2016). Adult Education Survey 2016: Survey data. Eurostat.
AET PL. (2020). *State of adult education in Poland*. https://countryreport.eaea.org/poland/poland-2020/A%20New%20Skills%20Strategy
AIVD. (2023). *Asociace institucí vzdělávání dospělých*. https://www.aivd.cz/
Albert, F. (2019). *ESPN thematic report on in- work poverty. Hungary*. European Commission.
Albert, C., García-Serrano, C., & Hernanz, V. (2010). On-the-job training in Europe: Determinants and wage returns. *International Labour Review, 149*(3), 315–341. https://doi.org/10.1111/j.1564-913X.2010.00089.x
Allmendinger, J. (1989). Educational systems and labor market outcomes. *European Sociological Review, 5*(3), 231–250. https://doi.org/10.1093/oxfordjournals.esr.a036524
Alvesson, M., & Käremman, D. (2011). *Qualitative research and theory development. Mystery as method*. Sage.
Ante, C. (2016). *The Europeanisation of vocational education and training*. Springer.
Archer, M. S. (1995). *Realist social theory: The morphogenetic approach*. Cambridge University Press.
Archer, M. S. (2013). *Social origins of educational systems*. Routledge.
Avlijaš, S. (2022). Explaining the contrasting welfare trajectories of the Baltic and Visegrád countries. In J. L. Garritzmann, S. Häusermann, & B. Palier (Eds.), *The world politics of social investment (volume II)* (pp. 209–227). Oxford University Press. https://doi.org/10.1093/oso/9780197601457.003.0009
Ball, S. J. (1995). Intellectuals or technicians? The urgent role of theory in educational studies. *British Journal of Educational Studies, 43*(3), 255–271.
Ball, S. J. (2009). The governance turn! *Journal of Education Policy, 24*(5), 537–538.
Bassanini, A., Booth, A., Brunello, G., De Paola, M., & Leuven, E. (2005). *Workplace training in Europe—IZA discussion paper 1640*. Institute for the Study of Labour.
Becker, G. S. (1993). *Human capital: A theoretical and empirical analysis with special reference to education*. University of Chicago Press.
Bell, D. (1973). *The coming of post-industrial society: A venture in social forecasting*. Basic Books.

Berend, I. (2009). *From the soviet bloc to the European Union. The economic and social transformation of central and Eastern Europe since 1973*. Cambridge University Press.

Bhaskar, R. (2008). *A realist theory of science*. Verso.

Blais, J.-G., Duqueite, A., & Painchaud, G. (1989). Deterrents to women's participation in work-related educational activities. *Adult Education Quarterly, 39*(4), 224–234. https://doi.org/10.1177/0001848189039004004

Blossfeld, H.-P. (1992). Is the German dual system a model for a modern vocational training systems? *International Journal of Comparative Sociology, 33*(3–4), 168–181.

Blossfeld, H.-P., & Stockmann, R. (1998). The German dual system in comparative perspective. *International Journal of Sociology, 28*(4), 3–28.

Blossfeld, H. P., & Stockmann, R. (1999). *Globalization and chances in vocational training systems in developing and advanced industrial societies*. Sharpe.

Blossfeld, H.-P., Kilpi-Jakonen, E., Vono de Vilhena, D., & Buchholz, S. (2014). *Adult learning in modern societies: An international comparison from a life-course perspective (EduLIFE lifelong learning)*. Edward Elgar Publishing.

Blossfeld, H.-P., Kilpi-Jakonen, E., Vono de Vilhena, D., & Buchholz, S. (2020). Is there a Matthew effect in adult learning? Results from a cross-national comparison. In J. Schrader, A. Ioannidou, & H.-P. Blossfeld (Eds.), *Monetäre und nicht monetäre Erträge von Weiterbildung–monetary and nonmonetary effects of adult education and training* (Edition ZfE) (Vol. 7, pp. 1–26). VS.

Blumer, H. (1969). *Symbolic interactionism: Perspective and method*. University of California Press.

Boeren, E. (2009). Adult education participation: The Matthew principle. *Filosofija—Sociologija, 20*(2), 154–161.

Boeren, E. (2011). Gender differences in formal, non-formal and informal adult learning. *Studies in Continuing Education, 33*(3), 333–346.

Boeren, E. (2016). *Lifelong learning participation in a changing policy context. An interdisciplinary theory*. Palgrave Macmillan.

Boeren, E. (2017). Understanding adult lifelong learning participation as a layered problem. *Studies in Continuing Education, 39*(2), 161–175.

Boeren, E. (2019). Being an adult learner in Europe and the UK: Persisting inequalities and the role of the welfare state. In E. Boeren & N. James (Eds.), *Being an adult learner in austere times. Exploring the contexts of higher. Further and community education* (pp. 21–45). Palgrave Macmillan.

Boeren, E. (2023). Conceptualizing lifelong learning participation—Theoretical perspectives and integrated approaches. In M. Schemmann (Ed.), *International yearbook of Adul education. Researching participation in adult education* (pp. 17–31). wbv Media Publikation.

Boeren, E., & Holford, J. (2016). Vocationalism varies (a lot): A 12-country multivariable analysis of participation in formal adult learning. *Adult Education Quarterly, 66*(2), 120–142. Available at: https://doi.org/10.1177/0741713615624207

Boeren, E., Holford, J., Nicaise, I., & Baert, H. (2012a). Why do adults learn? Developing motivational typology across twelve European countries. *Globalisation, Societies and Education, 10*(1), 247–269. https://doi.org/10.1080/14767724.2012.678764

Boeren, E., Nicaise, I., Roosmaa, E. L., & Saar, E. (2012b). Formal adult education in the spotlight: Profiles, motivation, and experiences of participants in 12 countries. In S. Riddel, J. Markowitsch, & E. Weeden (Eds.), *Lifelong learning in Europe: Equality and efficiency in balance* (pp. 63–86). Polity Press.

Boeren, E., Whittaker, S., & Riddell, S. (2017). *Provision of seven types of education for disadvantaged adults in ten countries: Overview and cross-country comparison* (ENLIVEN report, deliverable no. 2.1). https://h2020enliven.files.wordpress.com/2017/09/enliven-d2-1.pdf.

Bohle, D., & Greskovits, B. (2007). Neoliberalism, embedded neoliberalism and neocorporatism: Towards transnational capitalism in Central-Eastern Europe. *West European Politics, 30*(3), 443–466.

Bohle, D., & Greskovits, B. (2012). *Capitalist diversity on Europe's periphery*. Cornell University Press.

Boix, C. (2019). *Democratic capitalism at the crossroads: Technological change and the future of politics*. Princeton University Press.

Bondom, D., & Nemec, R. (2015). *Evaluation of selected structural funds and cohesion fund interventions using contrafactual impact evaluation methods*. Final report. KMPG.

Bonoli, G. (2007). Time matters: Postindustrialization, new social risks, and welfare state adaptation in advanced industrial democracies. *Comparative Political Studies, 40*(5), 495–520. https://doi.org/10.1177/0010414005285755

Bonoli, G., Cantillon, B., & Van Lancker, W. (2017). Social investment and the Matthew effect. In A. Hemerijck (Ed.), *The uses of social investment* (pp. 66–76). Oxford University Press.

Boshier, R. W. (1971). Motivational orientations of adult education participants: A factor analytic exploration of Houle's typology. *Adult Education, 21*(2), 3–26.

Boudard, E., & Rubenson, K. (2003). Revisiting major determinants of participation in adult education with a direct measure of literacy skills. *International Journal of Education Research, 39*(3), 265–281.

Bourdieu, P. (1984). *Distinction: A social critique of the judgement of taste*. Routledge.

Bourdieu, P. (1985). The social space and the genesis of groups. *Theory and Society, 14*(6), 723–744.

Bourdieu, P. (1990). *Logic of practice*. Polity Press.

Bourdieu, P. (2018). Social space and the genesis of appropriated physical space. *International Journal of Urban and Regional Research, 42*(1), 106–114. https://doi.org/10.1111/1468-2427.12534

Bourdieu, P., & Wacquant, L. J. D. (1992). *An invitation to reflexive sociology*. University of Chicago Press.

Boyadjieva, P., & Ilieva-Trichkova, P. (2021). *Adult education as empowerment: Re-imagining lifelong learning through the capability approach, recognition theory and common goods perspective*. Palgrave Macmillan.

Brown, P., Green, A., & Lauder, H. (2001). *High skills. Globalization, competitiveness, and skill formation*. Oxford University Press.

Brunello, G. (2001). *On the complementarity between education and training in Europe* (IZA Discussion Paper No 309). Institute for the Study of Labor.

Brunello, G., Garibaldi, P., & Wasmer, E. (2007). *Education and training in Europe*. Oxford University Press.

Bukodi, E., & Robert, P. (2007). *Occupational mobility in Europe (European Foundation for the improvement of living and working conditions report)*. Eurofound.

Bukodi, E., Eibl, F., Buchholz, S., Marzadro, S., Minello, A., Wahler, S., Blossfeld, H. P., Erikson, R., & Schizzerotto, A. (2018). Linking the macro to the micro: A multidimensional approach to educational inequalities in four European countries. *European Societies, 20*(1), 26–64.

Burns, T., & Köster, F. (Eds.). (2016). *Governing education in a complex world. Educational research and innovation*. OECD.

Busemeyer, M. R. (2015). *Skills and inequality. Partisan politics and the political economy of education reforms in western welfare states*. Cambridge University Press.

Busemeyer, M., & Trampusch, C. (Eds.). (2012). *The political economy of collective skill formation*. Oxford University Press.

Cabus, S., Ilieva-Trichkova, P., & Štefánik, M. (2020). Multi-layered perspective on the barriers to learning participation of disadvantaged adults. *Zeitschrift für Weiterbildungsforschungm, 43*(2), 169–196. https://doi.org/10.1007/s40955-020-00162-3

Campbell, M. (2012). *Skills for prosperity? A review of OECD and partner country skill strategies*. Centre for Learning and Life Chances in Knowledge Economies and Societies.

Capoccia, G. (2015). Critical junctures and institutional change. In J. Mahoney & K. Thelen (Eds.), *Advances in comparative-historical analysis* (pp. 147–179). Cambridge University Press.

Capoccia, G., & Kelemen, R. D. (2007). The study of critical junctures: Theory, narrative, and counterfactuals in institutional analysis. *World Politics, 59*(3), 341–369.

CEDEFOP. (2012). *Working and ageing: The benefits of investing in an ageing workforce*. Publications Office of the European Union. www.cedefop.europa.eu/files/3064_en.pdf

CEDEFOP. (2015). *Skills, qualifications and jobs in the EU: The making of a perfect match? Evidence from Cedefop's European skills and jobs survey*. Publications Office.
CEDEFOP. (2016). *Improving career prospects for the low-educated: The role of guidance and lifelong learning*. Publications Office. https://doi.org/10.2801/794545
CEDEFOP. (2018). *Insights into skill shortages and skill mismatch. Learning from Cedefop's European skills and job survey*. Publications Office.
CEDEFOP. (2022). *The future of vocational education and training in Europe* (Volume 2. Delivering IVET: Institutional diversification and/or expansion?). Publications Office.
Cerami, A., & Vanhuysse, P. (Eds.). (2009). *Post-communist welfare pathways. Theorising social policy transformations in central and Eastern Europe*. Palgrave Macmillan.
Chavance, B. (2008). *Institutional economics*. Routledge.
Chovanculiak, R. (2021). *Vzdelávanie dospelých stále nedospelo*. https://hnonline.sk/komentare/komentare/2334678-vzdelavanie-dospelych-stale-nedospelo.
Cincinnato, S., De Wever, B., Van Keer, H., & Valcke, M. (2016). The influence of social background on participation in adult education: Applying the cultural capital framework. *Adult Education Quarterly, 66*(2), 143–168.
Collier, B. R., & Collier, D. (1991). *Shaping the political arena: Critical junctures, the labor movement, and regime dynamics in Latin America*. Princeton University Press.
Cook, L. (2007). *Post-communist welfare states: Reforms politics in Russia and Eastern Europe*. Cornell University Press.
Cook, L., & Inglot, T. (2022). Central and eastern Europea countries. In D. Béland, K. J. Morgan, H. Obinger, & C. Pierson (Eds.), *The Oxford handbook of the welfare state* (pp. 881–898). Oxford University Press.
Cross, P. K. (1981). *Adults as learners: Increasing participation and facilitating learning*. Jossey-Bass.
Crouch, C., & Streeck, W. (Eds.). (1997). *Political economy of modern capitalism: Mapping convergence and diversity*. Sage.
Csanádi, G., Csizmady, A., & Róbert, P. (2014). Adult learning in Hungary: Participation and labor market outcomes. In H. P. Blossfeld, E. Kilpi-Jakonen, D. V. Vilhena, & S. Buchholz (Eds.), *Adult learning in modern societies: An international comparison from a life-course perspective* (pp. 264–282). Edward Edgar.
ČSÚ. (2013). *Česká republika od roku 1989 v číslech. Vzdělávání a kultura*. Český statistický úřad.
Culpepper, P. D., & Thelen, K. (2008). Institutions and collective actors in the provision of training. Historical and cross-National comparisons. In K. U. Mayer & H. Solga (Eds.), *Skill formation. Interdisciplinary and cross-National perspective* (pp. 21–49). Cambridge University Press.
Dacko-Pikiewicz, Z. (2013). Lifelong learning in Poland and the European experience. In Z. Dacko-Pikiewicz, K. Szczepańska-Woszczyna, & M. Walancik (Eds.), *Study about contemporary higher education* (pp. 89–94). Shaker Verlag Aachen.
Dahlen, M., & Ure, B. O. (2009). Low-skilled adults in formal continuing education: Does their motivation differ from other learners? *International Journal of Lifelong Education, 28*(5), 661–674.
Dämmrich, J., Vono, D., & Reichart, E. (2014). Participation in adult learning in Europe: The impact of country-level and individual characteristics. In H.-P. Blossfeld, E. Kilpi-Jakonen, D. Vono de Vilhena, & S. Buchholz (Eds.), *Adult learning in modern societies: Patterns and consequences of participation from a life-course perspective* (pp. 25–51). Edward Elgar.
Dämmrich, J., Kosyakova, Y., & Blossfeld, H. P. (2015). Gender and job-related non-formal training: A comparison of 20 countries. *International Journal of Comparative Sociology, 56*(6), 433–459.
Darkenwald, G. G., & Valentine, T. (1985). Factor of deterrents to public participation in adult education. *Adult Education Quarterly, 35*(4), 177–193. https://doi.org/10.1177/0001848185035004001

References

Decius, J., Knappstein, M., Schaper, N., & Seifert, A. (2023). Investigating the multidimensionality of informal learning: Validation of a short measure for white-collar workers. *Human Resources Quarterly.* https://doi.org/10.1002/hrdq.21461

Desjardins, R. (2011). Participation in adult learning. In K. Rubenson (Ed.), *Adult learning and education* (pp. 205–215). Elsevier.

Desjardins, R. (2013). The economics of adult education: A critical assessment of the state of adult education. In T. Nesbit & M. Welton (Eds.), *Adult learning in a precarious age, new directions for adult and continuing education* (pp. 81–90). Jossey-Bass.

Desjardins, R. (2014). *Rewards to skill supply, skill demand and skill match–Mismatch using direct measures of skills. Studies using the adult literacy and lifeskills survey* (Lund economic studies no 176). Lund University.

Desjardins, R. (2017). *Political economy of adult learning systems. Comparative study of strategies, policies, and constraints.* Bloomsbury.

Desjardins, R. (2018). Economics and the political economy of adult education. In M. Milana, S. Webb, J. Holford, R. Waller, & P. Jarvis (Eds.), *The Palgrave international handbook on adult and lifelong education and learning* (pp. 211–226). Palgrave Macmillan.

Desjardins, R. (2019). The relationship between attaining formal qualifications at older ages and outcomes related to active ageing. *European Journal of Education, 54*(1), 30–47. https://doi.org/10.1111/ejed.12315

Desjardins, P. (2020). *PIAAC thematic report on adult learning.* (OECD education working paper no. 223). OECD.

Desjardins, R. (2023a). Lifelong learning systems. In K. Evans, J. Markowitsch, W. O. Lee, & M. Zukas (Eds.), *Third international handbook of lifelong learning. Springer international handbooks of education* (pp. 353–374). Springer. https://doi.org/10.1007/978-3-030-67930-9_18-1

Desjardins, R. (2023b). Alternative approaches to the political economy of education and some of their implications. In L. I. Misiaszek, R. F. Arnove, & C. A. Torres (Eds.), *Comparative education: Emergent trends in the dialectic of the global and the local* (pp. 41–57). Rowman & Littlefield.

Desjardins, R., & Huang, H. (2023). Lifelong learning and skill formation over the life course. In E. Saar & P. Robert (Eds.), *Handbook on education and labour market.* Edward Elgar. in press.

Desjardins, R., & Ioannidou, A. (2020). The political economy of adult learning systems—Some institutional features that promote adult learning participation. *Zeitschrift für Weiterbildungsforschungm, 43*(1), 143–168. https://doi.org/10.1007/s40955-020-00159-y

Desjardins, R., & Kim, J. (2023). Inequality in adult education participation across national contexts: Is growing employer support exacerbating or mitigating inequality in participation? In M. Schemmann (Ed.), *Internationales Jahrbuch der Erwachsenenbildung / international yearbook of adult education 2023* (pp. 75–98). wbv Publikation. https://doi.org/10.3278/I73910W005

Desjardins, R., & Rubenson, K. (2013). Participation patterns in adult education: The role of institutions and public policy frameworks in resolving coordination problems. *European Journal of Education, 48*(1), 262–280.

Desjardins, R., Rubenson, K., & Milana, M. (2006). *Unequal chances to participate in adult learning: International perspectives.* UNESCO.

Desjardins, R., Melo, V., & Lee, J. (2016). Cross-national patterns of participation in adult education and policy trends in Korea, Norway, and Vietnam. *Prospects, 46*(1), 149–170.

Desjardins, R., Olsen, D. S., & Midtsundstad, T. (2019). Active ageing and older learners—Skills, employability and continued learning. *European Journal of Education, 54*(1), 1–4. https://doi.org/10.1111/ejed.12327

Dieckhoff, M., Jungblut, J. M., & O'Connell, P. J. (2007). Job-related training in Europe: Do institutions matter? In D. Gallie (Ed.), *Employment regimes and the quality of work* (pp. 77–103). Oxford University Press.

DiMaggio, P. J., & Powell, W. W. (1983). The iron cage revisited: Institutional isomorphism and collective rationality in organizational fields. *American Sociological Review, 48*(2), 147–160.

DiPrete, T. A., & Eirich, G. M. (2006). Cumulative advantage as a mechanism for inequality: A review of theoretical and empirical developments. *Annual Review of Sociology, 32*(1), 271–297.

Domonkos, S. (2016). *Economic transition, partisan politics and EU austerity: A case study of Slovakia's labour market policies.* European Trade Union Institute.

Drahokoupil, J., & Myant, M. (2011). *Transition economies: Political economy in Russia, Eastern Europe, and Central Asia.* Wiley.

EAEA HU. (2011). *Country report on adult education in Hungary.* Association for Education of Adults. https://eaea.org/wp-content/uploads/2018/01/hungary_country-report-on-adult-education-in-hungary.pdf

EAEA POL. (2011). *Country report.* Association for Education of Adults. www.eaea.org/country/poland

Ebenau, M. (2012). Varieties of capitalism or dependency? A critique of the VoC approach for Latin America. *Competition and Change, 16*(3), 206–223.

EC. (2001). *Making a European area of lifelong learning a reality*, COM(2001) 678 final. http://www.europarl.europa.eu/meetdocs/committees/cult/20020122/com(2001)678_en.pdf

EC. (2009). Strategic framework for European cooperation in education and training (ET 2020). *Official Journal of the European Union*, 2009/C119/02, 12 May 2009. http://eur-lex.europa.eu/legal-content/EN/TXT/?uri=celex:52009XG0528(01)

EC. (2012). *Rethinking education: Investing in skills for better socio-economic outcomes.* European Commission. https://www.cedefop.europa.eu/files/com669_en.pdf

EC. (2019). *Ageing Europe: Looking at the lives of older people in the EU.* European Commission.

EC. (2021). *Towards a sustainable Europe by 2030.* European Commission. https://ec.europa.eu/info/publications/towards-sustainable-europe-2030_en

EC CLA. (2016). *European Commission. Classification of Learning Activities. Manual. 2016 Edition.* Publications Office of the European Union.

Elfert, M., & Rubenson, K. (2023). Lifelong learning: Researching a contested concept in the twenty-first century. In K. Evans, W. O. Lee, J. Markowitsch, & M. Zukas (Eds.), *Third international handbook of lifelong learning* (pp. 1219–1234). Springer.

Elman, C. (2005). Explanatory typologies in qualitative studies of international politics. *International Organization, 59*(2), 293–326.

EPP. (2020). *Hodnotenie Verejnej Politiky Vzdelávania Dospelých na Slovensku.* Nova Academia.

Esping-Andersen, G. (1990). *Three worlds of welfare capitalism.* Princeton University Press.

Esping-Andersen, G. (1998). *The three worlds of welfare capitalism.* Princeton University Press.

Estevez-Abe, M., Iversen, T., & Soskice, D. (2001). Social protection and the formation of skills: A reinterpretation of the welfare state. In P. A. Hall & D. Soskice (Eds.), *Varieties of capitalism: The institutional foundations of comparative advantage* (pp. 145–183). Oxford University Press.

Eurostat. (2023). *Students enrolled in tertiary education by education level, programme orientation, sex, type of institution and intensity of participation.* https://ec.europa.eu/eurostat/databrowser/view/EDUC_UOE_ENRT01/default/table?lang=en&category=educ.educ_part.educ_uoe_enr.educ_uoe_enrt

Eurydice. (1999). *Structures of education, initial training and adult education.* Eurydice.

Eurydice CZ. (2022). *Czech Republic. Adult education and training.* https://eurydice.eacea.ec.europa.eu/national-education-systems/czech-republic/adult-education-and-training

Eurydice HU. (2022). *Hungary. Adult education and training.* https://eurydice.eacea.ec.europa.eu/national

Eurydice PL. (2022). *Poland. Adult education and training.* https://eurydice.eacea.ec.europa.eu/national-education-systems/poland/adult-education-and-training

Eurydice SK. (2022). *Slovakia. Adult education and training.* https://eurydice.eacea.ec.europa.eu/national-education-systems/slovakia/adult-education-and-training

References

Eyal, G., Szelényi, I., & Townsley, E. (1998). *Making capitalism without capitalists. The new ruling elites in Eastern Europe.* Verso.

Falleti, T. G. (2010). *Decentralization and subnational politics in Latin America.* Cambridge University Press.

Falleti, T. G., & Mahoney, J. (2015). The comparative sequential method. In J. Mahoney & K. Thelen (Eds.), *Advances in comparative-historical analysis* (pp. 211–239). Cambridge University Press.

Farkas, B. (2011). The central and eastern European model of capitalism. *Post-Communist Economies, 23*(1), 15–34.

Farkas, E. (2015). Financing the adult education system in Hungary. In B. Neméth (Ed.), *Research and development in adult learning and education in Hungary* (pp. 42–51). DVV International.

Farkas, B. (2016). *Models of capitalism in the European Union.* Palgrave Macmillan.

Field, J. (2012). Is lifelong learning making a difference? Research-based evidence on the impact of adult learning. In D. Aspin, J. Chapman, K. Evans, & R. Bagnall (Eds.), *Second international handbook of lifelong learning* (pp. 887–897). Springer.

Field, J., Künzel, K., & Schemmann, M. (2016). International comparative adult education research. Reflections on theory, methodology, and future developments. In M. Schemmann (Ed.), *Internationales Jahrbuch der Erwachsenenbildung/international yearbook of adult education 2016* (pp. 109–133). wbv Publikation.

Field, J., Künzel, K., & Schemmann, M. (2019). Revisiting the debate on international comparative adult education research: Theoretical and methodological reflection. In A. Fejes & E. Nylander (Eds.), *Mapping out the research Field of adult education and learning* (pp. 181–202). Springer.

Findesen, B. (2018). Learning in later adulthood: A critical perspective. In M. Milana (Ed.), *The Palgrave international handbook on adult and lifelong education and learning* (pp. 839–856). Palgrave Macmillan.

Findsen, B., & Formosa, M. (2011). *Lifelong learning in later life. A handbook on older adult learning.* Sense Publishers.

Flick-Takács, N. (2021). Is the secret to effective lifelong learning lurking in the views of prospective kindergarten teachers? Comparing German and Hungarian prospective kindergarten teachers' views on learning. *Journal of Pedagogy, 12*(2), 31–59. https://doi.org/10.2478/jpeg-2021-0009

Fodor, I. (2015). Facts and trends in adult education and training in Hungary. In B. Neméth (Ed.), *Research and development in adult learning and education in Hungary* (pp. 74–83). DVV International.

Garritzmann, J. L. (2016). *The political economy of higher education finance: The politics of tuition fees and subsidies in OECD countries, 1945–2015.* Palgrave Macmillan.

Garritzmann, J. L., Häusermann, S., Kurer, T., Palier, B., & Pinggera, M. (2022). Ïn the emergence of knowledge economies. In J. L. Garritzmann, S. Häusermann, & B. Palier (Eds.), *The world politics of social investment (Volume I)* (pp. 251–281). Oxford University Press. https://doi.org/10.1093/oso/9780197585245.003.0008

Geiss, M. (2020). In steady search for optimization: The role of public and private actors in Switzerland's political economy of adult education. *Zeitschrift für Weiterbildungsforschungm, 43*(2), 227–239. https://doi.org/10.1007/s40955-020-00157-0

Gerbery, D., & Džambazovič, R. (2018). Labour market inequalities and their reproduction from a class perspective: Class-based analysis of social stratification and social mobility. In M. Štefánik et al. (Eds.), *Labour market in Slovakia* (pp. 106–135). Centre of Social and Psychological Sciences, Slovak Academy of Sciences.

Green, A. (1991). The reform of post-16 education and training and the lessons from Europe. *Journal of Education Policy, 6*(3), 327–339.

Green, A. (2006). Models of lifelong learning and the knowledge society. *Compare, 36*(3), 307–325.

Green, A. (2011). Lifelong learning, equality and social cohesion. *European Journal of Education, 46*(2), 228–243.

Grek, S. (2008). From symbols to numbers: The shifting technologies of education governance in Europe. *European Education Research Journal, 7*(2), 208–218.

Groenez, S., Desmedt, E., & Nicaise, I. (2008). Participation in lifelong learning in the EU-15: The role of macro-level determinants. *International Journal of Contemporary Sociology, 45*(1), 51–83.

Habodászová, L., & Studená, I. (2020). *Marečku, podejte mi pero! Formálne vzdelávanie dospělých na Slovensku. Komentár 2021/16*. Ministerstvo financí SR.

Habodászová, L., & Studená, I. (2021). *Marečku, podejte mi pero. Formálne vzdelavanie dospelých na Slovensku.* Komentář 2021/21. Ministerstvo financí SR.

Hacker, J. S., Pierson, P., & Thelen, K. (2015). Drift and conversion: Hidden faces of institutional change. In J. Mahoney & K. Thelen (Eds.), *Advances in comparative-historical analysis* (pp. 180–208). Cambridge University Press.

Hahn, C. (2019). *Repatriating Polanyi. Market Society in the Visegrád States.* Central European University Press.

Hake, B. J. (2022). Negotiating border-crossings when 'adult education' meets 'vocational learning'. Comparative historical notes on defining the 'research object'. *Zeitschrift für Weiterbildungsforschungm, 45*, 491–511. https://doi.org/10.1007/s40955-022-00227-5

Hall, P. A. (2006). Systematic proces analysis: When a how to use it. *Management Review, 3*(1), 24–31.

Hall, P. A. (2007). The evolution of varieties of capitalism in Europe. In B. Hancké, M. Rhodes, & M. Thatcher (Eds.), *Beyond varieties of capitalism* (pp. 39–88). Oxford University Press.

Hall, P. A. (2018). Varieties of capitalism in light of the euro crisis. *Journal of European Public Policy, 25*(1), 7–30. https://doi.org/10.1080/13501763.2017.1310278

Hall, P. A. (2022). How growth strategies evolve in the developed democracies. In A. Hassel & B. Palier (Eds.), *Growth and welfare in the global economy: How growth regimes evolve.* Oxford University Press. https://scholar.harvard.edu/sites/scholar.harvard.edu/files/hall/files/hall2020_growthstrategies.pdf

Hall, P. A., & Gingerich, D. W. (2009). Varieties of capitalism and institutional complementarities in the political economy: An empirical analysis. *British Journal of Political Science, 39*(3), 449–482.

Hall, P. A., & Soskice, D. (Eds.). (2001). *Varieties of capitalism: The institutional foundations of comparative advantage.* Oxford University Press.

Hall, P. A., & Thelen, K. (2009). Institutional change in varieties of capitalism. *Socio-Economic Review, 7*(1), 7–34.

Haluš, M., Hlaváč M., Harvan, P., & Hidas, S. (2017). Odliv mozgov po slovensky. In *Analýza odchodov Slovákov do zahraničia od roku 2000.* Komentár 2017/1. Inštitút finančnej politiky.

Hämäläinen, R., De Wever, B., Malin, A., Cincinnato, S., Prieto, L. P., Persico, D., Villagrá-Sobrino, S. L., & Conlan, O. (2015). Education and working life: VET adults' problem-solving skills in technology-rich environments. *Comunicar, 88*(42), 38–47.

Hamplová, D., & Simonová, N. (2014). Adult learning in The Czech Republic: A youthand female-oriented system? In H. P. Blossfeld, E. Kilpi-Jakonen, D. Vono de Vilhena, & S. Buchholz (Eds.), *Adult learning in modern societies: Patterns and consequences of participation from a life-course perspective* (pp. 283–304). Edward Elgar.

Hansen, R. J., & Brady, E. M. (2016). Demographic and behavioral characteristics of Osher lifelong learning institute members. *The Journal of Continuing Higher Education, 64*(1), 42–50. https://doi.org/10.1080/07377363.2016.113154

Harangy, L., & Toth, J. S. (1996). Hungary. *International Review of Education, 42*(1/3), 59–74.

Hay, C. (2020). Does capitalism (still) come in varieties? *Review of International Political Economy, 27*(2), 302–319.

Hefler, G., & Markowitsch, J. (2008). To train or not to train: Explaining differences in average enterprises' training performance in Europe—A framework approach. In J. Markowitsch & G. Hefler (Eds.), *Enterprise training in Europe: Comparative studies on cultures, markets and public support initiatives* (pp. 24–63). Lit Verlag.

References

Hefler, G., & Markowitsch, J. (2010). Formal adult learning and working in Europe: A new typology of participation patterns. *Journal of Workplace Learning, 22*(1), 79–93.

Hefler, G., & Markowitsch, J. (2013). Seven types of formal adult education and their organisational fields: Towards a comparative framework. In E. Saar, O. B. Ure, & T. Roosalu (Eds.), *Lifelong learning in Europe: National patterns and challenges* (pp. 82–113). Edward Elgar.

Hemerijck, A. (Ed.). (2017). *The uses of social investment.* Oxford University Press.

Hemerijck, A. (2018). Social investment as a policy paradigm. *Journal of European Public Policy, 25*(6), 810–827.

Hemerijck, A., & Ronchi, S. (2022). Recent developments. Social investment reform in the twenty-first century. In D. Béland, K. J. Morgan, H. Obinger, & C. Pierson (Eds.), *The Oxford handbook of the welfare state* (pp. 112–130). Oxford University Press.

Hidas S., Vál'ková, K., & Havran, P. (2016). *Vel'a práce na úradoch práce: Efektivita a účinnost služeb zamestnanosti.* Ekonomická analýza 40.Inštitut Finančnej Politiky.

Hinzen, H., Klement, C., Klun, J., & Neméth, B. (2022). Local experience and global commitments in citizenship education and adult learning communities: Comparative perspective on Austria, Germany, Hungary and Slovenia. *SISYPHUS, Journal of Education, 10*(2), 129–155. https://doi.org/10.25749/sis.25450

Holford, J. (2023). Lifelong learning, the European Union, and the social inclusion of young adults: Rethinking policy. In J. Holford et al. (Eds.), *Lifelong learning, young adults and challenges of disadvantage in Europe* (pp. 3–39). Palgrave Macmillan.

Holford, J., & Millana, M. (2023). The European Union and lifelong learning policy. In K. Evans, J. Markowitsch, W. O. Lee, & M. Zukas (Eds.), *Third international handbook of lifelong learning. Springer international handbooks of education* (pp. 499–522). Springer. https://doi.org/10.1007/978-3-030-67930-9_18-1

Holford, J., & Mleczko, A. (2010). Lifelong learning: National policies in the European perspective. In E. Saar, O. B. Ure, & J. Holford (Eds.), *Lifelong learning in Europe: National Patterns and challenges* (pp. 25–45). Edward Elgar.

Holford, J., & Mohorčič-Špolar, V. A. (2012). Neoliberal and inclusive themes in European lifelong learning policy. In S. Riddell, J. Markowitsch, & E. Weedon (Eds.), *Lifelong learning in Europe: Equity and efficiency in the balance* (pp. 39–61). Policy Press.

Holford, J., & Mohorčič-Špolar, V. A. (2014). Adult learning: From the margins to the mainstream. In M. Milana & J. Holford (Eds.), *Adult education policy and the European Union. Theoretical and methodological perspectives* (pp. 35–50). Sense.

Holford, J., Riddell, S., Weedon, E., Litjens, J., & Hannan, G. (2008). *Patterns of lifelong learning, policy and practice in an expanding Europe.* Lit Verlag.

Holubec, S. (2009). *Sociologie světových systémů.* SLON.

Hordósy, R., & Szanyi, F. E. (2021). Moving through and moving away: (Higher) education strategies of Hungarian students. *Intersections EEJSP, 6*(4), 34–62. https://doi.org/10.17356/ieejsp.v6i4.600

Hovdhaugen, E., & Opheim, V. (2018). Participation in adult education and training in countries with high and low participation rates: Demand and barriers. *International Journal of Lifelong Education, 37*(5), 560–577. https://doi.org/10.1080/02601370.2018.1554717

Huber, E., & Stephens, J. (2001). *Development and crisis of the welfare state.* University of Chicago Press.

HUN DLL. (2008). *The development and the state of the art of adult learning and evaluation.* National Institute of Vocational and adult Training.

HUN LLS. (2006). *The strategy for lifelong learning in Hungary. An overview.* Ministry of Education of the Republic of Hungary.

Hwang, H., & Roehn, W. (2022). *Tackling the challenges of population ageing in the Slovak Republic* (OECD economics department working papers, no. 1701). OECD. https://doi.org/10.1787/03edcf77-en.

IALS. (1997). *International Adult Literacy Survey: Survey data.* OECD.

Illeris, K. (2003). Adult education as experienced by the learners. *Journal of Lifelong Education, 22*(1), 13–23.

Illeris, K. (2006). Lifelong learning and low-skilled. *International Journal of Lifelong Education, 25*(1), 15–28.

Iñiguez-Berrozpe, et al. (2020). Benefits of adult education for low-educated women. *Adult Education Quarterly, 70*(1), 64–88.

Ioannidou, A., & Parma, A. (2022). Risk of job automation and participation in adult education and training: Do welfare regimes matter? *Adult Education Quarterly, 72*(1), 84–109.

Isakjee, A. (2017). *Welfare state regimes: A literature review*. IRiS working paper series, no. 18/2017 (UPWEB working paper series, no. 5/2017). Institute for Research into Superdiversity.

ISCED. (2011). *International standard classification of education: ISCED 2011*. UNESCO Institute for Statistics.

Iversen, T., & Soskice, D. (2001). An asset theory of social policy preferences. *The American Political Science Review, 95*(4), 875–893.

Iversen, T., & Soskice, D. (2019). *Democracy and prosperity. Reinventing capitalism through turbulent century*. Princeton University Press.

Iversen, T., & Stephens, J. D. (2008). Partisan politics, the welfare state, and three worlds of human capital formation. *Comparative Political Studies, 41*(4–5), 600–637.

Janoušková, M., Škrabalová, S., & Veselý, M. (2008). *Dopady čerpání fondů Evropské unie na změny v organizační struktuře nestátních neziskových organizací*. Společnost pro studium neziskového sektoru.

Jarvis, P. (2004). *Adult education and lifelong learning*. Routledge.

Jelenc, Z. (2001). Lifelong learning policies in transition countries. In D. Aspin, J. Chapman, M. Hatton, & Y. Sawano (Eds.), *International handbook of lifelong learning* (pp. 259–284). Kluwer Academic.

Jenkins, A. (2006). Women, lifelong learning and transitions into employment. *Work, Employment & Society, 20*(2), 309–328. https://doi.org/10.1177/0950017006064116

Jenkins, A. (2021). Patterns of participation and non-participation in learning in mid-life and their determinants. *International Journal of Lifelong Education, 40*(3), 215–228. https://doi.org/10.1080/02601370.2021.1937357

Johnstone, J., & Rivera, R. (1965). *Volunteers for learning: A study of the educational pursuits of American adults*. Aldine.

Jungblut, J., Maltais, M., Ness, E. C., & Rexe, D. (2023). The politics of higher education policy in Canada, the U.S., and Western Europe—An introduction. In J. Jungblut, M. Maltais, E. C. Ness, & D. Rexe (Eds.), *Comparative higher education politics* (pp. 1–23). Springer. https://doi.org/10.1007/978-3-031-25867-1_1

Kadeřábková, A. (2005). The Lisbon strategy challenges to The Czech Republic human resources. *European Journal of Education, 40*(3), 323–336.

Kalenda, J. (2015). Development of non-formal adult education in The Czech Republic. *Proceedia—Social and Behavioral Sciences, 174*, 1077–1084.

Kalenda, J. (2021). *Vratký triumf: vývoj účasti na neformálním vzdělávání dospělých v České republice v letech 1997 až 2016*. Univerzita Tomáše Bati.

Kalenda, J. (2023). Participation in Non-formal Adult Education in the Czech Republic from 1997 to 2020. In M. Schemman (Ed.), *Internationales Jahrbuch der Erwachsenenbildung/International Yearbook of Adult Education 2023* (pp. 115–138). wbv Publikation. https://doi.org/10.3278/I73910W007

Kalenda, J., & Kočvarová, I. (2022a). Participation in non-formal education in risk society. *International Journal of Lifelong Education, 41*(2), 146–167. https://doi.org/10.1080/02601370.2020.1808102

Kalenda, J., & Kočvarová, I. (2022b). Enduring inequality: Long-term trends and factors in participation in adult education and learning among older adults. *Gerontology & Geriatrics Education*. https://doi.org/10.1080/02701960.2022.2156866

Kalenda, J., & Kočvarová, I. (2022c). Why do not they participate? Reasons for non-participation in adult learning and education from the viewpoint of self-determination theory. (RELA) *Journal of European Research of learning and education of Adults*. Pre-published, 1–16. https://doi.org/10.3384/rela.2000-7426.3535.

Kalenda, J., Kočvarová, I., & Vaculíková, J. (2020). Determinants of participation in non-formal education in The Czech Republic. *Adult Education Quarterly, 70*(2), 99–118. https://doi.org/10.1177/0741713619878391

Kalenda, J., Kočvarová, I., & Vaculíková, J. (2022). Barriers to Participation of Low-educated Workers in Non-formal Education. *Journal of Education and Work*. Pre-published, 1–16. https://doi.org/10.1080/13639080.2022.2091118

Kalenda, J., Boeren, E., & Kočvarová, I. (2023). Exploring attitudes towards adult learning and education: Group patterns among participants and non-participants. *Studies in Continuing Education*. https://doi.org/10.1080/0158037X.2023.2199201

Karger, T. (2021). The signs of a frenetic standstill: The concept of change in the discourse of lifelong learning and the tempo of the Czech National Qualifications Framework. *Time & Society, 30*(3), 423–444.

Karger, T., Kalenda, J., Kalenda, S., & Kroutilová Nováková, R. (2022). How disadvantaged groups legitimize non-participation in adult education and training: The situational logic of decision-making. *International Journal of Lifelong Education*. Pre-published. https://doi.org/10.1080/02601370.2022.2057606

Kaufmann, K. (2015). Non-formal education in international comparison: Patterns of participation and investment in selected European countries. *International Journal for Research in Vocational Education and Training, 2*(4), 239–267.

Kilpi-Jakonen, E., Vono de Vilhena, D., & Blossfeld, H.-P. (2015). Adult learning and social inequalities: Processes of equalisation or cumulative disadvantage? *International Review of Education, 61*, 529–546. https://doi.org/10.1007/s11159-015-9498-5

Kleisz, T. (2015). The state of profession-building in the field of andragogy in Hungary. In B. Neméth (Ed.), *Research and development in adult learning and education in Hungary* (pp. 16–25). DVV International.

Kondrup, S. (2015). Understanding unskilled work as a condition for participation in adult education training. *European Journal for Research on the Education and Learning of Adults, 6*(2), 159–173. https://doi.org/10.3384/rela.2000-7426.rela9064

Kopecký, M. (2014). Transnationalization of Czech adult education policy as glocalization of the world and European policy mainstream(s). *European Education, 46*(4), 9–24. https://doi.org/10.1080/10564934.2014.995534

Kopecký, M., & Šerák, M. (2015). Adult education and learning policy in the CZE. In M. Milana & T. Nesbit (Eds.), *Global perspectives on adult education and learning policy* (pp. 29–43). Palgrave Macmillan.

Kornái, J. (2008). *From socialism to capitalism. Eight essays*. Central European University Press.

Korpi, W. (1983). *The democratic class struggle*. Routledge.

Kosyakova, Y., & Bills, D. B. (2021). Formal adult education and socioeconomic inequality: Second chances or Matthew effects? *Sociology Compass*. https://doi.org/10.1111/soc4.12920

Koubek, J., & Brewster, C. (1995). Human resource management in turbulent times: HRM in The Czech Republic. *The International Journal of Human Resource Management, 6*(2), 223–247.

Koucký, J., Ryška, R., & Zelenka, M. (2014). *Reflexe vzdělávání a uplatnění absolventů vysokých škol. Výsledky šetření REFLEX 2013*. Univerzita Karlova v Praze.

Kozma, T., & Polonyi, T. (2004). Understanding education in Europe-East: Frames of interpretation and comparison. *International Journal of Educational Development, 24*(5), 467–477. https://doi.org/10.1016/j.ijedudev.2004.06.011

Kureková, L. M., Lenaerts, K., Studená, I., Štefánik, M., Tobback, I., & Vangeel, N. (2023). *Working paper on the role of industrial relations and social diaologue in improving adult learning outcomes and equity deliverable*. SAS.

Kwiek, M. (2014). Social perceptions versus economic returns of the higher education: The Bologna process in Poland. In T. Kozma, M. Rébay, A. Óhidy, & É. Szolár (Eds.), *The Bologna process in central and Eastern Europe* (pp. 147–182). Springer.

Kyndt, E., Govaerts, N., Keunen, L., & Dochy, F. (2013). Examining the learning intentions of low-qualified employees: A mixed method study. *Journal of Workplace Learning, 25*(3), 178–197. https://doi.org/10.1108/13665621311306556

Lakatos, I. (1978). *The methodology of scientific research programmes (philosophical papers)*. Cambridge University Press.

Langer, T. (2009). Vzdělávání dospělých pohledem laické i odborné veřejnosti. *Vzdělávání dospělých, 14*(1), 51–66.

Lawn, M. (2006). Soft governance and the learning space of Europe. *Comparative European Politics, 4*(2), 272–288.

Lawn, M., & Grek, S. (2012). *Europeanizing education: Governing a new policy space*. Symposium Books.

Lee, J. (2017). *Inequality in participation in adult learning and education (ALE): Effects of micro- and macro- level factors through a comparative study*. University of California. https://escholarship.org/uc/item/4jh4m92q

Lee, J. (2018). Conceptual foundations for understanding inequality in participation in adult learning and education (ALE) for international comparisons. *International Journal of Lifelong Education, 37*(3), 297–314. https://doi.org/10.1080/02601370.2018.1462265

Lee, J., & Desjardins, R. (2019). Inequality in adult learning and education participation: The effects of social origins and social inequality. *International Journal of Lifelong Education, 38*(3), 339–359.

Lee, J., & Desjardins, R. (2021). Changes to adult learning and education (ALE) policy environment in Finland, Korea and the United States: Implications for addressing inequality in ALE participation. *Compare: A Journal of Comparative and International Education, 51*(2), 221–239. https://doi.org/10.1080/03057925.2019.1610356

Levitsky, S., & Murillo, M. V. (2009). Variation in institutional strength. *Annual Review of Political Science, 12*(1), 115–133.

Levitsky, S., & Murillo, M. V. (2015). Not just what, but when (and how): Comparative-historical approaches to authoritarian durability. In J. Mahoney & K. Thelen (Eds.), *Advances in comparative-historical analysis* (pp. 97–120). Cambridge University Press.

LFS. (2022). *Labour Force Survey: Survey data*. Eurostat.

Li, J., & Wei, K. J. (2019). Polish vocational and adult education: Status Quo, Dilemma and Way O. In *Advances in social science, education and humanities research,* 341. 5th International Conference on Arts, Design and Contemporary Education.

Lichner, I. (2022). *30 rokov premien slovenského trhu práce*. Ekonomický ústav Slovenskej Akadémie vied.

Lieberman, E. S. (2005a). Nested analysis as a mixed-method strategy for comparative research. *American Political Science Review, 99*(3), 435–452.

Lieberman, E. S. (2005b). Nested analysis: Toward the integration of comparative-historical analysis with other social science methods. In J. Mahoney & K. Thelen (Eds.), *Advances in comparative historical analysis* (pp. 240–263). Cambridge University Press.

Lieberman, E. (2015). Nested analysis: Toward the integration of comparative-historical analysis: past, present future. In J. Mahoney & K. Thelen (Eds.), *Advances in comparative-historical analysis* (pp. 240–263). Cambridge University Press.

Little, D. (2006). Levels of the social. In S. Turner & M. Risjord (Eds.), *Handbook for philosophy of anthropology and sociology* (pp. 343–372). Elsevier.

Little, D. (2010). *New contributions to philosophy of history*. Springer.

LMP. (2019). *Labour market policy. Expenditure and participants. Data 2016*. European Commission.

Łobos, K., Malátek, V., & Szewczyk, M. (2020). Management practices in area of human resources and monitoring results as determinants of SME's success in Poland and The Czech

References

Republic. *E&M Economics and Management, 23*(2), 114–125. https://doi.org/10.15240/tul/001/2020-2-008
Lybeck, E. R. (2020). *Norbert Elias and the sociology of education*. Bloomsbury Academic.
Magnin, E., & Nenovsky, N. (2022). *Diversity of capitalism*. In central and Eastern Europe. Dependent economies and monetary regimes. Palgrave Macmillan.
Mahoney, J. (2000). Path dependence in historical sociology. *Theory and Society, 29*(4), 507–548.
Mahoney, J. (2001). *Legacies of liberalism: Path dependence and political regimes in Central America*. John Hopkins University Press.
Mahoney, J., & Goertz, G. (2004). The possibility principle: Choosing negative cases in comparative research. *American Political Science Review, 98*(4), 653–670.
Mahoney, J. S., & Goertz, G. (2006). A tale of two cultures: Contrasting quantitative and qualitative research. *Political Analysis, 14*(3), 227–249.
Mahoney, J., & Thelen, K. (Eds.). (2010). *Explaining institutional change. Ambiguity, agency, and power*. Cambridge University Press.
Mahoney, J., & Thelen, K. (Eds.). (2015). *Advances in comparative-historical analysis*. Cambridge University Press.
Maliszewski, T., & Solarczyk-Szwec, H. (2013). How? Where to? About the changes and challenges of adult education in Poland in the years 1989-2013. *Universal Journal of Educational Research, 2*(3), 256–261.
Mann, M. (1986). *The sources of social power: Volume 2. The rise of classes and nation-states, 1760–1914*. Cambridge University Press.
Magnin, E., & Nenovsky, N. (2022). Diversity of capitalism. In *Central and Eastern Europe. Dependent economies and monetary regimes*. Palgrave Macmillan.
Markowitsch, J., & Hefler, G. (2019). *Future developments in vocational education and training in Europe, report on reskilling and upskilling through formal and vocational education training*. European Commission.
Matysiak, A. (2003). *Kształcenie ustawiczne w Polsce Korzyści bariery rozwoju* [Lifelong learning in Poland, benefits and development barriers]. Polskie Forum Strategii Lizbońskiej.
May, C., Nölke, A., & ten Brink, T. (2019). Public-private coordination in large emerging economies: The case of Brazil, India and China. *Contemporary Politics*. https://doi.org/10.1080/13569775.2018.1555781
Mayer, K. U., & Solga, H. (Eds.). (2008). *Skill formation. Interdisciplinary and cross-national perspective*. Cambridge University Press.
McAdam, D., Tarrow, S., & Tilly, C. (2001). *Dynamic of contention*. Cambridge University Press.
Merton, R. K. (1976). *Sociological ambivalence and other essays*. Free Press.
MEYS. (2001). *Bílá kniha—Národní program rozvoje vzdělávání v ČR*. Ministerstvo školství mládeže a tělovýchovy.
MEYS. (2003). *Strategie rozvoje lidských zdrojů*. Ministerstvo školství mládeže a tělovýchovy.
MEYS. (2007). *Strategie celoživotního učení v ČR*. Ministerstvo školství mládeže a tělovýchovy.
MEYS. (2009). *Průvodce dalším vzděláváním*. Ministerstvo školství, mládeže a tělovýchovy.
MEYS. (2010). *Průvodce dalším vzděláváním*. Ministerstvo školství mládeže a tělovýchovy.
MEYS. (2017). *Výroční zpráva o stavu a rozvoji vzdělávání v České republice v roce 2017*. Ministerstvo školství, mládeže a tělovýchovy.
MEYS. (2020). *Strategie vzdělávací politiky do roku 2030+*. Ministerstvo školství, mládeže a tělovýchovy.
Milana, M. (2018). Research patterns in comparative and global policy studies on adult education. In M. Milana, S. Webb, J. Holford, R. Waller, & P. Jarvis (Eds.), *The Palgrave international handbook on adult and lifelong education and learning* (pp. 421–441). Palgrave Macmillan.
Milana, M., & Holford, J. (Eds.). (2014). *Adult education policy and the European Union*. Sense.
Milana, M., & Vatrella, S. (2020). Youth guarantee and welfare state regimes: Cross-countries considerations. In M. Milana et al. (Eds.), *Europe's lifelong learning markets, governance and policy* (pp. 419–429). Palgrave Macmillan.

Milana, M., et al. (Eds.). (2020). *Europe's lifelong learning markets, governance and policy*. Palgrave Macmillan.

Misiak-Kwit, S., Wlodarczyk, K., Mazur-Wievzbiska, E., Smerek, L., & Durian, J. (2023). The human resources management system in Slovakia and Poland—Chosen aspects. *European Research Studies Journal, 26*(1), 20–39.

Mlčoch, L., Machonin, P., & Sojka, M. (2000). *Ekonomické a společenské změny v české společnosti po roce 1989*. Karolinum.

MPP. (2020). *Monitorovanie Verejnej Politiky Vzdelávania Dospelých na Slovensku*. Nova Academia.

Mykhnenko, V. (2007a). Poland and Ukraine: Institutional structures and economic performance. In D. Lane & M. Myant (Eds.), *Varieties of capitalism in post-communist countries* (pp. 124–145). Palgrave Macmillan.

Mykhnenko, V. (2007b). Strengths and weaknesses of 'weak' coordination: Economic institutions, revealed comparative advantages, and socio-economic performance of mixed market economies in Poland and Ukraine. In B. Hancké, M. Rhodes, & M. Thatcher (Eds.), *Beyond varieties of capitalism: Conflict, contradictions and complementarities in the European economy* (pp. 351–378). Oxford University Press.

Nahalka, I. (2018). *Back to the past: The education system of Hungary after 2010*. Friedrich Ebert Stiftung.

Nastase, P. (2018). Institutional perspectives on lifelong learning: Evidence from Romania and Hungary. https://doi.org/10.21549/NTNY.24.2018.4.2

Neméth, B. (2010). The accelerating roles of higher education in regions through the European lifelong learning initiative. *European Journal of Education, 45*(3), 451–465.

Neméth, B. (2013). *The rise and fall of research on the history of adult education in contemporary Hungary: Trends and issues of historical research work from 1993 to 2013*. http://nevelestudomany.elte.hu/downloads/2014/nevelestudomany_2014_1_40-54.pdf

Neméth, B. (2014). Research and development of adult education through higher education institutions: A challenge and perspective for better adult learning and education. *Procedia Social and Behavioral Sciences, 142*, 97–103.

Newell, A. T., & Pastore, F. (2000). *Regional unemployment and industrial restructuring in Poland*. IZA. (Discussion paper no 194).

Nolke, A., & Vligenthart, A. (2009). Enlarging the varieties of capitalism. The emergence of dependent market economies in East Central Europe. *World Politics, 61*(4), 670–702. https://doi.org/10.1017/S0043887109990098

NSC. (2020). *Národní soustava kvalifikací*. https://www.narodnikvalifikace.cz/

NTF. (2017). *Dopady Průmyslu 4.0 na trh práce v ČR*. Národní vzdělávací fond.

OECD. (1999). *Towards lifelong learning in Hungary*. OECD.

OECD. (2000). *Literacy in the information age: Final report of the International Literacy Survey*. OECD.

OECD. (2003). *Beyond rhetoric: Adult learning policies and practices*. OECD.

OECD. (2005). *Promoting adult learning*. OECD.

OECD. (2013). *Higher education in regional and city development. Wroclaw, Poland 2012*. OECD.

OECD. (2014). *Education at a glance 2014*. OECD.

OECD. (2019a). *Getting skills right: Engaging low-skilled adults in learning*. OECD.

OECD. (2019b). *Getting skills right: Future-ready adult learning systems*. OECD.

OECD. (2020). *OECD skills strategy Slovak Republic: Assesment and recommendations. OECD skills studies*. OECD.

OECD. (2021). *SME and entrepreneurship policy in Slovak Republic*. OECD.

OECD. (2022). *Strengthening FDI and SME linkages in the Slovak Republic*. OECD.

OECD. (2023a). *Employment by activity (indicator)*. https://doi.org/10.1787/a258bb52-e. Accessed 23 June 2023.

OECD. (2023b). *Public spending on labour markets (indicator)*. https://doi.org/10.1787/911b8753-en. Accessed 23 June 2023.

References

OECD. (2023d). *Unemployment rate (indicator)*. https://doi.org/10.1787/52570002-en. Accessed 23 June 2023.
OECD. (2023e). *Population with tertiary education (indicator)*. https://doi.org/10.1787/0b8f90e9-en. Accessed 23 June 2023.
OECD PL. (2005). *Thematic review on adult learning. Poland*. Country Note. OECD.
Olsen, J. (2002). The many faces of Europeanization. *EJCMS, 40*(5), 921–952.
Palán, Z. (2013a). Další vzdělávání v nové ekonomické situaci. In T. Langer (Ed.), *Nová ekonomická situace: výzva ke vzdělávání* (pp. 31–40). Asociace institucí vzdělávání dospělých ČR.
Palán, Z. (2013b). Institucionalizace (?) vzdělávání dospělých v ČR. *Acta Andagogica, 3*(1), 141–146.
Palier, B., Garritzmann, J. L., & Häusermann, S. (2022). Toward a worldwide view on the politics of social investment. In J. L. Garritzmann, S. Häusermann, & B. Palier (Eds.), *The world politics of social investment (volume I)* (pp. 1–58). Oxford University Press. https://doi.org/10.1093/oso/9780197585245.003.0001
PIAAC. (2012). *Programme for the International Assessment of Adult Competencies: Survey data*. OECD.
Pierson, P. (2000). Increasing returns, path dependence, and the study of politics. *American Political Science Review, 94*(2), 251–267.
Pierson, P. (2004). *Politics in time: History, institutions, and social analysis*. Princeton University Press.
Pól, M., & Hloušková, L. (2008). Celoživotní učení a vzdělávání dospělých v politických dokumentech. In M. Rabušicová & L. Rabušic (Eds.), *Učíme se po celý život? O vzdělávání dospělých v české republice* (pp. 189–204). Masarykova univerzita.
Prokop, D., & Dvořák, T. (2019). *Analýza výzev vzdělávání v České republice*. Nadační fond Eduzměna.
Prudký, L., Pabián, P., & Šíma, K. (2010). *České vysoké školství na cestě od elitního k univerzálnímu vzdělávání 1989–2009*. Grada Publishing.
Rabušic, L., & Rabušicová, M. (2006). Adult education in The Czech Republic—Who participates and why. *Czech Sociological Review, 42*(6), 1195–1218.
Rabušicová, M., & Rabušic, L. (Eds.). (2008). *Učíme se po celý život? O vzdělávání dospělých v České republice*. Masarykova univerzita.
Rabušicová, M., Rabušic, L., & Šeďová, K. (2008). Motivace a bariéry ve vzdělávání dospělých. In M. Rabušicová & L. Rabušic (Eds.), *Učíme se po celý život? O vzdělávání dospělých v České republice* (pp. 97–112). Masarykova univerzita.
Rashid, M., Rutkowski, J., & Fretwell, D. (2005). Labor markets. In N. Barr (Ed.), *Labor markets and social policy in central and Eastern Europe. The accession and beyond* (pp. 45–56). World Bank.
Rees, G. (2013). Comparing adult learning systems: An emerging political economy. *European Journal of Education, 48*(2), 200–212.
Regmi, K. D. (2020). Social foundations of lifelong learning: A Habermasian perspective. *International Journal of Lifelong Education, 39*(2), 219–233. https://doi.org/10.1080/02601370.2020.1758813
Ricardo, R., Bora, B., Camilloni, F., Lizon, L., Cavaca, M., Sinha, P., Kandera, P., & Egetenmeyer, R. (2016). Participation and non-participation in adult education and learning: A comparative study between Portugal, Italy, Hungary, and India. In R. Egetenmeyer (Ed.), *Adult education and lifelong learning in Europe and beyond. Comparative perspectives from the 2015 Würzburg Winter School* (pp. 149–170). Peter Lang GmbH.
Riddell, E., Markowitsch, J., & Weedon, E. (Eds.). (2012). *Lifelong learning in Europe. Equity and efficiency in the balance*. Policy Press.
Roosmaa, E.-L., & Saar, E. (2010). Participating in non-formal learning. Patterns of inequality in EU-15 and the new EU-8 member countries. *Journal of Education and Work, 23*(3), 179–206. https://doi.org/10.1080/13639080.2010.486396

Roosmaa, E.-L., & Saar, E. (2012). Participation in non-formal learning in EU-15 and EU-8 countries: Demand and supply side factors. *International Journal of Lifelong Education, 31*, 477–501.

Roosmaa, E.-L., & Saar, E. (2017). Adults who do not want to participate in learning: A cross-national European analysis of their barriers. *International Journal of Lifelong Education, 36*(3), 254–277. https://doi.org/10.1080/02601370.2016.1246485

Rubenson, K. (1975). *Participation in recurrent education.* CERI/OECD.

Rubenson, K. (1999). The supply of lifelong learning opportunities. In A. Tuijnman & T. Schuller (Eds.), *Lifelong learning policy and research: Proceedings of an international symposium* (pp. 109–120). Portland Press.

Rubenson, K. (2006). The Nordic model of lifelong learning. *Compare, 36*, 327–341.

Rubenson, K. (2011). Barriers to participation in adult education. In K. Rubenson (Ed.), *Adult learning and education* (pp. 216–224). Elsevier.

Rubenson, K. (2018). Conceptualizing participation in adult learning and education. Equity issues. In M. Milana, S. Webb, J. Holford, R. Waller, & P. Jarvis (Eds.), *The Palgrave international handbook on adult and lifelong education and learning* (pp. 337–357). Palgrave Macmillan.

Rubenson, K., & Desjardins, R. (2009). The impact of welfare state requirements on barriers to participation in adult education: A bounded agency model. *Adult Education Quarterly, 59*(3), 187–207.

Saar, E., & Ure, B. (2013). Lifelong learning systems: Overview and extension of different typologies. In E. Saar, O. B. Ure, & J. Holford (Eds.), *Lifelong learning in Europe. National patterns and challenge* (pp. 46–81). Edward Elgar.

Saar, E., & Räis, M. L. (2017). Participation in job-related training in European countries: The impact of skill supply and demand characteristics. *Journal of Education and Work, 30*(5), 531–551. https://doi.org/10.1080/13639080.2016.1243229

Saar, E., Ure, O. B., & Desjardins, R. (2013a). The role of diverse institutions in framing adult learning systems. *European Journal of Education, 48*(2), 213–232.

Saar, E., Ure, O. B., & Holford, J. (2013b). Conclusion: Lifelong learning as a social field and entrance point to policy-making for education and. In E. Saar, O. B. Ure, & J. Holford (Eds.), *Lifelong learning in Europe. National patterns and challenges* (pp. 397–401). Edward Elgar.

Saar, E., Täht, K., & Roosalu, T. (2014). Institutional barriers for adults´ participation in higher education in thirteen European countries. *Higher Education, 68*, 691–710.

Saar, E., Roosalu, T., & Roosmaa, E. L. (2023). Lifelong learning for economy or for society: Policy issues in post-socialist countries in Europe. In K. Evans, J. Markowitsch, W. O. Lee, & M. Zukas (Eds.), *Third international handbook of lifelong learning. Springer international handbooks of education* (pp. 353–374). Springer. https://doi.org/10.1007/978-3-031-19592-1_28

Sabates, R., & Hammond, C. (2008). *The impact of lifelong learning on happiness and well-being.* National Institute for Adult and Continuing Education.

Scharpf, F. (2008). Negative and positive integration. In M. Höopner & A. Schäfer (Eds.), *Die Politische Ökonomie der europäischen Integration* (pp. 49–87). Campus.

Schedelik, M., Nölke, A., Mertens, D., & May, C. (2020). Comparative capitalism, growth models and emerging markets: The development of the field. *New Political Economy.* https://doi.org/10.1080/13563467.2020.1807487

Schemmann, M., Herbrechter, D., & Engels, M. (2020). Researching the political economy of adult learning systems. Theoretical amendments and empirical findings. *Zeitschrift für Weiterbildungsforschungm, 43*(2), 259–273. https://doi.org/10.1007/s40955-020-00163-2

Schmidt-Hertha, B., & Rees, S. L. (2017). Transitions to retirement—Learning to redesign one's lifestyle. *Research on Ageing and Social Policy, 5*(1), 32–56. https://doi.org/10.4471/rasp.2017.2426

Schroder, M. (2009). Integrating welfare and production typologies: How refinements of the varieties of capitalism approach call for a combination of welfare typologies. *Journal of Social Policy, 38*, 19–43.

References

Schroder, M. (2013). *Integrating varieties of capitalism and welfare state research. A unified typology of capitalisms*. Palgrave Macmillan.

Schuller, T. (1999). A research agenda for lifelong learning. In A. Tuijnman & T. Schuller (Eds.), *Lifelong learning policy and research: Proceedings of an international symposium* (pp. 23–32). Portland Press.

Schuller, T. (2019). Active ageing and older learners—Trajectories and outcomes. *European Journal of Education, 54*(1), 5–8. https://doi.org/10.1111/ejed.12316

Schuller, T., & Desjardins, R. (2010). The wider benefits of adult education. In P. Peterson, E. Baker, & B. McGaw (Eds.), *International encyclopedia of education* (pp. 229–233). Elsevier.

Schuller, T., & Watson, D. (2009). *Learning through life*. National Institute for Adult Continuing Education.

Šerák, M. (2012). Reflexe měnící se role dalšího vzdělávání optikou právních norem. In M. Šerák et al. (Eds.), *Celoživotní učení a sociální politika: vazby a přesahy* (pp. 70–80). AIVD.

Šilhár, L. (2013). Inštitucionalizácia ďalšieho vzdelávania na Slovensku. *Acta Andragogika, 3*(1), 157–166.

Šimek, D. (1996). *Andragogika*. UP Olomouc.

Simonová, N., & Hamplová, D. (2016). Další vzdělávání dospělých v České republice—kdo se ho účastní a s jakými výsledky? *Sociologický časopis, 52*(1), 3–25.

Singh, M. (2015). *Global perspectives in the recognition of non-formal and informal learning. Why recognition matters*. Springer Open.

Škerháková, V., Korba, P., Harničárová, M., & Ali Taha, V. (2022). Talent retention: Analysis of the antecedents of talented employees' intention to stay in the organizations. *European Journal of Interdisciplinary Studies, 14*(1), 56–67.

Sládkayová, M., & Krystoň, M. (2019). *Aktuálny stav občianskeho vzdelávánia dospelých v Slovenskej republike a České republike*. Conference paper. https://www.researchgate.net/publication/340829541_Aktualny_stav_obcianskeho_vzdelavania_dospelych_v_Slovenskej_republike_a_Ceskej_republike

Smerek, L., Vetráková, M., Smerková, Š., & Malátek, V. (2021). Comparison of the level of personnel work in The Czech Republic and Slovakia. *Sustainability, 13*, 287. https://doi.org/10.3390/su13010287

Šmídová, M., Šmídová, O., Kyllingstad, N., & Karlsen, J. (2017). Regional development: Lifelong learning as a priority in Norway and The Czech Republic? *Higher Education Policy, 30*(4), 499–516. https://doi.org/10.1057/s41307-017-0060-x

Spieser, C. (2007). Labour market policies in post-communist Poland: Explaining the peaceful institutionalisation of unemployment. *Politique européenne, 21*(1), 97–132. https://doi.org/10.3917/poeu.021.0097

Stachová, K., Stacho, Z., Raišienė, A. G., & Barokova, A. (2020). Human resource management trends in Slovakia. *Journal of International Studies, 13*(3), 320–331. https://doi.org/10.14254/2071-8330.2020/13-3/21

Stachová, K., & Smerek, L. (2023). *Managing human resources in Slovakia 1998–2018*. Oficyna Wydawnicza Stowarzyszenia Menedżerów Jakości i Produkcji.

Stark, D. (1992). Path dependence and privatization strategies in east Central Europe. *East European Politics and Societies, 6*(1), 17–53.

Štefánik, M. (2018). Active labour market policies in Slovakia—Overview of the available evidence. In M. Štefánik et al. (Eds.), *Labour market in Slovakia* (pp. 38–55). Centre of Social and Psychological Sciences, Slovak Academy of Sciences.

Streeck, W. (1992). *Social institutions and economic performance: Studies of industrial relations in advanced capitalist economies*. Sage.

Streeck, W. (1994a). *Social institutions and economic performance: Studies of industrial relations in advanced capitalist economies*. Sage.

Streeck, W. (1994b). Training and new industrial relations: A strategic role for unions? In M. Regini (Ed.), *The future of labour movements* (pp. 250–269). Sage.

Streeck, W. (2013). *Gekaufte Zeit: Die vertagte Krise des demokratischen Kapitalismus*. Suhrkamp.

Streeck, W., & Thelen, K. (2005). Introduction: Institutional change in advanced political economies. In W. Streeck & K. Thelen (Eds.), *Beyond continuity: Institutional change in advanced political economies*. Oxford University Press.

Studená, I. (2018). Slovak labour market—Selected trends. In M. Štefánik et al. (Eds.), *Labour Market in Slovakia* (pp. 7–20). Centre of Social and Psychological Sciences, Slovak Academy of Sciences.

Studená, I., & Habodászová, L. (2020). *Vzdelávanie dospelých na Slovensku*. https://epale.ec.europa.eu/sites/default/files/02_vzdelavanie_dospelych_v_sr_-_zakladne_fakty_data_a_zistenia_v_roku_2020.pdf

Studená, I., & Polačková, Z. (2020). The Slovakian Rejoinder to youth guarantee. In M. Milana, G. Klatt, & S. Vatrella (Eds.), *Europe's lifelong learning markets, governance and policy. Palgrave studies in adult education and lifelong learning*. Palgrave Macmillan. https://doi.org/10.1007/978-3-030-38069-4_10

Swidler, A. (1986). Culture in action: Symbols and strategies. *American Sociological Review, 51*(2), 273–286.

Szelenyi, I., & Wilk, K. (2010). Institutional transformation in European post-communist regimes. In G. Morgan et al. (Eds.), *The Oxford handbook of comparative institutional analysis* (pp. 698–712). Oxford University Press.

Szelewa, D., & Polakowski, M. (2020). The "ugly" face of social investment? The politics of childcare in central and eastern Europe. *Social Policy and Administration, 54*(1), 14–27.

Szelewa, D., & Polakowski, M. (2022). Explaining the weakness of social investment policies in the Visegrád countries. In J. L. Garritzmann, S. Häusermann, & B. Palier (Eds.), *The world politics of social investment (volume II)* (pp. 186–208). Oxford University Press. https://doi.org/10.1093/oso/9780197601457.003.0008

Szikra, D. (2014). Democracy and welfare in hard times: The social policy of the Orban government in Hungary between 2010 and 2014. *Journal of European Pocial Policy, 24*(5), 486–500.

Thelen, K. (1991). *Union of parts. Labour politics in postwar Germany*. Cornell University Press.

Thelen, K. (2004). *How institutions evolve: The political economy of skills in comparative-historical perspective*. Cambridge University Press.

Thelen, K. (2007). Skill formation and training. In G. Jones & J. Zeitlin (Eds.), *The Oxford handbook of business history* (pp. 558–580). Oxford University Press.

Thelen, K. (2014). *Varieties of liberalization and the new politics of social solidarity*. Cambridge University Press.

Tilly, C. (1984). *Big structures, large processes, huge comparisons*. Russell Sage Foundation.

Tilly, C. (2001). Mechanisms in political processes. *Annual Review of Political Science, 4*(1), 21–41.

Tilly, C. (2006). *Regimes and repertoires*. University of Chicago Press.

Tilly, C. (2008). *Explaining social processes*. Routledge.

Timmermans, S., & Tavory, I. (2012). Theory construction in qualitative research: From grounded theory to abductive analysis. *Sociological Theory, 30*(3), 167–186. https://doi.org/10.1177/0735275112457914

Tóth, J., Szirmai, É., Merkovity, N., & Pongó, T. (2021). Promising or compelling future in Hungary? In N. Kersh et al. (Eds.), *Young adults and active citizenship* (pp. 121–137). Springer. https://doi.org/10.1007/978-3-030-65002-5_7

Trajlinková, K. (2001). Review of Slovakia's accession to the OECD. Liberalization progress comparison between Slovakia, The Czech Republic, Poland, and Hungary. *BIATEC, 9*(2), 33–36.

Trampusch, C. (2009). Employers, the state, and politics of institutional change: Vocational educational training in Austria, Germany, and Switzerland. *European Journal of Political Research, 49*(4), 545–573.

Tuijnman, A. C. (1999). Research agenda for lifelong learning: A report by the task force of the international academy of education. In A. Tuijnman & T. Schuller (Eds.), *Lifelong learning policy and research: Proceedings of an international symposium* (pp. 1–22). Portland Press.

UNESCO. (2019). *GRALE IV. 4th global report on adult learning and education. Leave no one behind: Participation, equity and inclusion*. UNESCO Institute for Lifelong Learning.

References

UNESCO. (2020). *Embracing a culture of lifelong learning. Contribution to the future of education initiative*. UNESCO Institute for Lifelong Learning.

UNESCO. (2022). *5th global report on adult learning and education. Citizenship education: Empowering adults for change*. UNESCO Institute for Lifelong Learning.

Ure, O. B., & Aaslid, B. E. (2013). In search of building blocks for lifelong learning: Motivation and institutional support in Norwegian education and training. In E. Saar, O. B. Ure, & J. Holford (Eds.), *Lifelong learning in Europe. National patterns and challenges* (pp. 206–231). Edward Elgar.

Vaculíková, J., Kalenda, J., & Kočvarová, I. (2021). Hidden gender differences in formal and non-formal adult education. *Studies in Continuing Education, 43*(1), 33–47. https://doi.org/10.1080/0158037X.2020.1732334

Valentine, T., & Darkenwald, G. G. (1990). Deterrents to participation in adult education: Profiles of potential learners. *Adult Education Quarterly, 41*(1), 29–42. https://doi.org/10.1177/0001848190041001003

van Nieuwenhove, L., & De Wever, B. (2021). Why are low-educated adults underrepresented in adult education? Studying the role of educational background in expressing learning needs and barriers. *Studies in Continuing Education*. https://doi.org/10.1080/0158037X.2020.1865299

Van Nieuwenhove, L., & De Wever, B. (2023). Psychosocial barriers to adult learning and the role of prior learning experiences: A comparison based on educational level. *Adult Education Quarterly*. https://doi.org/10.1177/07417136231147491

van Ours, J. C., & Lubyová, M. (1999). Effects of active labour market programmes on the transition rate from unemployment into regular jobs in the Slovak Republic. *Journal of Comparative Economics, 27*(1), 90–112.

Vanhuysse, P. (2006). *Divide and pacify: Strategic social policies and political protests in post-communist democracies*. Central European University Press.

Večerník, J. (1999). Střední vrstvy v české transformaci. *Sociologický časopis, 35*(1), 33–51.

Večerník, J. (2022). *Social stratification in Central Europe. Long-term developments and new issues*. Springer.

Večerník, J., & Matějů, P. (1998). *Zpráva o vývoji české společnosti 1989*. Academia.

Verdier, E. (2017). How are European lifelong learning systems changing? An approach in terms of public policy regimes. In R. Normand & J.-L. Derouet (Eds.), *A European politics of education. Perspectives from sociology, policy studies, and politics* (pp. 194–215). Routledge.

Verdier, E. (2018). Europe: Comparing lifelong learning systems. In M. Milana, S. Webb, J. Holford, R. Waller, & P. Jarvis (Eds.), *The Palgrave international handbook on adult and lifelong education and learning* (pp. 461–483). Palgrave Macmillan.

Veselý, A. (2013). Vzdělávací politika: rozdílné vymezení, předpoklady a implikace. *Pedagogická orientace, 23*(3), 279–297.

Veselý, A. (2017). Education officials between hierarchies and networks. *Studia paedagogica, 22*(4), 118–133.

Walker, J. (2020). Comparing adult education systems: Canada and Aotearoa New Zealand. *Zeitschrift für Weiterbildungsforschungm, 43*(2), 241–257. https://doi.org/10.1007/s40955-020-00158-z

WB. (2023). *UNESCO (2023). Lower secondary completion rate (indicator)*. World Bank. Available at: https://data.worldbank.org/indicator/SE.SEC.CMPT.LO.ZS

Widany, S., Christ, J., Gauly, B., Massing, N., & Hoffmann, M. (2019). The quality of data on participation in adult education and training. An analysis of varying participation rates and patterns under consideration of survey design and measurement effects. *Frontiers in Sociology, 4*, 71. https://doi.org/10.3389/fsoc.2019.00071

Wilder, K. (2023). Getting a worker: Recruiters, culture, and on-the-job skilling. *Sociological Forum*. https://doi.org/10.1111/socf.12893

Wilkins, A., & Olmedo, A. (2018). Introduction: Conceptualizing education governance: Framings, perspectives and theories. In A. Wilkins & A. Olmedo (Eds.), *Education governance and social theory. Interdisciplinary approaches to research* (pp. 1–17). Bloomsbury Academic.

Wiśniewski, J. (2008). *The development and state of adult learning and education (ALE)*. The National Report of Poland. Centre for Social and Economic Research.

Witt, M. A., & Jackson, G. (2016). Varieties of capitalism and institutional comparative advantage: A test and reinterpretation. *Journal of International Business Studies, 47*, 778–806. https://doi.org/10.1057/s41267-016-0001-8

Wolbers, M. H. J. (2005). Initial and further education: Substitutes or complements? Differences in education and training over the life-course of European workers. *International Review of Education, 51*(5/6), 458–478.

Wotschack, P. (2020). When do companies train low-skilled workers? The role of institutional arrangements at the company and sectoral level. *British Journal of Industrial Relations, 58*, 587–616. https://doi.org/10.1111/bjir.12503

Wren, A. (Ed.). (2013). *Political economy of the service transition*. Oxford University Press.

Yamashita, T., López, E. B., Keene, J. R., & Kinney, J. M. (2015). Predictors of adult education program satisfaction in urban community-dwelling older adults. *Educational Gerontology, 41*(11), 825–838. https://doi.org/10.1080/03601277.2015.1050909

Yamashita, T., López, E. B., Soligo, M., & Keene, J. R. (2017). Older lifelong learners' motivations for participating in formal volunteer activities in urban communities. *Adult Education Quarterly, 67*(2), 118–135. https://doi.org/10.1177/0741713616688957

Zounek, J., Novotný, P., Knotová, D., & Čiháček, V. (2006). Vzdělávací nabídka pro dospělé v České republice. *Pedagogika, 56*(2), 152–163.

Printed by Printforce, United Kingdom